SHAKESPEARE AND SCIENCE

SHAKESPEARE AND SCIENCE

A Study of Shakespeare's interest
in, and literary and dramatic use
of, natural phenomena; with an
account of the astronomy, astrology,
and alchemy of his day, and his
attitude towards these sciences.

BY

CUMBERLAND CLARK, F.R.A.S.

Vice-President of the Shakespeare Reading Society.

HASKELL HOUSE PUBLISHERS Ltd.

Publishers of Scarce Scholarly Books

NEW YORK. N. Y. 10012

1970

First Published 1929

HASKELL HOUSE PUBLISHERS Lᴛᴅ.
Publishers of Scarce Scholarly Books
280 LAFAYETTE STREET
NEW YORK, N. Y. 10012

Library of Congress Catalog Card Number: 79-92956

Standard Book Number 8383-0965-8

Printed in the United States of America

CONTENTS

Shakespeare and Science

I.

SHAKESPEARE'S INTEREST IN NATURAL PHENOMENA.

THE miracle of Shakespeare is the unrivalled power of a country-bred Warwickshire lad, with a rural education, to observe, absorb, retain, and deck in the garb of superb poetry for the delectation of his fellows, so much that pertains to life and nature. Books have been written by experts in their various fields on his knowledge of the birds, of the flowers, of law, of medicine, of the Scriptures, of sculpture, of precious stones, of folklore, of printing, of seamanship, of military tactics, and a host of other subjects. All of them have helped us to appreciate and understand better the man who is not only conceded to be the greatest figure of English literature, but the crowning poet of all time.

Many admirers of Shakespeare's works have found it impossible to believe that a boy with his limited opportunities, with only those educational facilities which the Stratford-on-Avon Grammar School was able to afford, could possibly have attained to his high standard of erudition and amassed his almost inexhaustible fund of knowledge. In their dilemma they have searched round wildly for another possible author for the plays and alighted upon Francis Bacon. But to the unprejudiced mind it seems even more impossible for Bacon to have written them than the unlearned, untutored Shakespeare. Bacon sought to explain the causes of phenomena :

the dramatist was content to describe their beauty. Bacon
dived into scientific experiment : the dramatist borrowed
picturesque simile and metaphor. Bacon revealed in his
astronomical researches a dry, legal, scientific mind : the
dramatist's mind glowed with poetry, beauty, and romance.
Bacon could not have been the dramatist.

Almost beyond credence though it may be, there is no
doubt to-day that Shakespeare actually was responsible for
most of the works that bear his name. The proofs are too
numerous and too strong to be denied. The wonder happened;
and the country boy, by exercise of his keen perceptive
faculties, his tireless study of books, and the stocking of his
mental storehouse with material to be polished later into
literary gems, perfected his native genius and gained a throne
unchallenged through the ages.

The books that have been written on the many different
sides of his learning show that he amassed a wealth of
knowledge, much of which was outside the ordinary man's
ken. In matters, then, that enter the experience of every one
of us, the poet's interest must have been keen indeed. Except
for such emotions as love, there are no influences in human
lives exceeding those of natural phenomena. The sun, the
moon, the stars, rain, snow, and hail, the seasons, the winds,
thunder and lightning, the tides, and so forth, engage the
attention of the most dull-witted and raise even the gross-
minded to thoughts above the material and mundane. To
those gifted with imaginative minds and the power of expression they have been a source of inspiration since the dawn of
literature. The author was prompted, therefore, to make an
exhaustive study of the attitude and feeling of the master-
poet towards them, and found illuminating self-revelation
in the lines of Theseus in " Midsummer Night's Dream "
(V.1. 12-17) :

> The poet's eye, in a fine frenzy rolling,
> Doth glance from heaven to earth, from earth to heaven ;
> And, as imagination bodies forth
> The forms of things unknown, the poet's pen
> Turns them to shapes, and gives to airy nothing
> A local habitation and a name.

So Shakespeare, turning to the wonders and beauties of the universe, and acknowledging, " Thou, Nature, art my goddess " (" King Lear " I.2. 1), explores the field of natural science and mines abundant treasure in apt metaphor, simile, comparison, and allegory. As he writes in "As You Like It " (II.1. 16-17), he

> Finds tongues in trees, books in the running brooks,
> Sermons in stones, and good in every thing,

and reaps parallel rewards for his observation when scanning the broad face of the heavens. When he basked in the sun, blinked at the stars, shuddered at the thunder, or battled with the wind, he stored up impressions that blossomed later into literary figures and became the pearls of great price in the English language. It is difficult in any Shakespearian study to distinguish between the poet's own views and those which he attributes to his characters, but in the passages on natural phenomena, some of the finest he ever penned, we can rest confident that it is the soul of the poet speaking. He shows no reticence here, but pours forth his golden thoughts in a stream of prodigal loveliness.

Not only did Shakespeare turn to the manifestations of Nature to adorn his poetry : he availed himself of them as a dramatist and was fully aware of their value in enhancing tragedy, suspense, fear, disaster. Happily for English literature, scenery on the Elizabethan stage was primitive in the extreme, and the poet was compelled to win his effects by word-descriptions. How successfully he achieved this and with what treasures he enriched our language thereby, form an interesting side of our study.

Quite apart from Shakespeare's work and genius, the Elizabethan age was one of first importance in the development of scientific discovery. In the realm of astronomy it witnessed a complete reversal of all preconceived ideas ; and the theories of Ptolemy, which had held the field for fourteen centuries, were overthrown by the discoveries of Copernicus, Kepler, and Galileo. Coincident with this astronomical advance came the first challenge to the whole position of astrology, which had been deeply entrenched in the superstition of the world since the days of Babylon. The old art did not surrender at once to the new science. Indeed, the struggle was long and bitter. But truth finally vanquished superstition, and the astrologers are no more. Again, the work of the alchemists, whose high-falutin claims had been for some years increasingly discredited, was at length taking that turn that enabled its practitioners to lay the foundations of the science of chemistry as we know it to-day. Shakespeare's attitude to these changes, both privately as a philosopher and publicly as a dramatist, is an investigation which appealed to the author as likely to interest all admirers of the poet.

A natural question that suggests itself is : Did Shakespeare, who plainly gave the closest attention to natural science and phenomena, adopt any cosmic theory or explanation of the universe ? Sir Sidney Lee has handled this query in dealing with the Sonnets. This great Shakespearian scholar points out that the poet toyed with ideas on this obscure and difficult problem which were found in his favourite poet, Ovid. The Latin poet's " Metamorphoses," available to Shakespeare in Golding's English translation, was responsible for the speculation which, says Lee, he " wove dispersedly into the

texture of his sonnets." Frequently he expresses his fear
that nothing is new, that that which is hath been before,
and that there is no new thing under the sun, as we read in
" Ecclesiastes." Time, according to this theory, is in a state
of revolution, merely reproducing past events and old
experiences, and that what seems novel and strange to the
circumscribed human mind, is only repetition from some
distant past to be repeated again at some distant future.
Shakespeare's particular application of the theory is to his
love for his friend, which he fears may not be original nor
individual, but a recurrence of something that has already
been. Sonnet LIX presents this view-point :

> If there be nothing new, but that which is
> Hath been before, how are our brains beguiled,
> Which, labouring for invention, bear amiss
> The sacred burthen of a former child !
> O, that record could with a backward look,
> Even of five hundred courses of the sun,
> Show me your image in some antique book,
> Since mind at first in character was done.
> That I might see what the old world could say
> To this composed wonder of your frame ;
> Whether we are mended, or whether better they,
> Or whether revolution be the same.
>   O, sure I am, the wits of former days
>   To subjects worse have given admiring praise.

Shakespeare does not identify himself with this idea. He
merely asks the question. Nor did it arise independently
in his own mind, but was introduced to his thoughts by the
study of Ovid. There is not data enough to justify us in
concluding that the poet had formed any theory on mysteries
that have baffled man since he existed as a reasoning creature.

II.

NATURAL PHENOMENA ON THE SHAKESPEARIAN STAGE.

EVERY practised playwright is fully aware of the value of the imitative uses of natural phenomena to intensify the most dramatic moments of his plot. He can so handle the elements as to harmonize them with the mental processes of his characters and strengthen the impression he desires to convey. Fire, air, earth, and water may thus appear in the guise of the objectified thought-forces of the men and women in his play. For example, if a dramatist wishes to depict a happy and contented state of mind, he can surround his characters with golden sunshine, gentle zephyrs, scent and colour, peaceful skies and seas. Doubt and anxiety can be portrayed by dark and scurrying clouds, by concealing mists or banks of fog. Anger, fear, and superstitious dread of the supernatural have a fitting accompaniment in storm, hurricane, thunder, and lightning. Vice and crime are well suited to the shrouding blackness of night. Romance has long enjoyed an almost undisputed claim upon the moonlight, while those unfortunate people, who are unjustly disinherited, are invariably turned out into the snow. The seasons are identified with particular human emotions—spring with hope, summer with joy, autumn with sadness, winter with pain—and often the time of year with its appropriate climatic conditions is indicated to emphasize certain traits of character or aspects of the dramatized story. These devices of the playwright may seem to us to have been employed rather crudely in ages past. The modern dramatist is more subtle in their uses, but he avails himself of them nevertheless, though he is careful that they do not obtrude with too obvious an artificiality.

Although the art of playwriting is constantly progressing, the improved use of natural phenomena on the stage is not to be laid wholly to the credit of the dramatist. He has received incalculable aid from a non-literary quarter. This is a mechanical age, and the inventor has found in the theatre a most favourable opportunity for the exercise of his talents. Device has followed device, not only with the object of increasing the realistic effect produced by sound and colour, but also with the admirable aim of simplifying and accelerating the laborious duties falling on scene-shifters, stage-hands, electricians, and their fellows. This advance has enabled more wonderful and astonishing spectacles than ever before to be presented on the limited compass of the stage. Our forefathers would have rubbed their eyes in astonishment at to-day's achievements, while we, rendered indifferent by the more elaborate and realistic thrills of the motion-picture, are rarely moved to unrestrained applause.

As far as the portrayal of natural phenomena is concerned, the dramatist of our time has been assisted by our modern proficiency in lighting systems more than by any other mechanical improvement. If he wants a day of sunshine, a moonlight night, a breaking dawn, or a gradual sunset, he can have it merely by demanding it from the management. Mechanically he can have gales of wind, realistic lightning and thunderstorms, fires, earthquakes, and a reasonable imitation of a rough sea, by indicating them on his script. He is thus spared a great deal of work which the old dramatist had to shoulder, when plays were produced in broad daylight and the only device to be relied upon was a crashing noise that indifferently represented tempests, alarums and excursions, and like upheavals. The playwright of Shakespeare's day had to rely on the effect of spoken descriptions for his settings, and the modern author enjoys the inestimable advantage of having transferred these descriptions from the dialogue to the stage directions. From a literary point of view we rejoice that the Elizabethan stage was so deficient of scenic devices, for had it possessed modern equipment, a large number of the beautiful descriptive passages in Shakespeare would never have been penned.

Like all great dramatists, Shakespeare was fully alive to the value and importance of the introduction of natural phenomena into his plays. In order to appreciate his method of doing so, it is necessary to bear in mind some of the leading features of Elizabethan theatre-construction.

The precise architecture of the Shakespearian playhouse is still a matter of controversy, but enough is known to elucidate the particular investigation we have in hand. Most of the theatres were built of wood in a circular shape—" this wooden O," as Shakespeare calls it in the prologue to " Henry V." Round the circle ran covered galleries or boxes in tiers or stories. The arena in the centre was open to the sky. Certain of these playhouses were used alternatively for the drama and for bear-baiting and kindred sports. Others, like the " Globe," were reserved solely for the production of plays.

The stage was a large platform which projected into the arena—the cheapest part of the theatre, where the people stood throughout the performance, exposed to whatever weather the skies chose to pour down upon them. Above the back of the platform or stage proper was an upper stage or balcony running out from the first tier of boxes. Here the actors appeared when the stage directions read " enter

above " or " aloft "—directions we find so frequently in
Shakespeare. This upper stage served for Juliet's balcony,
Jessica's window, the walls of Flint Castle in " Richard II,"
of Angiers in " King John," or Harfleur in " Henry V," the
Tower of London in " 2 Henry VI," Cleopatra's monument,
a bedchamber in the Induction to " The Taming of the
Shrew," and many other purposes.

What the upper stage was meant to represent was, unless
indicated by a board, deduced by the audience from the
dialogue. The beautiful scenery of to-day, of course, leaves
no doubt in the audient mind and does not require it to
conjecture whether it is viewing Juliet's bedroom or the
walls of Flint.

When the upper stage was not required in the particular
play down for presentation, it was allotted to the spectators
like the rest of the gallery of which it formed a part. Very
frequently it was filled with the musicians, who provided the
music before the play began and commonly between the acts
as well. It was not unusual, however, for actors, musicians,
and a few spectators into the bargain to crowd into the upper
stage together during the course of a performance.

Beneath the upper stage was another distinctive feature of
the Elizabethan theatre known as the recess or rear-stage.
This was formed by curtains hung from the outer edge of the
upper-stage, which fell in such a way as to leave the side
doors to the main platform clear. The front curtains, known
as traverses, slid back, revealing the recess beyond. Thus the
Elizabethan producers provided themselves with an interior ;
and the common stage direction " within " indicated clearly
where it was to be used. The rear stage became in turn the
tomb of the Capulets, the caves of Timon and Belarius,
Prospero's cell, Benedict's arbour, a bed-chamber, a cavern,
and so forth. As in the case of the upper stage, the audience

B

was informed of its present character by descriptive sentences inserted into the dialogue.

High above the stage was a sloping thatched canopy, known in theatrical language as the " shadow " or the " heavens," which protected the actors from the weather. Thus the stage would escape a rain shower, which would drench the standing throng—the groundlings, as they were called—in the arena. From this " shadow " or canopy it was customary to hang tapestries ; and if a tragedy was to be presented, these tapestries would be black. Bedford's words, which open the first part of " Henry VI," " Hung be the heavens with black," refer to this theatrical usage.

Such was the primitive scenery of the Elizabethan play-house. It afforded little help to the dramatist, whose skill was tested to the full in making the best of it. From the religious plays of the Middle Ages the stage of Shakespeare's day had inherited the use of certain stock properties. Beds to signify a chamber, tables, benches, and flagons of wine to designate an ale-house, an altar to portray a church, and such objects as could be easily recognized, were in general service. But often no such simple method of indicating a scene was possible. When there was constant change, such as occurs in "Antony and Cleopatra " and " Pericles," recourse was had to a notice board, which bore the name of the place where the action was supposed to be taking place. The use of this board, however, was not so general as is supposed.

Indeed, Mr. William Archer and Mr. W. J. Lawrence point out in " Shakespeare's England " that the dramatist quite frequently had no particular place in mind when writing some of his scenes, and the attempt to supply a definite location immediately brings one in conflict with the dialogue. Again, the actors entering the stage doors at the back of the platform may be spoken of as in a certain named spot, while as they walk to the front of the long stage, they may be considered as having passed to another place altogether. And this may easily occur in the one scene. In fact, it does so occur in " Julius Cæsar." Artemidorus, the soothsayer, it will be remembered, tries to waylay Cæsar with a warning of his peril, and is commanded to " come to the Capitol." Immediately afterwards Cæsar is spoken of as having entered the Capitol where the other events of the scene take place.

The rough and simple scenery was often, then, of little help to the audience in recognizing in what country or setting the play was supposed to be laid. Sir Philip Sidney in his "Apology for Poetry " sneered at the failure of the theatre to explain the geography of its drama with any lucidity. His criticism was biting and derisive. He laughed at the actor's necessity of telling the audience where he was before the plot of the play could be understood. He jeered at the feeble devices of showing a few flowers to represent a garden, four or five men to import an army, a monster to signify a cave, and the news of a shipwreck to imply a rocky sea-coast. Shakespeare himself was conscious of the shortcomings of the stage mechanics. In the prologue to " Henry V " he apologises for bringing so mighty a personage on " this unworthy scaffold." " Can this cockpit," he asks, " hold the vasty fields of France ? Or may we cram within this wooden O the very casques that did affright the air at Agincourt ? " He sighs for " a kingdom for a stage," for " princes to act," and an audience of monarchs. Such might be worthy of his theme. But fettered as he is by the limitations of the theatre, he confesses that he must work on the imagination of his audience. They must " piece out " the theatre's " imperfections with their thoughts." They must divide one man into a thousand parts, believe they see horses when the actors speak of them, " make imaginary puissance," and with their thoughts deck out their kings and " carry them here and there."

If scenic resources were so meagre that the audience had to be acquainted through the actors' mouths of the location of the scene and its main features, then, obviously, the representation of natural phenomena could only be satisfactorily given by word-pictures. Shakespeare, be it remembered, had none of the ingenious lighting devices that make appropriate settings so easy for the modern dramatist to obtain. He could not even avail himself of the simple expedient of plunging his stage into total darkness. The performances of his plays began at two or three o'clock in the afternoon, after the mid-day dinner. They would be over before daylight began to wane. Indeed, they appear to have lasted only about two hours, judging by the prologues to " Henry VIII " and " Romeo and Juliet." The Prologue to " Henry VIII " promises the audience, if they be still and willing, he'll undertake that they shall have their money's worth " richly in two short hours." The Chorus in " Romeo and Juliet " announces that the tragedy is " now the two hours' traffic of our stage." It is difficult to see how a five-act drama could be completed in that time. There can have been no waits nor intervals, and an abbreviated form, or a portion only, must have been presented. From our point of view, however, it is important to understand that, his plays being performed in the afternoon, Shakespeare had no help whatsoever from artificial lighting with its illusory possibilities and power to affect and influence an audience.

Such being the limitations of theatrical production, the poet was forced to rely upon the might of his pen and the enunciation of the actor to convey a convincing picture to his hearers of brilliant sunshine, the fading light of evening, the breaking of the dawn, cold winds, moonlight, or gathering clouds. Besides these incidental concomitants, he had to put scenery into his lines to describe the heath, palace, sea-coast, ship, street, wood, or battlefield where his players were supposed to be. Further, he had to describe the battle, shipwreck, storm, or earthquake, which was a material incident of his plot. Hence we have those long, and often very beautiful, passages setting forth atmosphere, circumstance, and attendant phenomena, which would have been lost to literature had the dramatist lived in an age when the mechanical side of the theatre was far developed.

Only in one direction did Shakespeare receive any outside assistance. The Elizabethans experimented to a considerable extent in sound effects. Flourishes on the trumpets announced the approach of the great ones of the earth, and " alarums and excursions " were indicated throughout the plays to present the noise and clatter of battle. The rumblings of thunder and the fury of the storm were simulated in the tyring-house, which was located in that part of the gallery behind the stage. The noise was sometimes produced by the beating of drums : sometimes by the discharge of small cannon. It was the careless firing of two such cannon that caused the destruction of the Globe Theatre during the performance of " Henry VIII " on 29th June, 1613. The flame set fire to the thatch of the roof over the galleries, and the theatre was burned to the ground in two hours.

These realistic imitations of storm and battle seem to have been popular with a certain class of playgoer. The Prologue to " Henry VIII " warns the audience that the entertainment to follow will not please those who come to hear a " noise of targets." The common appreciation of the sound effects appears to have annoyed the dramatists, for Ben Jonson in " Every Man in his Humour " treats such theatrical appliances with contempt and dispenses with them :

Nor nimble squib is seen to make afeard
The gentlewoman, nor roll'd bullet heard
To say, it thunders ; nor tempestuous drum
Rumbles, to tell you the storm doth come.

An amusing skit on the limitations of stage expedients occurs in "Midsummer Night's Dream" (III.1. 48-73). Quince, Bottom, and company meet in the wood to rehearse the interlude, Pyramus and Thisby, which they are to play before Theseus and Hippolyta, the Duke and Duchess of Athens, in the great chamber on their wedding night. The problem of scenic effects confronts them :

> *Quince :* . . . But there is two hard things ; that is, to bring the moonlight into a chamber ; for, you know, Pyramus and Thisby meet by moonlight.
>
> *Snout :* Doth the moon shine the night we play our play ?
>
> *Bottom :* A calendar, a calendar ! look in the almanac ; find out moonshine, find out moonshine.
>
> *Quince :* Yes, it doth shine that night.
>
> *Bottom :* Why, then may you leave a casement of the great chamber window, where we play, open, and the moon may shine in at the casement.
>
> *Quince :* Ay ; or else one must come in with a bush of thorns and a lantern, and say he comes to disfigure, or to present, the person of moonshine. Then, there is another thing : we must have a wall in the great chamber ; for Pyramus and Thisby, says the story, did talk through the chink of a wall.
>
> *Snout :* You can never bring in a wall. What say you, Bottom ?
>
> *Bottom :* Some man or other must present wall : and let him have some plaster, or some loam, or some rough-cast about him, to signify wall ; and let him hold his fingers thus, and through that cranny shall Pyramus and Thisby whisper.

Now that we have a clear idea of the scenic limitations of the Elizabethan stage, the next step is to gain a due appreciation of Shakespeare's genius in overcoming them with the might of his pen. We shall confine ourselves to a consideration of the presentation of natural phenomena—the special subject of our study.

Except for efforts to reproduce realistic sound effects, the use of simple properties, and the somewhat crude device of a notice board, the dramatist was compelled to rely wholly upon his dialogue to convey setting and atmosphere. Examples of his skill and success could be quoted *ad infinitum*. They occur in every play. We must, therefore, restrict ourselves to a wise selection from the abundant material available. Let us begin by citing a few instances where Shakespeare felt the need of reference to natural phenomena in the opening lines of a play in order to prepare the minds of his audience for what was to follow and ensure the appropriate psychological reaction.

" Hamlet " opens on the sentries' platform before the bleak castle of Elsinore. We learn at once that it is past midnight and " bitter cold." The night is eerie and silent— " not a mouse stirring." The sentry is " sick at heart." So, in a few short sentences, the dramatist conveys a set of circumstances suitable for the terrifying appearance of a ghost. All that is necessary to word-paint the scene is contained in those few scraps of dialogue.

Take another tragedy from the years of the poet's matured powers—" Macbeth." The opening stage direction indicates " thunder and lightning," produced, no doubt, by the mechanical means we have discussed. But the dialogue is needed to complete the picture. The reference to meeting " in thunder, lightning, or in rain . . . upon the heath " is followed by the lines :

> Fair is foul, and foul is fair,
> Hover through the fog and filthy air.

Macbeth on his entry says : " So fair and foul a day I have not seen "—fair because of his victory, foul because of the weather. Here Shakespeare has recourse to the elements to intensify that weird, gruesome influence resulting from the presence of the supernatural. Thunder is associated with fear, fog with the mysterious unknown. Thus is struck at once that solemn note of black, superstitious terror that drones through the whole tragedy of " Macbeth."

" The Tempest," as the name implies, is overshadowed by the elements. Again the opening lines give the key to the dramatic setting. "A tempestuous noise of thunder and lightning heard," read the stage directions at the head of scene one. The first call, " Boatswain ! " and the answer, "Here, master," show that we are on a ship at sea. The master's order to the mariners to bestir, " or we run ourselves aground," at once reveals the peril they are in. There follows the instructions to " take in the top-sail," " down with the topmast," etc., revealing once again Shakespeare's faculty for absorbing knowledge and ability to draw upon it when occasion required. He had learned a little of how a ship was managed in a storm, and in a few crisp phrases conveyed the whole picture with its dismay, fury, raging seas, howling wind and thunder, and threat of death. Probably the poet was never in such a predicament as were his characters, but his age was one of adventure and bold enterprise on the seas, when England disputed with her mighty imperial rival the freedom of the Spanish Main. Many stirring tales and vivid descriptions must have fallen upon Shakespeare's ears from the lips of sea-faring men. Indeed, it is widely believed by scholars that " The Tempest " itself was inspired by the accounts of the wreck of Sir George Somers' ship on the Bermudas in 1609 and the subsequent life of the crew marooned on the storm-girdled island. The opening tempest returns later in the play, and thunder recurs at intervals throughout. By contrast the centre of the island is calm and peaceful, " the air breathes most sweetly," it is perfumed, the grass is a lovely green.

Other plays open with references to natural phenomena. The speech of Bedford in " 1 Henry VI " commences, " Hung be the heavens with black,"—which also had the theatrical significance already described—" yield day to night ! " Comets, " importing change of times and states," are invoked to scourge with their " crystal tresses " the " bad revolting stars," which have consented to the death of Henry V. These erratic, celestial wanderers were accounted fitting companions for so tragic an event. (Shakespeare's part in this drama was only revisionary, and probably he found these opening lines and allowed them to stand.)

The above extracts seem to imply that the dramatist had a predilection for commencing his plays on a somewhat gloomy and sinister note. We must not forget, however, that " Hamlet " and " Macbeth " are very dark tragedies, " The Tempest " treats of the magical and supernatural, and " 1 Henry VI " covers one of the saddest reigns in English history. Not all dramas, not even tragedies, had so forbidding an introduction. " Richard III," a play as full of horrors as the greatest gourmand for sensation could desire, commences with a good specimen of happy metaphor, suggesting that all is well :

> Now is the winter of our discontent
> Made glorious summer by this sun of York ;
> And all the clouds that lour'd upon our house
> In the deep bosom of the ocean buried.

" Julius Cæsar," another soul-tearing tragedy, is introduced in a strain of gaiety, with witty artisans stealing an unauthorized holiday and crowding the streets to welcome back the great conqueror to Rome.

Beautiful descriptions of the weather conditions and the caprices of the elements are an integrant part of Shakespeare's lines from prologue to epilogue. In some plays we are made aware of the passage of time by the introduction of casual remarks on the temperature, climate, and seasonable phenomena. In " Hamlet," for example, the " bitter cold " of Act I, scene 1, is evidence of winter conditions, while the flowers gathered by Ophelia, Act IV, scene 5, show that June has come. In like manner Shakespeare would insert unobtrusive remarks into his dialogue, which indicated the passage of days or hours by references to dawn, noon, sunset, moonlight, midnight, which the audience absorbed without conscious concentration on the point.

Perhaps " Romeo and Juliet " illustrates as well as any play could how the master dramatist was able to embody the sense of time into his plot by references of a scientific nature. Night follows day and day night with their identities clearly defined. When the drama opens it is day. Romeo, we learn, has been missing since an hour before sunrise. On his appearance, Benvolio tells him it has " but new struck nine." The day, we imagine, is warm and sunny, for it is the middle of July—" a fortnight and odd days to Lammas-tide," according to Lady Capulet. In the evening Romeo is present at the banquet in Capulet's house, and there he and Juliet meet and fall in love with each other at first sight. On the way home Romeo finds he cannot leave the house where his lovely Juliet is and rashly leaps the wall into Capulet's orchard.

The beautiful balcony scene follows, and the poet with a few deft touches presents a setting all aglow with romance. We learn that the moon is shining—envious of Juliet's beauty, as Romeo declares, when his love appears. In his rapture he readily compares her eyes to two of the fairest stars shining

in the sky above him and avows they put them to shame
" as daylight doth a lamp." Beneath their gaze " birds would
sing and think it were not night." When Romeo speaks,
apparently from the orchard's shadows, Juliet asks what
man is there " be-screened by night." Discovering it is
Romeo, she fears for his safety, till he reassures her with the
fact that he has " night's cloak " to hide him. Juliet is herself glad to have the " mask of night " to cover her embarrass-
ment, for she has unintentionally spoken her heart in her
lover's hearing. Never would she have allowed him to come
by such knowledge had not the dark night discovered it.
Romeo has cause to thank the " blessed blessed night," and
is about to swear by " yonder moon," when Juliet stays
him, holding the moon to be inconstant. After their long,
stolen interview, " it is almost morning."

The next scene in Friar Laurence's cell reveals plainly that
day has dawned, " the grey-eyed morn smiles on the frowning
night, chequering the eastern clouds with streaks of light."
At nine o'clock Juliet despatches the nurse with an enquiry
to Romeo as to his true intentions. At noon the nurse
returns to Juliet in the orchard with Romeo's plans for
elopement and marriage that very afternoon. The marriage
takes place, and the hot day, " the fiery-footed steeds of
Phœbus," draws on. Juliet, pacing her father's orchard, is
impatient for the " close curtain " of " love-performing
night." Meanwhile Romeo has slain Tybalt and taken
refuge in Friar Laurence's cell, where he hears that sentence
of banishment has been passed upon him. From Capulet's
lips we learn that this fateful day is Monday ; and in the
darkest hours of its night Romeo and Juliet are found
spending the precious moments in each other's arms. Dawn
is to separate them, for Romeo must fly for his life to Mantua.
The song of the lark disturbs the stillness. Romeo recognizes

it as " the herald of the morn," but Juliet, jealous of every minute, declares it was the nightingale who sang. But " envious streaks do lace the severing clouds in yonder east," " night's candles are burnt out, and jocund day stands tiptoe on the misty mountain tops." A few lines later Romeo exclaims, " More light and light it grows." Then enters the nurse to say, " the day is broke."

Romeo and Juliet are separated, and the days draw on toward that dreaded Thursday, when Juliet is to be married to Paris according to her father's desire. The final morning of the tragedy, after that sad night in the churchyard among the yew trees, dawns in appropriate gloom. The Prince of Verona talks of " a glooming peace this morning brings," when the " sun for sorrow will not show its head."

This tragedy illustrates how Shakespeare with cunning and clever strokes of his pen produced the effect for which the theatrical world of to-day looks to the electrician.

A beautiful picture of a lovely night and the gradual coming of dawn is painted by Shakespeare in the last act of " The Merchant of Venice." It is an instructive example of his skill in the dramatic use of natural phenomena. The scene is Portia's beautiful garden at Belmont, and Lorenzo and Jessica are alone. Lorenzo opens the scene with the words, " The moon shines bright " and the " sweet wind " doth " gently kiss the trees." Such a night is made for romance, and in the entrancing silence the lovers surrender to the ecstasy of the moment. " How sweet the moonlight sleeps upon this bank ! " exclaims Lorenzo ; and then bids Jessica " look how the floor of heaven is thick inlaid with patines of bright gold."

Through the " soft stillness " of the night come the returning Portia and Nerissa. They see the candle shining in Portia's hall through the door left open by the musicians.

Says Nerissa, " When the moon shone, we did not see the candle." The moon has gone behind a cloud. It peeps in and out, for later Portia cries, " The moon sleeps with Endymion." The first pale streaks of dawn are now stabbing the darkness. " This night methinks is but the daylight sick," is Portia's comment as the women's husbands and Antonio enter. " It looks a little paler ; 'tis a day, such as the day is when the sun is hid." After the fun over the rings is done with, " it is almost morning," " two hours to-day," though the moon apparently is still visible in the sky. The modern playgoer, accustomed to gradations and subtle changes of lighting, can hardly appreciate how difficult a task the Elizabethan playwright had to convey correct impressions to a by-no-means-highly-educated audience. Only a genius could do it.

Many instances could be added to those selected above of the clever technique displayed by Shakespeare in his use of natural phenomena the more surely to convey his meaning and sway the minds of his audience. A drizzling rain is falling on the night that Borachio and Conrade, the villainous henchmen of Don John, discuss their plot against Hero. (" Much Ado About Nothing," III.3.) The moon looks with " a watery eye " upon Titania and her fairies and Bottom in the wood (" Midsummer Night's Dream," III.1) ; and later Puck is commanded by Oberon to " overcast the night " and cover the stars with " drooping fog as black as Acheron." Such tricks of dramatic writing were very effective on a daylight stage, devoid of scenery, when the spoken word was practically everything.

Elizabethan playwrights made wide use of thunder, lightning, storms, earthquakes, shipwrecks, and strange appearances in the heavens, partly because noise was one of the stage effects at their disposal, and partly because the audience, being by nature superstitious, were moved most easily by the uncanny, supernatural, ominous, and terrifying. Shakespeare was no exception to the general trend of his age and enlisted these strange phenomena in his service to accompany and reflect the turbulence, mental stress, passions, and sinister designs of his characters. How fitting an attendant to that wild, barbaric tragedy of " King Lear " is the foul weather, the storm with thunder and lightning sweeping over the desolate heath in Act III ! What a setting for the terror, disloyalty, cruelty, villainy, and insanity that pervade the drama ! How the fury of the elements agree with the tempestuous states of mind of mad old Lear and the other outcasts, whom they buffet and tear in their anger ! Hurricanes, cataracts, lightning, and thunderbolts are the wild music of this play.

What a night of blinding rage and deafening noise is that which precedes the dastardly murder of Julius Cæsar ! Some of the conspirators are deeply moved by the strange sights they have witnessed. The superstitious Roman had an unholy dread of the weird, and the imperturbable Cassius is in strong contrast to most of his fellows.

Storm, darkness, fog, and filthy air overshadow the great tragedy of " Macbeth." We have seen how the opening appearance of the weird sisters predict the gloom to come. By way of contrast Shakespeare makes Duncan arrive at Macbeth's castle during a peaceful evening. " The castle has a pleasant seat," says Duncan. The air is sweet to the gentle senses. The little martlet flits to and from its nest beneath the eaves. To the audience, knowing so much, this calm is unnatural, terrifying. Horrible is the night that follows, the night when foul murder is committed on the sacred person of the king. The moon goes down leaving impenetrable darkness behind her. The unearthly screeching of the owl causes even the innocent to shudder. The winds are unruly, chimneys are blown down, and strange screams of death and lamentation are heard in the air. A vile night it was. " Remembrance " could not " parallel a fellow to it " —"A sore night " that " trifled former knowings." Congruous conditions these in a tragedy in which murder is the central act and the supernatural element looms large.

Shipwrecks were often convenient to the dramatist in developing his plot or working out a dénouement, and accompanied, as they invariably were, with storm of gale or thunder, formed a popular attraction with certain classes of the theatre-going public. We have already discussed the wreck in the opening scene of " The Tempest." Two other sea disasters occur in " Pericles." The first is described by Gower, the chorus, in the Prologue to Act II. Pericles then enters, wet from the sea, and gives a graphic account of his experiences. The second time the action is staged on the doomed ship, the setting being described by Gower in the Prologue to Act III. Pericles is on board his ship with his wife, Thaisa, and her nurse Lychorida, and is sailing from Pentapolis to Tyre when the storm overtakes them. Pericles prays to the " god of this great vast " to still the " deafening, dreadful thunders " and gently quench the " nimble sulphurous flashes." Thaisa dies in giving birth to a daughter (Marina), and the superstitious sailors demand that the dead body be thrown overboard. (This old seaman's superstition, noted by Shakespeare, is by no means dead to-day.) The storm is also felt at Ephesus ; and later in the play the child Marina describes to Leonine the fury of the night on which she was born.

Other shipwrecks enter into Shakespeare's plots. " The Winter's Tale " tells of the loss of the vessel which brought Antigonus and the baby Perdita to the shore of Bohemia

(Shakespeare's notorious geographical error). A few sentences foretell the storm, and the clown describes it. Storm and disaster at sea also play a part in the action of " Othello." It is described by Montano and other gentlemen near the quay of a Cyprus sea-port. A hurricane is blowing and a terrific sea running. The Turkish fleet is dispersed, and fears are entertained for the safety of Othello, servant of the state of Venice, whose ship has been parted from its escort in the tempest. But the pilot and his stoutly timbered ship bring him safe to port.

Terrifying phenomena invariably accompany the super-natural—a useful trick for the playwright appealing to so superstitious an audience as the Elizabethans. The most famous example of Shakespeare's use is the storm and thunder that attend the weird sisters of " Macbeth." In " Cymbeline " Jupiter descends in thunder and lightning, sitting on an eagle, and hurling a thunderbolt. Ghosts always appear in eerie, hair-raising circumstances, most usually at dead of night.

Shakespeare found weather conditions and celestial portents of great assistance in foreshadowing thrilling events to come. We have noted how often he opened his play with reference to such phenomena. I have quoted the ungovern-able rage of the tempest preceding Cæsar's murder, the uncanny silence of the night that introduces the tragedy of Hamlet, the unnatural calm of the evening before Duncan's assassination. There are many others. Battles were often foretold by heavenly omens and fought to the accompaniment of celestial fury. It was a mysterious night and a drowsy dawn that ushered in the day of Agincourt. A stormy, red-sky morning preceded the struggle at Shrewsbury. Richard III met a black dawn, sunless, when the sky frowned and loured upon him, before his defeat on Bosworth field.

Sometimes Shakespeare uses sultry heat and scorching sun-shine to intensify and influence the cruel passions of men. In "King John" Philip Faulconbridge remarks that the day grows hot, "some airy devil hovers in the sky and pours down mischief" (III.2. 2-3).

Because natural phenomena are common knowledge and enter into the experience of every man, woman, and child, soothing, delighting, disturbing, terrifying, as the case may be, they are important weapons in every dramatist's armoury. The foregoing remarks have attempted to show how the master-dramatist handled them, receiving but little assistance from ingenious mechanical device and extraneous effects, and relying almost wholly on his unrivalled command of language.

C

III.

THE SCIENCE OF ASTRONOMY IN
SHAKESPEARE'S DAY.

THE life of Shakespeare coincided with a period of astronomical discovery and progress that is without parallel in the
history of the science. Until the sixteenth century the
Ptolemaic system was the basis upon which all the astronomers
of Europe worked. It was accepted without question as true,
for it appeared to bear out ocular observation and harmonized
with cherished ideas that man had held ever since he began
to think.

The Ptolemaic system received its name from its pro-
pounder, Claudius Ptolemæus of Alexandria. A native of
Egypt, Ptolemy became the leading mathematician, astronomer,
and geographer of his time. The date of his birth is unknown,
but his working years extended from A.D. 127 to 151. Efforts
have been made to prove that he was of the kingly race of
the Ptolemies, but no evidence is forthcoming. The name was
a common one in the Egypt of his day.

The conclusions of Ptolemy were the fruits of centuries of
astronomical study and observation; and the discoveries
and deductions of Pythagoras, Heraclides, Aristarchus,
Hipparchus, and others were freely drawn upon and adopted
in the compilation of his system. His teaching, briefly, was
as follows : The earth was stationary and occupied the
central point of the universe. Round it moved, in their
several orbits, eight transparent crystal spheres. Each of

these spheres contained a heavenly body : (1) The Moon ; (2) Mercury ; (3) Venus ; (4) The Sun ; (5) Mars ; (6) Jupiter ; (7) Saturn ; (8) The Fixed Stars. There was a ninth sphere called " primum mobile," or first cause of motion, whose function was to give motion to all the others. These spheres revolved round the earth in twenty-four hours at different distances from it and with varying velocities. The friction of one sphere upon another produced a sound poetically called " the music of the spheres."

Ptolemy set forth his system in his " Syntax of Astronomy," to which the Arabian scholars gave the name of the "Almagest." Written in Greek and later translated into Latin, the theories it discussed were received with little demur by astronomers for nearly 1,500 years. The book circulated throughout the world and was regarded as an unchallengeable authority. Approved by the scientists, it was not surprising that its principles were adopted by the rest of cultured society, who appreciated the ingenuity of its reasoning, and blindly accepted by the uneducated, coming, as it did, within the bounds of their comprehension. The importance of astronomy was patent to all classes, for everybody was affected by the moods of external nature. The value of reliable data was appreciated and the worth of accurate forecast undisputed. Poets wrote of the wonder of the heavens, mariners steered by the stars, shepherds found their clock in the skies, farmers worked by the weather portents. All and sundry were astronomers in a greater or less degree ; and the Ptolemaic explanations were universally regarded as reliable, satisfactory, and true.

This wholesale loyalty to Ptolemy began, after fourteen centuries, to be questioned by a few—a very few—doubting and enquiring minds. Flaws had been noted in the doctrine by careful observers, and attempts were made from time

to time to rectify them. It was not revision, however, but
wholesale rejection and substitution that was to be the fate
of the system of Ptolemy.

The advent of the New Learning in Italy, which gave birth
to the Renaissance, not only rekindled man's interest in the
fine arts, but transformed all philosophy, religion, and
science. The awakened thought was no more inclined to
accept a dictatorship in astronomy than in any branch of
knowledge; and the Egyptian's system, with its patent
mistakes and miscalculations, was no longer slavishly and
blindly regarded as inviolable. Certain ideas regarding the
earth's motion, attributed to Pythagoras, but dropped on
account of their inherent difficulties, were more and more discussed in secret; and among those who eagerly embraced
these original and revolutionary speculations was one
destined to earn the name of the father of modern astronomy.

Nicolas Copernicus was by birth a Pole. As a young man he
became a professor of mathematics at Rome, and on his
return to his own country was given a canonry by his uncle,
the Bishop of Warmia. The appointment afforded him ample
leisure for the pursuit of his scientific studies, whence he
evolved an entirely original basis and built thereon an
astronomical design that was wholly new. He rejected
the long-cherished theory that the earth was the fixed,
unmoving centre of our universe and transferred this distinction to the sun. He taught that the earth was merely one
of a number of planets revolving round the sun, at different
speeds and at widely differing distances from it. He asserted
that the moon revolved round the earth and accompanied
our planet on its yearly journey round the sun. Further, he
declared that the apparent motion of the heavenly bodies from
east to west was caused by the actual motion of the earth
upon its axis from west to east. The discernment of these

truths by the Polish astronomer was one of the most amazing miracles of the human mind.

Copernicus set forth his discoveries in his work, " De Revolutionibus Orbium Coelestium " (the author owns a copy of the original edition), but he was in no hurry to give his solar system to the world. He realized its amazing originality and its reversal of all preconceived notions and ingrained ideas. He foresaw that there would be a stubborn resistance to a theory so antagonistic to popular beliefs ; and when he did publish his scientific conclusions, he did so tentatively, making no extravagant claims for their truth and merely presenting them as a topic for interesting discussion. Even so, the great pioneer was actually on his deathbed when the first number of his epoch-making treatise appeared in print, 1543.

All the efforts of Copernicus might have been in vain, so strong was popular prejudice against his theories, had he not been followed by three great men, Kepler, Galileo, and Newton. The Copernican discoveries aroused the fury of the Church of Rome, which conceived them to be in conflict with its own teachings and the word of the Bible. But no amount of bigoted opposition could stay the advance of astronomical knowledge. In 1609 Kepler, mathematician to the Emperor of Austria, published his great work, " De Motibus Stellæ Martis," setting forth the laws of planetary motion. This eminent German scientist, regarded as the link between Copernicus and Newton, had certain of his books banned by the Church and was compelled to fight hard to prevent his mother from being burned as a witch. But he won immortal honour. When he died in 1630, he had established for all time the truth of the Copernican system.

Giordano Bruno, that philosopher and original thinker, who was burned by the Inquisition for heresy in 1600, also subscribed to the theories of Copernicus. But it was from Galileo that the next striking corroborative evidence was to come. This great astronomer was born in the same year as Shakespeare (1564) at Pisa. After years of scientific study, he possessed himself of the new invention of the telescope, which led him to fresh exciting and wonderful revelations. He discovered Jupiter's satellites, Saturn's ring, the sun's spots, and the fact that the Milky Way was composed of stars. His investigations convinced him that Copernicus had found the truth, and he supported him unequivocally in his " Sidereus Nuncius " published in 1610. He was compelled by the persecution of the Inquisition to abjure his real opinions and state in public that he believed the earth to be stationary. Twice recantation was forced upon him, but his own convictions never wavered.

Galileo died in 1642, the year which saw the birth of Newton. Educated at Grantham and Cambridge, Newton's early studies led him to new theories on light and colour. But it was his momentous discovery of the laws of gravitation that finally established the Copernican doctrine on a foundation that could not be shaken. Newton's system was published in his " Philosophiæ Naturalis Principia Mathematica," 1687, and scientific honours were showered upon him. He died in 1727.

The foregoing historical and biographical facts show that Shakespeare's working career coincided with the great change-over from the ancient to the modern system of astronomy. Although Copernicus's great work was issued twenty-one years before Shakespeare was born, his ideas only gained ground slowly. The English astronomers, it is true, were not backward in studying the new theory. Robert Recorde referred to it in his treatise, " The Castle of Knowledge," 1556. John Field, a talented student of astronomy, confessed that he thought the Copernican hypotheses were true (1557). John Dee, highly honoured as astrologer and alchemist, gave his support (1557). Thomas Digges followed suit (1571). William Gilbert, another eminent English scientist, who published his " De Magnete " in 1600, was also an able champion of Copernicus. When Shakespeare was at the height of his power and success, the astronomers of England were in constant touch with the finest brains in the scientific world abroad and playing no small part in the astonishing progress that was being made.

Beyond scientist circles, however, this revolution in accepted astronomical truths did not attract very much notice. Most of the Copernican ideas were too original to be palatable. Men who had been educated to regard their own earth as the centre of the universe did not readily take to a theory that labelled it merely one of several planets revolving round a fixed sun. Moreover, the Churches confirmed them in their conservative attitude. Herein lies the explanation why Shakespeare makes no reference to one of the greatest scientific discoveries of all time, though it occurred in his own age. In only one instance is there a passage which could be interpreted, at a stretch, as acceptance of the fact that the sun and not the earth is the fixed centre round which the other heavenly bodies revolve. It occurs in " Troilus and Cressida " (I.3. 85-91) :

> The heavens themselves, the planets, and this centre,
> Observe degree, priority, and place,
> Insisture, course, proportion, season, form,
> Office and custom in all line of order :
> And therefore is the glorious planet Sol
> In noble eminence enthron'd and spher'd
> Amidst the other . . .

This is the only reference—if, indeed, it can be so interpreted—to the new Copernican system in the whole of

Shakespeare's plays. We shall find in our study that the old ideas of the Ptolemaic astronomy, on the contrary, occur repeatedly, though in a poetic and metaphorical sense, and not in a descriptive and scientific sense. For example, we have the following lines in " Titus Andronicus " (II.1. 5-8):

> As when the golden sun salutes the morn,
> And, having gilt the ocean with his beams,
> Gallops the zodiac in his glistering coach,
> And overlooks the highest-peering hills.

Also Ptolemaic is the following reference to the spheres :

> She's (the Queen) so conjunctive to my life and soul,
> That, as the star moves not but in his sphere,
> I could not but by her.
> > " Hamlet " (IV.7. 14-16).

Shakespeare looked at the skies with the eye of the poet. He approached astronomy in general with the mind of the poet. True, he studied the heavens closely. He knew the stars. He was familiar with the common or garden practical astronomy of the everyday people about him. But to him the sun was Phoebus with his fiery steeds, the moon was Diana the chaste, dawn was the goddess Aurora, Jupiter, Mars, and Venus were personalities, and comets were messengers of evil omen. To the inhabitants of the celestial universe he assigned the attributes of their namesakes in classical mythology. Legend interested him more than scientific fact, though both were useful to him in his poetry. But the scientific fact must be that generally accepted and understood—not some incomprehensible, newly-propounded theory of a learned astronomer. He had no use for rigid science or competing theories ; and, to judge from a passage in " Love's Labour's Lost " (I.1. 84-91), was tempted to be somewhat sarcastic at the expense of their authors :

Study is like the heaven's glorious sun,
 That will not be deep-search'd with saucy looks :
Small have continual plodders ever won,
 Save base authority from others' books.
These earthly godfathers of heaven's lights,
 That give a name to every fixed star,
Have no more profit of their shining nights
 Than those that walk and wot not what they are.

Shakespeare's indifference to astronomical systems was not shared by his literary contemporaries. In " Doctor Faustus " Marlowe gives a very fair description of the Ptolemaic doctrine in the form of a dialogue between the doctor and Mephistopheles (lines 644-678). Spenser, again, gave more than a poet's heed to the wonders of the skies, for he noted in " The Faerie Queen " (Book V, stanzas 5-6) the fact that the principal stars of certain constellations, recorded by Ptolemy as being in his day in one zodiacal sign, had by the sixteenth century wandered into another, neighbouring sign. These changes, caused by that slow motion known astronomically as the precession of the equinoxes, were set down by the scientists of the age and the correct adjustments made. In Spenser's case, what absorbed the astronomers was also understood by, and attracted, the poet. Ben Jonson, also, took a technical interest in the study of the heavens and refers in " Volpone," 1605, to the new star in the constellation Serpentarius discovered by Kepler in the previous year.

Among the literary giants of Shakespeare's day the new theories received most attention from Bacon, whose scientific mind could more easily grasp their importance and implication. Although he was aware that the Ptolemaic system offered no satisfactory explanations or proofs in the light of modern knowledge, yet he could not accept the theories of Copernicus either, and even visited them with derisive comment. He devised a system of his own, but since he clung to Ptolemy's main tenet of the fixity of the earth and the revolution of the planets round it, he merely wasted his time and labour. One useful fact has emerged from his astronomical studies, however, They reveal the matter-of-fact mind of the lawyer and the scientist, concentrated on the crucible and the test tube in its endeavours to explain the causes of phenomena—a mind, in short, which never could have glowed with the warmth, light, romance, and beauty that radiate from the poetic fancy of Shakespeare. They prove, beyond doubt, that a Baconian authorship of the plays is incredible and impossible.

Shakespeare's disregard of the mighty, competing astronomical systems is not difficult to understand. Outside the select band of scientists, the old ideas were still generally and firmly held. Opposed by the Church and declared in conflict with the Bible and the wisdom of Aristotle, the new theories could only make slow headway. Indeed, we find Milton in " Paradise Lost," written after 1660, still sitting on the fence and quite unable to make up his mind which of the two contradictory propositions is true. Shakespeare was content to leave the explanation of causes to the astronomers, and confine himself to the observation of effects, the praise of their beauty, the charm of their mystery, and the knowledge of their practical uses. How expert this knowledge was is evident from the following quotation from " Othello " (II.1. 13-15) :

> The wind shak'd surge, with high and monstrous mane,
> Seems to cast water on the burning bear,
> And quench the guards of the ever-fixed pole.

The " burning bear " is the constellation of Ursa Minor, and the guards, two stars of the constellation. According to the astronomer Recorde, the lesser bear, the most northerly constellation, was the chief guide to Elizabethan mariners. The name of " guards " for the two stars comes, says this authority, from the Spanish word " guardare," meaning " to look," i.e., looked at by the seamen captains.

While Shakespeare was aware of the sailors' practice of navigating by close observance of the heavens, " sailing by the star " (" Much Ado About Nothing," III.4. 58), he was also familiar with the trick of landsmen of telling the time by similar means. A reference occurs in " 1 Henry IV " (II.1. 1-3).

> *First Carrier :* Heigh ho ! an it be not four by the day, I'll be hanged : Charles' wain is over the new chimney, and yet our horse not packed !

(Charles' wain was the popular name for the stars of the Great Bear). Another reference occurs in " Julius Cæsar " : Brutus says, " I cannot, by the progress of the stars, give guess how near to-day " (II.1. 2-3).

In addition to the spontaneous appreciation of the beauty of the heavens, and apart from the superstitious beliefs in planetary influence and the reliability of celestial portents, the Elizabethans, we note, had a practical use for celestial phenomena. Shakespeare refers to them repeatedly in this connection, and only in such degree can he be considered an astronomer. Primarily he was the poet, who did not look at the skies with the cold eye of the scientist, but with the joy of the nature-lover. There are three direct references in the plays to the astronomer, but in each case it is the astrologer of whom the dramatist is thinking. The terms seem to have been used indifferently by the writers of the age ; and it is not difficult to believe that astrology would make the greater appeal to Shakespeare's imagination.

One small matter of interesting conjecture requires notice before these remarks on the astronomy of Shakespeare's

day are concluded.   For the first time the astronomers had
the aid of that wonderful invention, the telescope.   Without
it such a golden era of astronomical discovery would have
been impossible.   It is debatable to whom the real credit
for the invention is due, but English scientists were using
an instrument they called " perspective glasses " before the
turn of the century.   Many believe that Shakespeare was
referring to the early telescope in the following quotation
from "All's Well That Ends Well " (V.3. 47-49) :

> Where the impression of mine eye infixing,
> Contempt his scornful perspective did lend me,
> Which warp'd the line of every other favour.

Another reference occurs in " Richard II " (II.2. 16-20) :

> For sorrow's eye, glazed with blinding tears,
> Divides one thing entire to many objects ;
> Like perspectives, which, rightly gazed upon,
> Show nothing but confusion, eyed awry,
> Distinguish form.

The word " perspective " also appears in " Twelfth Night "
(V.1. 224).   The Temple Shakespeare, dealing with the first
quotation, describes " perspective " as " a glass so cut as
to produce an optical deception " ; and it is possible that the
poet was not referring to the telescope at all, but, as
" Shakespeare's England " suggests, to a toy popular at the
time.

IV.

THE ASTROLOGY OF THE ELIZABETHANS.

THE science of astrology was founded on the belief that the heavenly bodies exerted a direct influence upon the lives of men and women ; and its practice consisted of endeavours to read human destiny from the positions and indications of sun, moon, and planets. To call astrology a science is really a misnomer, for it possessed no fixed principles and was unable to offer convincing demonstrations of its claims. Even its fundamental proposition was not established, and experience proved that certain phenomena could not confidently be relied upon as predicting certain events. Astrology never, therefore, fulfilled the requirements of a science, and vanished in the dawn of our modern scientific age.

Although discredited in the light of modern knowledge, astrology is far older than the science of astronomy. When astronomy was born and grew in honour and importance, it was not looked upon as superseding astrology, but merely as a sister science. The name astrology was, in fact, retained to cover both branches ; and the term " judicial astrology " was introduced to distinguish the study of the fateful influence of the stars in human history, while " natural astrology " was used to refer to the observation of ordered phenomenon, predicting the movements of the planets, the dates of eclipses, and matters purely astronomical. The sixteenth century, with its wonderful scientific discoveries, made the word " astronomy " widely known. It passed into popular use, and was often employed incorrectly in cases where astrology

pure and simple was meant. Shakespeare was guilty of this confusion of terms as the following quotations will show :
   " Cymbeline " (III.2. 27-29) :

> O, learn'd indeed were that astronomer
> That knew the stars as I his characters ;
> He'ld lay the future open.

Shakespeare is here thinking of the astrologer and his predictions, and not of the scientist. The word " astronomer " is used in a similar sense in the following lines :
   " Troilus and Cressida " (V.1. 99-101) :

> But when he performs, astronomers foretell it ; it is prodigious, there will come some change ; the sun borrows of the moon when Diomed keeps his word.

In " King Lear," when Edmund is pretending to believe the predictions of an astrologer relating to recent eclipses of the sun and moon, Edgar asks (I.2. 164-165), " How long have you been a sectary astronomical ? " That is, " How long have you been a disciple of astrology ? "

Again, in Sonnet XIV, the poet writes :

> Not from the stars do I my judgment pluck ;
> And yet methinks I have astronomy,
> But not to tell of good or evil luck,
> Of plagues, of dearths, of seasons' quality.

In all these instances Shakespeare refers to judicial astrology, the reading of future events from the stars, which has nothing to do with the pure science of astronomy pursued by Copernicus and his disciples.

It is not difficult to understand how the universal belief in astrology arose. Ever since man learned to observe and reason, he noted the beneficial effect of the sunlight on the earth, the increase in the fertility of the soil after the rains—in Egypt the overflowing Nile was of first importance to the annual harvest—the drying properties of the winds and their aids to navigation, and the many instances in which the human race was directly affected by the activities of the heavens. In contrast to these good influences, he saw the terrible havoc wrought by hurricane, storm, flood, and fire. It was natural that he should imagine that superhuman, divine powers existed in the heavenly bodies, some kindly and well-disposed, others hostile and requiring to be propitiated, but all exercising control over the destiny of man.

The beginnings of astrology are, therefore, sought and found in that cradle of civilization, Mesopotamia. Records of extensive and careful astronomical observations by the Babylonian priests date back to 3,000 B.C. They made accurate notes of the movements of the sun, moon, and five of the planets—Jupiter, Venus, Saturn, Mercury, and Mars—which they identified with their various heathen gods. They recorded their different positions and exact appearances, and noted the events of human history that occurred simultaneously. The activity of the heavenly bodies were thought to be the activity of their gods, and close scrutiny of the heavens was made to reveal the divine intentions. Special occurrences, such as eclipses, intensified the earnestness of the work. Human events and celestial phenomena were associated ; and similar phenomena would be followed, it was assumed, by similar events. But the priests, with their mass of data to consult, did not insist that identical events would come to pass, but only events of a like nature. They were definite, however, as to whether an association were good or bad.

The Babylonians only made predictions concerning the welfare of the nation as a whole and its rulers. It was left to the Greeks, who learned their astrology from Babylon in the fourth century B.C., to develop the science and apply it to the fate of the individual—the reading of the horoscope, as it came to be called. Great advances in both judicial and natural astrology were made by the Greek philosophers and scientists, who carried a more perfected system to Rome and Egypt. The Arab astronomers borrowed from them wholesale, and the Greek ideas were adopted by the Jews and Christians of the Middle Ages, who made them their own, and dignified them with the name of science.

At the European courts astrologers were persons of great power and influence in the fourteenth and fifteenth centuries. Educated men believed in them, as we may learn from Chaucer. Kings and princes consulted them regularly on matters of policy, and were governed by their answers. They inspired terror among the ignorant and superstitious. It is during this period that we find the anxiety to link all other sciences to astrology, the aim in every case being to read the future and gain helpful and guiding foreknowledge. Metals, for instance, had long been allotted to the various heavenly bodies—gold to the sun, silver to the moon, copper to Venus, etc. For this reason the more-recently discovered metal was given the name of Mercury. Animals, again, were placed under one or other of the planets. Certain colours were associated with them—grey with Saturn, white with Jupiter, etc. Days of the week were named after them. Even parts of the body were ruled by them, the brain by Saturn, the liver by Mercury, and so on. (A Shakespearian reference to this old belief occurs in "Twelfth Night," and will be quoted later.) The influence of astrology had therefore been steadily increasing in the pre-Shakespearian centuries, and taken firm hold of human credence.

There was little serious effort to challenge the position of astrology during the days of Elizabeth. A few isolated voices were raised against its structure of superstition, consequent upon the tremendous strides that astronomy was making amongst the disciples of Copernicus. But so deeply rooted were the beliefs of planetary influence and faith in celestial portents that astrology successfully resisted all attack, whether by way of argument or ridicule, until the sixteenth century was past. Even those well versed in pure astronomy did not neglect the astrological branch. Tycho Brahe, the great Danish astronomer and Kepler's teacher, practised it. In fact, his prediction of future events on the appearance of the comet of 1577 was one of those rare cases where all the important details of the prophecy were fulfilled. He foretold that a prince would be born in the north, who would lay waste Germany, and vanish in 1632. Gustavus Adolphus was born in Finland, overran Germany, and died in 1632. But the writer in the "Encyclopædia Britannica" suggests that Tycho may have relied more upon political prescience than astrology for his remarkable forecast.

In Elizabethan England the mass of folklore and superstition, the universal belief in witchcraft and occult practices, and the widespread ignorance and illiteracy were ideal conditions for the success of astrology. Indeed, we find it deeply rooted and universally honoured, not only among the poor and uneducated, but as highly by the cultured and wealthy. This latter class, in fact, produced most of the practitioners of astrology, and its learned votaries were made welcome at the court. Most of the well-to-do had their horoscopes read, an important ritual observed by all who could afford it. Nor was the English court alone in this. In France astrology's position was no more strongly disputed, and even the great Richelieu tolerated it.

Among eminent Englishmen several have left a record of their interest in, and practice of, astrology. Robert Fludd, physician and philosopher and a contemporary of Shakespeare, elaborated in all seriousness a set of astrological rules

D

for the detection of thieves. John Dee is a famous name among English devotees. Elizabeth is said to have consulted him as to the most propitious date for her coronation. She is believed to have retained him at a salary and employed him on secret missions, often visiting him at his house in Mortlake. One of the achievements attributed to Dee is the magical discovery of the Gunpowder Plot. Men like Bacon and Sir Thomas Browne, the renowned antiquary, certainly attacked astrologers, but this they did on charges of trickery and incapacity, and did not question the truth of astrology itself. Another famed English astrologer was William Lilly, who is reported to have received £500 from Charles I for his advice on the flight from Hampton Court. Lilly, however, favoured the Parliament party. He read the horoscope of Cromwell, and was of immense use to the Protector in influencing the ignorant soldiery and the common people. Even to the days of Milton astrological beliefs continued to hold their ground, and many references to planetary influence occur in the works of the blind poet. But by his time the position of the science had been rudely shaken, and the ridicule later poured upon it by Swift largely discredited it among the learned classes.

It is surprising to us that in face of the scientific discoveries of Copernicus, Kepler, Galileo, and Newton, astrology was able to maintain its footing at all. The truth is that, although a few like Philip Stubbes, the exposer of current abuses, denounced astrology, the astronomers themselves were not hostile. They believed that the general interest in astrology was good for their own science. Kepler said, " Astrology is the foolish daughter of a wise mother, and for one hundred years past, this wise mother could not have lived without the help of her foolish daughter." As the truths of astronomy became more widely promulgated, so the sister science declined. But it cannot even now be said to be defunct, and has a characteristic successor in palmistry. The language we speak to-day is sprinkled with words born in the practice of the astrologers. We have the days of the week named after the planets. We employ freely such adjectives as jovial, mercurial, and saturnine. We still speak of things as " disastrous," astra meaning the stars, and we still " consider " our plans, the literal translation of the Latin words, " *con sidere*," being " with the star." Which of us, again, when his affairs turn out well, does not " thank his lucky stars " ?

In studying the question of Shakespeare's astrology, we are faced with a dual aspect of the problem : What was his private attitude as a man of learning, and what was the attitude he assumed as a popular dramatist ? I shall hope to show that these two attitudes were very different.

As a working dramatist out to please his public, Shakespeare, like the clever business man he was, adopted the current astrological beliefs. This course would be popular with his audience, and on popularity depended his financial success and literary reputation. This course he usually pursued, whether dealing with ghosts, witches, fairies, folklore, or other cherished ideas and superstitions ; and it is often difficult to detect the dramatist's own convictions among those he attributes to his various characters. Here and there, however, we feel sure that we are face to face with the real Shakespeare, and not with one of his puppets.

A study of the plays reveals unmistakably that planetary influence, the main point of the astrological creed, is accepted by Shakespeare the dramatist. (We shall consider Shakespeare the man and thinker later.) The belief that men and women are the helpless playthings of the stars is repeated over and over again in his works, and the heavenly bodies are acknowledged to be the dispensers of good and evil. The following quotations are typical :

"King Lear" (IV.3. 34-35) :

Kent :   It is the stars,
      The stars above us, govern our conditions.

Ibid. (I.1. 111-115) :

Lear :   For, by the sacred radiance of the sun,
      The mysteries of Hecate, and the night ;
      By all the operation of the orbs
      From whom we do exist and cease to be ;
      Here I disclaim. . . .

"The Winter's Tale" (I.2. 424-429) :

Camillo :   Swear his thought over
      By each particular star in heaven and
      By all their influences, you may as well
      Forbid the sea for to obey the moon,
      As or by oath remove or counsel shake
      The fabric of his folly.

The astrologers affirmed that the fate of men and women depended upon the planet or star under which they were born and its relation to other stars and planets at the time. Thus, the first step in reading the horoscope was to ascertain the date of birth. Some great men concealed their true natal day until they heard what the astrologers had to say about it. An unfavourable prediction sometimes brought death to the court astrologer from an irate prince. Shakespeare's references to birth under a lucky or evil star are numerous. In "Cymbeline" we learn from Jupiter himself that Posthumus was born under "Our Jovial star" (V.4. 105), and that happy times are in store for him. Equally fortunate was Beatrice, who declares in "Much Ado About Nothing," "There was a star danced, and under that I was born" (II.1. 348-350). In "Two Gentlemen of Verona" (II.7. 73-75), we read :

> Base men, that use them to so base effect !
> But truer stars did govern Proteus' birth :
> His words are bonds. . . .

In " The Winter's Tale " (IV.3. 24-26), Autolycus says of himself :

> My father named me Autolycus ; who being, as I am, littered under Mercury, was likewise a snapper-up of unconsidered trifles.

Helena attributes Monsieur Parolles' immersion in the wars to the fact that he was born under Mars. " All's Well That Ends Well " (I.1. 204-214) :

> *Helena :* Monsieur Parolles, you were born under a charitable star.
> *Parolles :* Under Mars, I.
> *Helena :* I especially think under Mars.
> *Parolles :* Why under Mars ?
> *Helena :* The wars have so kept you under, that you must needs be born under Mars.
> *Parolles :* When he was predominant.
> *Helena :* When he was retrograde, I think, rather.
> *Parolles :* Why think you so ?
> *Helena :* You go so much backward when you fight.

To be born when the heavenly signs were unpropitious was a terrible fate for the unlucky child and presaged a life of storm and disaster. Pericles' daughter, Marina, had the " rudeliest welcome " to the world, for she was born on her father's ship at the height of the tempest. Pericles prays for a quiet life for his daughter in spite of these evil omens :

> Happy what follows !
> Thou hast as chiding a nativity
> As fire, air, water, earth and heaven can make,
> To herald thee from the womb.
>
> ("Pericles," III.1. 31-34.)

This is in contrast to circumstances attending the birth of Antiochus's daughter in the same play (I.1. 10-11). Then, we learn :

> The senate-house of planets all did sit
> To knit in her their best perfections.

According to the astrologers, if at one's birth good stars were opposite, in opposition, that is to say, good fortune would be denied one. Good planets in opposition brought unavoidable disaster. Richard III, in the play of that name (IV.4. 215-217), says of the little Princes :

> Lo, at their births good stars were opposite
>
> . . . . . .
>
> All unavoided is the doom of destiny.

The same idea is referred to again farther on in the same scene (401-405), when Richard exclaims :

> Day, yield me not thy light ; nor, night, thy rest !
> Be opposite all planets of good luck
> To my proceedings, if, with pure heart's love,
> Immaculate devotion, holy thoughts,
> I tender not thy beauteous princely daughter.

Planetary influence continued to regulate the human life long after birth, and even to the grave. The stars would pour down good or evil fortune on the individual according to their disposition. All events, rank, state, health, success, defeat, and being were under their control. A lucky man must continue to worship his star or its protection and good influence would be withdrawn. An evil star it was necessary to try to propitiate. Prospero is one of those fortunate men to whom the heavenly powers are kind, but instinct tells him that he must not neglect them.

" The Tempest " (I.2. 180-184) :

> And by my prescience
> I find my zenith doth depend upon
> A most auspicious star, whose influence
> If now I court not, but omit, my fortunes
> Will ever after droop.

The stars determine rank, wealth, and position. The ridiculous Malvolio reads in the letter, which, he believes, comes from the high-born Olivia, " In my stars I am above thee " (" Twelfth Night," II.5. 155-156). But he is assured that his Fates open their hands.

Obedience and resignation to whatever one's controlling star chooses to send may bring reward.

Sonnet XXVI (9-10) :

> Till whatsoever star that guides my moving,
> Points on me graciously with fair aspect.

To oppose the stars was the act of madness. Witness the fate of Romeo and Juliet, described in the prologue to the play as a pair of " star-crossed lovers." In " The Winter's Tale " (V.1. 44-46), Paulina remarks in surprise, " 'Tis your counsel my lord should to the heavens be contrary, oppose against their wills." Such advice would sound unbelievable folly to an Elizabethan audience.

It would seem that astrology taught that the stars were more inclined to be hostile than friendly towards the inhabitants of the earth. In the following passages they were plainly in inimical mood, and to this were attributed the misfortunes through which the speakers were passing.

" The Winter's Tale " (II.1. 105-107) :

> There's some ill planet reigns :
> I must be patient till the heavens look
> With an aspect more favourable.

" Twelfth Night " (II.1. 3-7) :

> *Sebastian :* My stars shine darkly over me : the malignancy of my fate might perhaps distemper yours ; therefore I shall crave of you your leave that I may bear my evils alone.

" 1 Henry VI " (I.1. 23-24) :

> What ! shall we curse the planets of mishap
> That plotted thus our glory's overthrow ?

Sometimes the stars intervened to strike a felling blow at man, either at his physical body or his reason.

"Titus Andronicus" (II.4. 14-15):

> If I do wake, some planet strike me down,
> That I may slumber in eternal sleep !

"Othello" (II.3. 181-184):

> *Iago* (describing the duel) :   And then, but now,
>   As if some planet had outwitted men,
>   Swords out, and tilting one at other's breast,
>   In opposition bloody.

On other occasions it happened that the good stars, which had guided and protected a man through the better part of his life, at length deserted him.

"Antony and Cleopatra" (III.13. 145-147):

> *Antony* : . . . my good stars that were my former guides
>   Have empty left their orbs and shot their fires
>   Into the abysm of hell.

In referring to the influence exerted by stars and planets upon the fate of mankind, Shakespeare often mentioned the heavenly body by name. The moon, for example, was supposed to exercise wide powers, a belief that arose, no doubt, from its known influence on the tides—" the governess of floods," as it is called in " Midsummer Night's Dream." From this came the theory that vegetable growth depended on lunar moisture, and the poet uses the phrase, " as plantage to the moon " in the same breath as " true as steel " to represent the constancy of true love (" Troilus and Cressida," III.2. 184). On the other hand, to Juliet the moon, with her frequent changes, rather stood for inconstancy, and she begs Romeo to swear his love for her by something more stable (II.2. 109) It was commonly believed that the satellite had a baneful influence on human beings generally. The following is from " Othello " (V.2. 109-111):

> It is the very error of the moon ;
> She comes more nearer earth than she is wont
> And makes men mad.

This idea is perpetuated in such words as lunacy, lunatic, and moon-struck.

According to that old rascal, Falstaff, the moon was the ruler over thieves. He says, " We that take purses go by the moon and seven stars, and not by Phœbus " (" I Henry IV," I.2. 14-16). The position of the moon was closely recorded by all astrologers investigating a case of theft or robbery. Further, one born when the moon was unfavourably placed as regards Mars and Mercury was certain to inherit a dishonest nature. The seven stars mentioned by Falstaff are the Pleiades, which also exerted an influence tending to make men rogues and thieves.

Those born under Mars were likely to be in the wars in all senses of the word, and, according to Parolles in " All's Well," it was not a charitable star. In Shakespeare we have the conventional view of Mars as the old Roman war-god, and such phrases as " Mars's armour," " mailed Mars," are common enough. Astrology declared Mars fiery, choleric, quarrelsome, the sender of wars, treasons, and murders.

Jupiter, the king of heaven in the old classical mythology, is a favourite with the poet, and actually enters in person into " Cymbeline." Such expressions as " Jove shield thee," " Jove bless thee," indicate a kindly-disposed planet, and the adjective " jovial " derived from his name is a good indication of his character. From his own speech in " Cymbeline " (V.4. 101-108), we gather that Jupiter means well by mankind :

> Whom best I love I cross ; to make my gift,
> The more delay'd, delighted. Be content ;
> Your low-laid son our godhead will uplift :
> His comforts thrive, his trials are well spent.

> Our Jovial star reign'd at his birth, and in
> Our temple he was married. . . .
> He shall be lord of lady Imogen,
> And happier much by his affliction made.

Two planets of somewhat opposite dispositions may next be considered in conjunction, since Shakespeare twice mentions them together—Venus, associated from earliest religious history with love, and Saturn, god of the power of reason. Astrology taught that Venus governed the emotions, and Saturn the brain. In " Romeo and Juliet " we learn that " Venus smiles not in a house of tears " (IV.1. 8) ; and in " Much Ado About Nothing " (I.3. 11-13) Don John says to Conrade, " I wonder that thou, being born under Saturn, goest about to apply a moral medicine to a mortifying mischief." These two planets of contrasted influences are first mentioned together in " Titus Andronicus " (II.3. 30-31), where Aaron says to Tamora :

> Madam, though Venus govern your desires,
> Saturn is dominator over mine.

The second dual mention occurs in " 2 Henry IV " (II.4. 286-287). Prince Henry and Poins enter behind, disguised, and discover Falstaff and Doll Tearsheet together.

> *Prince* : Saturn and Venus this year in conjunction !
> what says the almanack to that ?

The adjective " mercurial " indicates astrology's conception of the influence of the planet Mercury. He was associated with subtlety, trickery, craft, perjury. " Mercury endue thee with leasing " is a sentence from " Twelfth Night " (I.5. 105). Autolycus, we have seen, was born under Mercury, to which accident the scamp's character must be attributed.

The Signs of the Zodiac were familiar to a people so interested in astrology. Shakespeare talks of the sun which " gallops the zodiac in his glistering coach." In " Love's

Labour's Lost " the Princess speaks of staying remote from the world " until the twelve celestial signs have brought about the annual reckoning " (V.2. 806-808). The most interesting astrological fact, however, is the influence that each sign was supposed to exert over different parts of the body. The Ram governed the head, Pisces the feet, and each intervening part was placed under one or other of the twelve signs. Shakespeare has an amusing reference to this in "Twelfth Night," (I.3. 147-151) :

> *Sir Toby :* Were we not born under Taurus ?
> *Sir Andrew :* Taurus ! That's sides and heart.
> *Sir Toby :* No, sir ; it is legs and thighs.

As a matter of astrological fact, both knights are wrong, for Taurus was supposed to govern the neck and throat. The dramatist obviously caused his characters to make these mistakes for the entertainment of the audience.

Astrologers, closely watching the heavens, were deeply impressed by the settled order of the stars and planets, moon and sun. Although of the opinion that evil planetary influence predominated, practitioners were inclined to be more optimistic in their predictions when the revolutions of the heavens proceeded without untoward occurrence. Bodies that moved calmly and correctly in their proper spheres might be hoped to tilt the scales of destiny towards good. Says Philip Faulconbridge in " King John " (V.7. 74-78) :

> Now, now, you stars that move in your right spheres,
> Where be your powers ? show now your mended faiths,
> And instantly return with me again,
> To push destruction and perpetual shame
> Out of the weak door of our fainting land.

When, on the contrary, disorder was observed in the heavens and strange phenomena were noted, then gloomy indeed were the prophecies, and disasters in the affairs of

men were confidently predicted. In " Troilus and Cressida "
Shakespeare deals with this point. After speaking of the
ordered movements of the heavenly bodies with the planet
Sol enthroned and controlling " ill aspects of planets evil "
—a condition of affairs that all wise men must desire—he
continues (I.3. 94-101) :

> . . . . but when the planets
> In evil mixture to disorder wander,
> What plagues and what portents, what mutiny,
> What raging of the sea, shaking of the earth,
> Commotion in the winds, frights, changes, horrors,
> Divert and crack, rend and deracinate
> The unity and married calm of states
> Quite from their fixture !

Plagues were widely believed to be sent to earth from the
planets. In " Timon of Athens " the phrase, " a planetary
plague " occurs (IV.3. 108) ; and in " Love's Labour's
Lost " we read, " Thus pour the stars down plagues for
perjury " (V.2. 394).

The special harbingers of evil were those rare or un-
explained phenomena, which appeared to interfere with the
even tenor of celestial activity. Great apprehensions were
caused by the appearance of comets, meteors, and eclipses,
which were regarded as very special portents of evil. It is
on record that the comet of 1618 so frightened the profligate
court of James I that repentance and gravity sobered for a
while the frivolous men and women.

Comets were believed to foretell the deaths of kings, and
this deeply-intrenched superstition was long in yielding to
more enlightened views. Shakespeare makes dramatic use of
this belief in " Julius Cæsar." On the night before the
assassination the elements were convulsed with terrifying
fury, and dreadful signs and portents filled the sky. Even
the most hardened were deeply moved by the rage of the

storm ; and Calphurnia, Cæsar's wife, in fear and trembling, said (II.2. 30-31) :

> When beggars die, there are no comets seen ;
> The heavens themselves blaze forth the death of princes.

Horatio, in " Hamlet," recalls this awesome night, referring to the " stars with trains of fire " that foretold the tragedy. A further reference to this aspect of the comet's appearances occurs in " 1 Henry VI " (I.1. 2-5), where the Duke of Bedford exhorts the heavens :

> Comets, importing change of times and states,
> Brandish your crystal tresses in the sky,
> And with them scourge the bad revolting stars
> That have consented unto Henry's death.

Small wonder that the appearance of comets were regarded with awe and dread, when such a calamity was expected to follow. Shakespeare makes Henry IV say (" 1 Henry IV," III.2. 47), " Like a comet I was wondered at." The poet, no doubt, mixed with the shivering crowds that gazed in fear at these apparitions of the sky.

Like comets, meteors—falling stars, as they are also called— were dreaded messengers of evil. Unusual and not understood, they lit the flame of superstitious fear. The contrast between the disorder which the meteor suggested and the regular government of the heavens which was an omen of good, is well illustrated in the following passage from " 1 Henry IV " (V.1. 15-21). The King is chiding Worcester for his part in the rebellion against him and says :

> . . . will you again unknit
> This churlish knot of all-abhorred war ?
> And move in that obedient orb again,
> Where you did give a fair and natural light,
> And be no more an exhaled meteor,
> A prodigy of fear, and a portent,
> Of broached mischief to the unborn times,

A further striking reference to meteors occurs in " Richard II." Richard was depending on the support of an army of Welshmen, but his return from Ireland was long delayed, and the superstitious Welsh, frightened by unusual portents, declared that the king was dead, and hurriedly dispersed to their homes. Their captain told the Earl of Salisbury (II.4. 7-10, 15) :

> 'Tis thought the king is dead ; we will not stay.
> The bay-trees in our country are all wither'd,
> And meteors fright the fixed stars of heaven ;
> The pale-faced moon looks bloody on the earth.
>
> .   .   .   .   .
>
> These signs forerun the death or fall of kings.

Since the sun and the moon are the most conspicuous heavenly bodies, and since their light and radiance, the solar life-giving properties, and the lunar control of the seas have been noted since man first commenced to gaze wonderingly at the skies, it may be imagined with what terror and foreboding their eclipses were viewed by the ignorant and superstitious. Although by Elizabethan days the astronomers knew a great deal about eclipses and these phenomena were accurately reported by the dramatists, the common people still regarded them with awe, while their prophetic character was credited even by the educated. There was a wild scene in Edinburgh during the eclipse of 1597. Cries and screams of terror were heard in the streets, and men and women ran in panic into the churches. Even so deep a thinker as Shakespeare had an antipathy to this phenomenon. " Clouds and eclipses stain both moon and sun," he writes in Sonnet XXXV ; and in Sonnet CVII he says, " The mortal moon hath her eclipse endured." In his dramatic work once again he adopted the popular belief. " These late eclipses in the sun and moon portend no good to us," declares

Gloucester in "King Lear" (I.2. 112-113). The eclipses referred to occurred both in October, 1605, and that of the sun was practically total in England. This evil omen is referred to once more in "Antony and Cleopatra" (III.13. 153-155):

Antony: Alack, our terrene moon
    Is now eclipsed; and it portends alone
    The fall of Antony.

Othello, too, in that horrible moment after he has murdered the innocent Desdemona, cries:

   O, insupportable! O heavy hour!
   Methinks it should be now a huge eclipse
   Of sun and moon, and that the affrighted globe
   Should yawn at alteration.
       (V.2. 97-100).

Although Shakespeare for literary and dramatic reasons was compelled to adopt the old and still firmly held astrological beliefs, he was not deaf to the challenge to astrology that was sounded by the few more progressivy minds. Although we find in the plays more astrologe than scientific astronomy, Shakespeare was sufficiently impressed by the exposures of Philip Stubbes and the sober arguments of the new, practical school of thought to take considerable notice of them in his writings. Thus we find in "King Lear," a play very full of astrology, the old and new ideas set forth, compared, and contrasted. The Earl of Gloucester clings to the old faith, while his son Edmund holds advanced ideas. "Thou, nature, art my goddess," Edmund declares; "to thy law my services are bound" (I.2. 1-2). The following quotations from the same scene illustrate the difference of outlook (112-115; 116-119; 122-124; 128-144):

Gloucester : These late eclipses in the sun and moon portend no good to us : though the wisdom of nature can reason it thus and thus, yet nature finds itself scourged by the sequent effects : . . . in cities, mutinies ; in countries, discord ; in palaces, treason ; and the bond cracked 'twixt son and father. . . .

We have seen the best of our time : machinations, hollow-ness, treachery and all ruinous disorders follow us disquietly to our graves. . . .

(Exit.)

Edmund (in soliloquy) : This is the excellent foppery of the world, that when we are sick in fortune—often the surfeit of our own behaviour—we make guilty of our disasters the sun, the moon, and the stars : as if we were villains by necessity, fools by heavenly compulsion ; knaves, thieves and treachers, by spherical predominance ; drunkards, liars and adulterers, by an enforced obedience of planetary influence ; and all that we are evil in, by a divine thrusting on : an admirable evasion of whoremaster man, to lay his goatish disposition to the charge of a star ! My father compounded with my mother under the dragon's tail, and my nativity was under Ursa major ; so that it follows I am rough and lecherous. Tut, I should have been that I am, had the maidenliest star in the firmament twinkled on my bastardizing.

Gloucester's legitimate son, Edgar, approaches. He stands in Edmund's path to ownership of the Gloucester estates, and the bastard is determined to play him false and deprive him of his inheritance. He laughs to himself, sarcastically murmuring, " O, these eclipses do portend these divisions ! " (I.2. 148-149). When Edgar reaches him, he assumes a doleful expression and simulates a belief in an astrologer's terrible prognostications in regard to the recent eclipses. " Do you busy yourself about that ? " asks Edgar in surprise. " I promise you, the effects he writ of succeed unhappily," replies the deceitful Edmund, and instances a string of disasters, until Edgar remarks, " How long have you been a sectary astronomical (a disciple of astrology) " ? (I.2. 155-157, 164).

In any Shakespearian study there is always the difficulty of distinguishing between the dramatist's own beliefs and opinions and those which he attributes to his characters. A careful reading of this scene in " King Lear," however, leaves one convinced that the progressive, enlightened views of Edmund were Shakespeare's own. We know that he was responsive to new ideas, and the argument in these lines rings true. Moreover, we have strong corroborative evidence from other plays. There are Cassius's famous lines in " Julius Cæsar " (I.2. 140-141) :

> The fault, dear Brutus, is not in our stars,
> But in ourselves, that we are underlings.

This is a very unlikely remark to have been made by a Roman. As a race the Romans were superstitious, and thorough believers in predestination and celestial influences. Plainly, it is the dramatist himself here voicing a great, fundamental truth. It is interesting to recall that these lines inspired a fine play by a leading modern dramatist.

In the same play, in the midst of credulous Rome, we find Casca, who is awestruck and fearful on account of the strange prodigies of the unparalleled storm, answered by Cicero in those calm and matter-of-fact tones that denote the clear, scientific thinker. " Are you not moved ? " Casca asks in trembling surprise. Cicero seems to shake his head, and, while acknowledging that " it is a strange-disposed time," adds (" Julius Cæsar," I.3. 34-35) :

> But men may construe things after their fashion,
> Clean from the purpose of the things themselves.

Another very significant passage is put into the mouth of Helena in " All's Well " (I.1. 231-234) :

E

> Our remedies oft in ourselves do lie,
> Which we ascribe to heaven : the fated sky
> Gives us free scope ; only doth backward pull
> Our slow designs when we ourselves are dull.

Shakespeare's own scepticism of the old teaching is revealed in Sonnet XIV :

> Not from the stars do I my judgement pluck ;
> And yet methinks I have astronomy,
> But not to tell of good or evil luck,
> Of plagues, of dearths, of seasons' quality ;
> Nor can I fortune to brief minutes tell,
> Pointing to each his thunder, rain and wind,
> Or say with princes if it shall go well,
> By oft predict that I in heaven find :
> But from thine eyes my knowledge I derive. . . .

Not only do the above lines give an indication of the trend of the poet's own thought, but they are an interesting commentary on the practice of the astrologers of the day. Against these same astrologers a biting satire occurs in the words of Cardinal Pandulph in "King John" (III.4. 153-159) :

> No natural exhalation in the sky,
> No scope of nature, no distemper'd day,
> No common wind, no customed event,
> But they will pluck away his natural cause
> And call them meteors, prodigies and signs,
> Abortives, presages and tongues of heaven,
> Plainly denouncing vengeance upon John.

Finally, we may quote from the scene in the first part of " Henry VI," where Glendower, the Welsh leader, and the impulsive Hotspur almost come to an open quarrel over these old beliefs. Glendower says (III.1. 13-17) :

> . . . at my nativity
> The front of heaven was full of fiery shapes,
> Of burning cressets ; and at my birth
> The frame and huge foundation of the earth
> Shaked like a coward.

To which Hotspur irreverently replies that so it would have done if his mother's cat had kittened. Glendower angrily repeats that the earth trembled at his birth, and Hotspur as stoutly affirms that the trembling was due to natural causes. The argument becomes heated. Glendower holds tenaciously to the old superstitions, and Hotspur stands as firmly for practical common-sense. It is all the peace-making Mortimer can do to calm them down. Shakespeare would surely never have allowed one of his characters to ridicule the hoary, time-honoured beliefs, as he makes Hotspur do in this passage, had he one shred of reverence left for them. Clearly, he had arrived at the stage when he regarded them as nonsense.

Our final conclusion must be, then, that as a poet and a working dramatist he adopted and accepted the affirmations of astrology, but that as the progressive, practical philosopher and thinker that he really was, he knew that self-responsibility and the power of each individual to work out his own salvation, revolutionary though the ideas might sound in his age, were the truths of the universe.

V.

THE ART OF THE ALCHEMIST.

In its narrow sense, the art of the alchemist consisted of an attempt to change base metals into gold. Some claimed to be able to do this ; others, more honest, were engaged in research to discover how it could be done. The idea appears to have originated among the Greeks of Alexandria. The jewellers in Egypt had developed great skill in making imitation gold and silver from inferior material for use in their manufacture. These workers, however, made no claim to transmutation. They did not deny that the results of their work, realistic as they appeared, were counterfeit. Their success, however, gave impulse to the question whether it were not possible actually to change one metal into another.

In this way there grew up an art, which was practised assiduously throughout the Middle Ages, and which attracted men of diverse character to a study of its secrets. The opportunity it afforded for dishonest dealing induced more rogues than honest investigators to style themselves alchemists ; and we find Chaucer moved to expose their roguery in the " Canterbury Tales." Nevertheless, the alchemists were extremely popular with all classes of credulous society, who were inclined to take them at their own valuation. Some were given official positions at the royal courts, where, as a rule, all that the monarchs gained in return for their favour was a great increase in the circulation of spurious coins.

The art of alchemy was based on the hypothesis that the *prima materia*, that is primary or primitive matter, filled all space and composed all substances. This primary matter took to itself certain qualities, namely, hot or cold, dry or moist. In any given substance the combinations could be hot and dry, hot and moist, cold and dry, cold and moist. So were recognized four classes of matter : fire, air, earth, and water, known as the four elements. The hope of the alchemist was to find a means of taking away the added qualities, and so obtaining the primary matter itself ; then by the infusion of qualities selected at will to produce the substance or compound desired.

The perfect compound was that in which the elements were so ideally proportioned that no one predominated. Among inanimate bodies this perfection was reached in gold. All metals consisted of earth, fire, and water in varying degree. They also contained the qualities of sulphur, mercury, and salt. But, apart from gold, the metals were defective or diseased in some particular, and the aim of the alchemist was to cure this disease, and so make the base metal perfect—in other words, turn it into gold. The metals recognized, and the planets to which they were astrologically assigned, were as follows : gold (Sun), silver (Moon), copper (Venus), lead (Saturn), tin (Jupiter), iron (Mars), and quicksilver (Mercury).

The much-desired transmutation of those base metals, in which the qualities of sulphur, mercury, and salt were not perfectly blended, into gold, where the proportion was exactly right, was to be effected by what was termed the Philosophers' Stone. This Philosophers' Stone was a medicine, an element, mixture, or solid substance which, when applied, would cure the disease or defect in any metal and so produce the perfect—gold. The discovery of the exact nature and composition of the Philosophers' Stone was the great aim of all alchemy.

Analogous to the idea that the baser metals were chemically imperfect was the belief that a diseased human body resulted from a wrong mixture of the elements. As lead, copper, and the like were to be turned into gold by the application of a medicine, so was the sick body to be made healthy by a similar process. In this connection the Philosophers' Stone was called the Elixir of Life. Although the idea of a universal medicine was an old one and had originally come from China, it did not engage the minds of the alchemists to the same extent as the transmutation of metals until the coming of Paracelsus.

Paracelsus was the name assumed by a theosophist, physician, and chemist, who was born near Zurich in 1493. He was taught alchemy, astrology, and medicine by his father, and became a wandering scholar to all parts of Europe. He made some fortunate cures, which enabled him to claim to have found the precious Elixir of Life, which healed all ailments and prolonged life indefinitely. His reputation grew to an enormous extent, and, but for the vileness of his private life, he would have reached a position of power and wealth. Despite his mistakes and the extravagance of his claims, however, he was right in asserting that the real aim of alchemy should be to promote bodily health and not to convert base metals to gold. It is eloquent of his influence on the art, that since his day chemistry has occupied an important place in all medical education.

By the reign of Elizabeth alchemy in England had passed its most palmy days. These occurred during the Wars of the Roses. The practice of the art was now forbidden by statute, but, despite this embargo, the alchemists continued to search for the Philosophers' Stone and Elixir of Life, or to deceive gullible folk with the assertion that they held the secret. The dishonest tricksters, who far outnumbered the honest enquirers, concentrated more on the conversion of all kinds of metals to gold than on the cure of disease. They found this much more profitable. They attracted the notice of the gamblers, the adventurers, the ambitious, the get-rich-quicks, the disappointed, and those down on their luck. They did not claim, like the astrologers, to possess supernatural powers. They were emphatic that their art was practised according to the discovered laws of nature. Nor were their clients deceived without reason. Extremely clever tricks were played by the rogues, who had a certain amount of chemical and metallurgical knowledge, through the aid of which the dupes were easily imposed upon. For example, a piece of gold would be covered by a layer of silver or copper, and would be shown to the sceptic as solid silver or copper. The application of certain powders then burned away the thin coating, revealing the gold beneath ; and the un-initiated onlooker imagined that the whole lump had been transmuted. Many of these crooks rose suddenly to fame and amassed great fortunes, only to sink to poverty again when they met with exposure or end their careers in gaol on being sentenced for coining.

A censure on the sharp practices of the pseudo-alchemists, and a satire on the amazing credulity of their victims, form the theme of one of the best of Ben Jonson's comedies, actually entitled " The Alchemist." In this splendid play we have the typical fraudulent alchemist in Subtle, and a good specimen of the credulous dupe in Sir Epicure Mammon. The clever, scheming Subtle, speaking an impressive and unintelligible jargon, plays on the avaricious and profligate longings of Mammon, and with plausible argument induces him to put more and yet more money into the experiments, sedulously keeping the glittering end in view. Excuses for delaying the final projection, as the last stage of the transmutation was called, are framed with convincing ingenuity. Mammon is urged to bring all his brass, pewter, iron, and every kind of metal for Subtle to turn into gold. But the matter is never completed. Mammon is trapped into an immoral intrigue, which causes the alchemist's furnace to blow up at the critical moment, leaving nothing but a peck of coals.

Although men like Ben Jonson poured ridicule on the alchemist's claims, and exposed the mass of trickery that had been fostered by the art, yet encouragement was forthcoming from influential people like the Earl of Leicester. Even Elizabeth herself took practitioners under her protection, and gave them special permission to conduct their experiments. There was the case of Cornelius de Alveto, or de Lannoy, who was given accommodation at Somerset House on the understanding that he would make gold for the Queen, and was apparently in high favour until discovered in an intrigue to restore the fortunes of a Swedish princess exiled in England. The learned John Dee, again, whom we have already noticed in connection with astronomy and astrology, devoted many years to alchemy, and became involved with a clever impostor named Kelly, who had been arrested for forgery and coining. They were joined by a ruined nobleman from Bohemia named Laski. Their magical practices and crystal-gazing were pursued actively for a few years, until Dee thought it prudent to dissolve a partnership that was proving anything but a credit to him. Many adventurers, who determined to live by their wits, found that the sphere of alchemical research gave them a glorious opportunity for exercising their peculiar gifts. Meteoric rises to fame and sudden falls to poverty or disgrace were the common fate of the Elizabethan alchemists. Nevertheless, it must not be forgotten that the serious students, though working upon false hypotheses, laid the foundations on which was to be built the structure of modern chemistry, a science which did not exist in Tudor days.

Now we may turn to the plays of Shakespeare and discover what the poet knew of alchemy, and what attitude he adopted towards it. With his wonderful fund of general knowledge and astonishing powers of observation, we should scarcely suppose that so prevalent a foible of the time would escape reference. Nor, indeed, does it. The quotations given below show that the poet had more than a superficial acquaintance with the alchemical art. At the same time his references are mostly metaphorical, and we find nothing in the satirical vein of Ben Jonson.

The main purpose of the alchemist, the changing of something base and worthless into something else, beautiful and precious, provided Shakespeare with a ready poetical simile. He uses it in Sonnet CXIV :

> Or whether shall I say, mine eye saith true,
> And that your love taught it this alchemy,
> To make of monsters and things indigest
> Such cherubins as your sweet self resemble,
> Creating every bad a perfect best,
> As fast as objects to his beams assemble ?

What is, perhaps, a more striking reference to the art occurs in " Julius Cæsar " (I.3. 157-160), where the conspirators are anxious to win the noble Brutus to their cause. Casca says of him :

> O, he sits high in all the people's hearts ;
> And that which would appear offence in us
> His countenance, like richest alchemy,
> Will change to virtue and to worthiness.

The chief fascination of alchemy for most minds was turning other metals into the all-precious gold, and Shakespeare has a number of specific references to this. King Henry V, in the play of that name (II.2. 96-102), says to the traitorous Lord Scroop :

> Thou that didst bear the key of all my counsels,
> That knew'st the very bottom of my soul,
> That almost mightst have coin'd me into gold,
> Wouldst thou have practised on me for thy use,
> May it be possible that foreign hire
> Could out of thee extract one spark of evil
> That might annoy my finger ?

In the sense of transmuting things to gold, the sun to Shakespeare's poetic fancy seemed the greatest alchemist of them all. The following beautiful passages express this thought :

Sonnet XXXIII :

> Full many a glorious morning have I seen
> Flatter the mountain-tops with sovereign eye,
> Kissing with golden face the meadows green,
> Gilding pale streams with heavenly alchemy.

" King John " (III.1. 77-80) :

> To solemnize this day the glorious sun
> Stays in his course and plays the alchemist,
> Turning with splendour of his precious eye
> The meagre cloddy earth to glittering gold.

The only reference to alchemy that could be construed as antagonistic occurs in " Timon of Athens " (V.1. 115-118), where the angry Timon beats the Painter and the Poet from his presence.

> *Timon :* Hence, pack ! there's gold ; you came for gold, ye slaves :
> (To Painter) : You have work for me, there's payment : hence !
> (To Poet) : You are an alchemist, make gold of that ; Out, rascal dogs !

The Philosophers' Stone is mentioned in " Timon of Athens " (II.2. 115-117), where the Fool, describing a certain bad character, says, " Sometime 't appears like a lord ; sometime like a lawyer ; sometime like a philosopher, with two stones moe than's artificial one." Falstaff also makes a direct reference to this instrument of wonderful power in " 2 Henry IV " (III.2. 354-355). " And it shall go hard," he says, " but I will make him a philosopher's two stones to me." The " two stones " refer, of course, to the Philosophers' Stone and the Elixir of Life. A remark relating to the effect of the stone in multiplying the amount of gold occurs in the speech of the King in " All's Well " (V.3. 101-104) :

> Plutus himself,
> That knows the tinct and multiplying medicine,
> Hath not in nature's mystery more science
> Than I have in this ring.

In an old licence granted in 1456 for making the Elixir of Life and Philosophers' Stone, occur the words :

> In former times wise and famous philosophers in their writings and books have left on record and taught under figures and coverings that from wine, precious stones, oils, vegetables, animals, metals, and minerals can be made many glorious and notable medicines, and chiefly . . . . the Philosophers' Stone and Elixir of Life.

With this it is interesting to compare the following lines from " Pericles " (III.2. 31-38) :

> 'Tis known I ever
> Have studied physic, through which secret art,
> By turning o'er authorities, I have,
> Together with my practice, made familiar
> To me to my aid the blest infusions
> That dwell in vegetives, in metals, stones ;
> And I can speak of the disturbances
> That nature works, and of her cures. . . .

In " 2 Henry IV " (IV.5. 161-163) we find another mention of the Elixir of Life.

> Therefore, thou best of gold art worst of gold :
> Other, less fine in carat, is more precious,
> Preserving life in medicine potable.

Alonso's remark in " The Tempest " (V.1. 279-280), " Where should they find this grand liquor that hath gilded 'em ? ", though more obscure, is probably also a reference to the universal medicine.

In addition to these picturesque uses of alchemical terms, it is clear that Shakespeare had some acquaintance with the theories which the alchemists held. The four elements, fire, air, earth, and water, which, we have seen, were the four classes of matter distinguished, are employed frequently by the dramatist. " Does not our life consist of the four elements ? " asks Sir Toby in " Twelfth Night " (II.3. 9-10). And in the same play (I.5. 293-294), we read : " O, you should not rest between the elements of air and earth." In " Hamlet " the four elements are mentioned by Horatio, when he speaks of the ghost, and says that at the warning of the cock crow :

> Whether in sea or fire, in earth or air,
> The extravagant and erring spirit hies
> To his confine.
>
> (I.1. 153-155.)

In " Troilus and Cressida," again, (I.3. 41), sea and air are spoken of as " the two moist elements." Shakespeare's uses of these words were not strictly accurate in the alchemical sense, but, nevertheless, they reveal a scholarly interest in the art.

The following passage from " Coriolanus " calls for comment under our study of alchemy in Shakespeare :

If you see this in the map of my microcosm, follows it
that I am known well enough, too?

(II.1. 68-70.)

The explanation of this passage is given by Robert Steele
in "Shakespeare's England." He writes: "Mediæval
science was founded almost entirely on analogy. Man, the
microcosm, was compared to the great universe, the macro-
cosm, and, as his body was thought to be formed and secreted
from blood in its interior, so the stones and metals were
formed in the interior "veins o' th' earth " (Temp. I.2. 255);
"but, as the life of the earth was incalculably longer than
the life of man, so the time taken in the formation of a metal
was thousands of years."

The above quotations reveal once again the many-sided
mind of Shakespeare, who allowed nothing to escape his
observation, absorption, and retention for future use. He
was interested, like most of his contemporaries, in the claims
and practice of alchemy, but he is not a satirical antagonist
of the Ben Jonson type, nor, it seems, a sympathetic sub-
scriber to the beliefs like Leicester and even the Queen herself.
Though he had some knowledge of the theories of the
alchemists and understood what they hoped or pretended to
do, he found their art chiefly useful to him as a source of
picturesque metaphor or poetic simile.

VI.

THE FIRMAMENT.

IN modern language the word " firmament " means the expanse of heaven, the sky.

The Hebrew word used in Genesis, "And God called the firmament Heaven," is " raqiya," which literally means " expanse." It is derived from a verb signifying " to beat out," and thus clearly and accurately describes the heavens as an expanse, a beaten out, or extended arch of the sky. The Greeks translated the word by a verb meaning to make firm or solid. The Romans retained this meaning by using their equivalent word, " firmare." Thus we get the noun " firmamentum," literally, a strengthening or support, which in English became firmament.

The change from the Hebrew description of the heavens as an expanse to the Greek and Latin interpretations as something that makes firm or strong, can be traced to the old Ptolemaic system of astronomy. It will be remembered that according to Ptolemy the vault of heaven was the eighth sphere, which contained the fixed stars and revolved outside the spheres of the sun, moon, and planets. This conveyed the idea of firm support, consolidating the whole system.

Although according to the ancient astronomers the Latin " firmamentum " was the more scientifically accurate description of the heavens, to-day the Hebrew " expanse " seems more correct. Firmament gives a wrong idea in the light of modern knowledge. The heavens are not firm, fixed, and solid, but in reality continually moving in space in obedience to the laws of motion.

Shakespeare does not employ firmament in an accurate scientific sense as the eighth sphere of Ptolemy's system, but uses it loosely as a synonym for the sky. In the following quotation the old Hebrew conception of a vast roof or arch seems to be in his mind.

"Hamlet" (II.2. 311-315):

> This most excellent canopy, the air, look you, this brave o'erhanging firmament, this majestical roof fretted with golden fire, why, it appears no other thing to me than a foul and pestilent congregation of vapours.

Certain quotations might be read as evidence of the poet's concurrence in Ptolemy's dictum that the fixed stars were contained in the firmament or eighth sphere.

"Richard II" (II.4. 19-20):

> I see thy glory like a shooting star
> Fall to the base earth from the firmament.

"Julius Cæsar" (III.1. 60-62):

> But I am constant as the northern star,
> Of whose true fix'd and resting quality
> There is no fellow in the firmament.

"King Lear" (I.2. 142-144):

> *Edgar :* I should have been that I am, had the maidenliest star in the firmament twinkled on my bastardizing.

In the next quotation the firmament is used to signify the sky above, exclusively, without any thought of spheres or astronomical theories.

"Titus Andronicus" (V.3. 17-18):

> *Saturninus :* What, hath the firmament more suns than one?
> *Lucius :* What boots it thee to call thyself a sun?

The old idea of the heavens as a roof is returned to again in the Clown's description of the storm which wrecked Antigonus.

" The Winter's Tale " (III.3. 85-87) :

> But I am not to say it is a sea, for it is now the sky : betwixt the firmament and it you cannot thrust a bodkin's point.

Often Shakespeare uses synonyms for firmament.

" 2 Henry IV " (II.3. 18-19) :

> . . . it stuck upon him, as the sun
> In the grey *vault of heaven*.

Again, we may take that beautiful description of Lorenzo in the moonlit garden of Belmont.

" The Merchant of Venice " (V.1. 58-59) :

> . . . Look how the *floor of heaven*
> Is thick inlaid with patines of bright gold.

VII.

THE MUSIC OF THE SPHERES.

In discussing in a previous chapter the science of astronomy in Shakespeare's day, we saw that the Ptolemaic theory was still the one generally accepted outside the ranks of the scientists. Ptolemy's main thesis was a fixed earth, round which revolved at varying distances and varying velocities, concentric, transparent crystal spheres, each containing a heavenly body. Whatever his opinions as a scholar and philosopher, Shakespeare, we saw, adopted these astronomical explanations in his work as a dramatist. The natural, regular, ordered movement of sun, moon, and planet was within its own prescribed sphere.

" Hamlet " (IV.7. 14-16) :

> She's so conjunctive to my life and soul,
> That, as the star moves not but in his sphere,
> I could not but by her.

" Romeo and Juliet " (II.2. 15-17) :

> Two of the fairest stars in all the heaven,
> Having some business, do intreat her eyes
> To twinkle in their spheres till they return.

In " Midsummer Night's Dream " the Fairy makes a special reference to the revolution of the moon :

> I do wander everywhere,
> Swifter than the moon's sphere.

> (II.1. 6-7.)

In the case of the sun, moon, and planets each body had its own sphere, which could not be invaded by any other body. The fixed stars had a sphere to themselves. This idea is most poetically expressed by Shakespeare in the following lines :

" 1 Henry IV " (V.4. 65-66) :

> Two stars keep not their motion in one sphere ;
> Nor can one England brook a double reign.

"All's Well That Ends Well " (I.1. 96-100) :

> Helena :   . . . 'Twere all one
> That I should love a bright particular star
> And think to wed it, he is so above me :
> In his bright radiance and collateral light
> Must I be comforted, not in his sphere.

When all the spheres were revolving with their native order and regularity, harmony was expressed ; and the sound produced by their contacts was described as the music of the spheres. An English Franciscan friar, named Bartholomew de Glanville, who was an authority on natural philosophy in the fourteenth century, wrote a most popular work about 1360, entitled " De Proprietatibus Rerum." An English translation written by Trevisa in Chaucer's day was published in London in 1533. It was republished, considerably enlarged, by Stephen Batman, a physician, in 1582. On the subject of the music of the spheres de Glanville writes : " Wise men tell that of meeting of roundnesses, and of contrary movement of planets cometh a sweet harmony . . . In putting and moving of these round worlds cometh sweet sound and accord." In the philosophy of Pythagoras this music was held to be inaudible to human ears and heard by the gods alone. It is the Pythagorean theory that Shakespeare is referring to in that superb speech of Lorenzo in " The Merchant of Venice " (V.1. 54-65) :

How sweet the moonlight sleeps upon this bank !
Here will we sit, and let the sounds of music
Creep in our ears : soft stillness and the night
Become the touches of sweet harmony.
Sit, Jessica. Look how the floor of heaven
Is thick inlaid with patines of bright gold :
There's not the smallest orb which thou behold'st
But in his motion like an angel sings,
Still quiring to the young-eyed cherubins ;
Such harmony is in immortal souls ;
But whilst this muddy vesture of decay
Doth grossly close it in, we cannot hear it.

This heavenly music is referred to by Shakespeare on a number of occasions. Pericles believes that he hears it (V.1. 228-234) :

Pericles :	But, what music ?
Helicanus :	My lord, I hear none.
Pericles :	None !
	The music of the spheres ! List, my Marina.
Lysimachus :	It is not good to cross him ; give him way.
Pericles :	Rarest sounds ! Do ye not hear ?
Lysimachus :	My lord, I hear.
Pericles :	Most heavenly music !

Two further passages may be cited.
" Twelfth Night " (III.1. 120-121) :

I had rather hear you to solicit that
Than music from the spheres.

"Antony and Cleopatra " (V.2. 83-84) :

. . . his voice was propertied
As all the tuned spheres. . . .

That discord could ever disturb this heavenly harmony was unthinkable. Duke Senior says of Jaques in "As You Like It " (II.7. 5-6) :

If he, compact of jars, grow musical,
We shall have shortly discord in the spheres.

According to Ptolemy, the laws of stellar motion required that each star should revolve harmoniously round the earth, keeping within its allotted sphere. When this happened, mankind could expect good.

"King John" (V.7. 74-78):

> Now, now, you stars that move in your right spheres,
> Where be your powers? show now your mended faiths,
> And instantly return with me again,
> To push destruction and perpetual shame
> Out of the weak door of our fainting land.

Shakespeare makes hyperbolic use of the mad idea of stars leaving their spheres.

"Midsummer Night's Dream" (II.1. 150-154):

> (I) heard a mermaid on a dolphin's back,
> Uttering such dulcet and harmonious breath,
> That the rude sea grew civil at her song,
> And certain stars shot madly from their spheres,
> To hear the sea-maid's music.

"Tempest" (II.1. 182-184):

> You are gentlemen of brave mettle; you would lift the moon out of her sphere, if she would continue in it five weeks without changing.

In our study of the astrological beliefs of Elizabethan times, we saw that a disturbance of the settled order of the universe was associated with evil and disaster. For stars to stray from their spheres was thought to be an unnatural occurrence inevitably followed by direful consequences. Antony attributes his fall to the fact that his " good stars " which were his " former guides have empty left their orbs " ("Antony and Cleopatra," III.13. 145-146). Orb in this passage, as in that from " The Merchant of Venice," quoted above, is only another name for sphere. In the same play, Cleopatra in the hour of her terrible sorrow at the loss of Antony, exclaims:

> O sun,
> Burn the great sphere thou movest in ! darkling stand
> The varying shore o' the world !
>
> (IV.15. 9-11.)

In " Hamlet " (I.5. 17) the ghost tells his son that he could unfold to him a tale that would make his two eyes, " like stars, start from their spheres." So, it was thought, any disturbance of the natural motion, on which depended the harmony or music of the spheres, was certain to be reflected in discordant human conditions.

Modern language has retained the expression originated by the old astrological belief. To speak of one as being " out of his proper sphere " is to-day common enough. Its old association, however, is smothered by its new meaning of occupation, position, and terrestrial surroundings. Shakespeare uses it in our present signification in " Hamlet " (II.2. 141). Polonius tells the King and Queen that he has warned Ophelia that, though the lord Hamlet has offered her his love, yet he is a prince, " out of her sphere," and she must entertain no thoughts of him. This is yet another example, to add to the thousands of others, where our language has been enriched by the poet's coining of a phrase, which has become an every-day figure of speech.

VIII.

THE SUN.

THE most conspicuous extra-terrestrial object is the sun. It is likewise the most important, influential, and necessary to the existence and well-being of the earth. These facts have been recognized since the dawn of human intelligence. Man's first impulse was to worship the sun as the giver of all good things. Under various names, therefore, the sun-god (Helios, Phœbus Apollo, Hyperion, etc.) held a high and honoured place in the polytheism of many ancient races, a polytheism that was generally the personification of natural phenomena.

After many ages of worshipping the sun, men next tried to explain it. We have seen that for generations the theory that the sun was one of a number of planetary bodies revolving round a fixed earth met with universal acceptance. This theory was shattered by Copernicus and the new astronomy, which completely reversed existing ideas and proved their exact opposite to be the truth, namely, that our earth was merely one of a family of planets which revolved round, and depended on, the sun. Scientists have now established that the sun, the centre of light, heat, and attraction of our universe, is 1,300,000 times the size of the earth, 867,000 miles in diameter, and 93,000,000 miles away !

These cold, mathematical statements, wonderful as their ascertainment is, make little appeal to the poetic mind, which prefers to regard the sun as an intelligent personality, one of the gods of the old classical mythology. Shakespeare adopted

78

this attitude. To him the sun was the spirit of good, pouring down his blessings upon mankind, sustaining and infusing life, and giving light, warmth, and increase to the earth. Note some of the significant adjectives he applies to it. He calls it " the blessed sun," " the beneficial sun." He endows it with divine properties—" the holy sun," " the sacred radiance of the sun " ; and confesses, " I adore the sun," " I worship a celestial sun." Its glory, majesty, and magnificence arouse his reverential love and praise. He sings of " the beauty of the sun," " the glorious sun," " the golden sun," " the sun enthroned." He refers again and again to its cheery and heartening influence—" thou sun, that comfortest," " all the world is cheered by the sun," " the all-cheering sun." He speaks often of the " sun's hot beams " ; and " fiery," " scorching," " radiant," " parching," " fair," " garish," are some of the epithets he applies to it.

The sun and its various synonyms are mentioned some 250 times in Shakespeare's works, and only a selected number of quotations can be given here. A reference to its daily passage through the arc of heaven is mentioned by way of simile in " Timon of Athens " (III.4. 12-13) :

> You must consider that a prodigal course
> Is like the sun's ; but not, like his, recoverable.

An acknowledgment of the sun as king of all the heavenly bodies is contained in the following lines from " Pericles " (II.3. 37-40) :

> Yon king's to me like to my father's picture,
> Which tells me in that glory once he was ;
> Had princes sit, like stars about his throne,
> And he the sun for them to reverence.

The action of the sun in causing evaporation is one of the few Shakespearian solar references that can be classified as scientific :

" Timon of Athens " (IV.3. 1-2) :

> O blessed breeding sun, draw from the earth
> Rotten humidity.

Ibid (IV.3. 439-440) :

> The sun's a thief, and with his great attraction
> Robs the vast sea. . . .

" Tempest " (II.2. 1-2) :

> All the infections, that the sun sucks up
> From bogs, fens, flats. . . .

The common spectacle of the sun playing hide-and-seek among the clouds provided the poet with an obvious simile. Two quotations will suffice to illustrate his clever use of it.

" I Henry IV " (I.2. 221-227) :

> Yet herein will I imitate the sun,
> Who doth permit the base contagious clouds
> To smother up his beauty from the world,
> That, when he please again to be himself,
> Being wanted, he may be more wonder'd at,
> By breaking through the foul and ugly mists
> Of vapours that did seem to strangle him.

" Rape of Lucrece " (372-375) :

> Look, as the fair and fiery-pointed sun,
> Rushing from forth a cloud, bereaves our sight ;
> Even so, the curtain drawn, his eyes begun
> To wink, being blinded with a greater light.

That curious phenomenon known as " Parhelia " was also noted by Shakespeare. A parhelion is a mock sun, which appears in the form of a bright light, a duplication of the real sun, and close to it. Two or more parhelia are sometimes seen, their apparent existence being due to ice-crystals in the air. Shakespeare introduces this celestial apparition into " 3 Henry VI " (II.1. 25-32), and correctly places it in the morning, for mock suns are usually seen when the sun is at a low altitude. Like all unusual phenomena, the parhelion was regarded as an omen, and is seen here by Edward and Richard at Mortimer's Cross shortly before they hear of their father's death.

> *Edward :* Dazzle mine eyes, or do I see three suns ?
> *Richard :* Three glorious suns, each one a perfect sun ;
> Not separated with the racking clouds,
> But sever'd in a pale clear-shining sky.
> See, see ! they join, embrace, and seem to kiss,
> As if they vow'd some league inviolable :
> Now are they but one lamp, one light, one sun.
> In this the heaven figures some event.

The dramatist, no doubt, obtained his information about the parhelia from his authority, Holinshed, who wrote : "At which tyme the sun (as some write) appeared to the Earl of March like *three sunnes*, and sodainely joyned altogether in one, upon whiche sight hee tooke such courage, that he fiercely setting on his enemyes put them to flight."

The poet often spoke of the sun by one of its old names in pagan worship. Sol, the Latin word for sun and the name of the old Italic sun-god, occurs in " Troilus and Cressida " (I.3. 89) : " The glorious planet Sol in noble eminence enthroned and sphered." But by far the most popular with Shakespeare among solar synonyms was Phœbus. The later Greek mythology identified the god Apollo with the sun. In this connection they added to his name the epithet " phœbus," meaning " bright "—Phœbus Apollo. More shortly the sun became known as Phœbus ; and he was picturesquely described as riding in a wheeled chariot and driving his fiery steeds across the heavens, his course representing the day, dawn to sunset. Shakespeare delighted in this poetical figure of the sun. It appears in fourteen of his plays, sometimes more than once. Such phrases as " the radiant fire of flickering Phœbus' front," " carbuncled like holy Phœbus' car," are typical.

At dawn "the youthful Phœbus" is represented as starting off on his daily journing.

" Much Ado About Nothing " (V.3. 25-27) :

> . . . and look, the gentle day,
> Before the wheels of Phœbus, round about
> Dapples the drowsy east with spots of grey.

" Cymbeline " (II.3. 21-24) :

> Hark, hark ! the lark at heaven's gate sings,
> And Phœbus 'gins arise,
> His steeds to water at those springs
> On chaliced flowers that lies.

" I Henry IV " (III.1. 221-222) :

> The hour before the heavenly-harness'd team
> Begins his golden progress in the east.

Phœbus' passage to noon is imaged as a climb up a steep hill : " Now is the sun upon the highmost hill of this day's journey " (" Romeo and Juliet," II.5. 9-10). Thence the way towards the sea and sunset is downward. To Shakespeare's fancy a long and wearisome day called up a picture of footsore horses in the god's chariot.

" Tempest " (IV.1. 30-31) :

> . . . I shall think, or Phœbus' steeds are founder'd (i.e., footsore),
> Or Night kept chain'd below.

A beautiful poetic description of the transit of Phœbus, ending with a "weary car " that " reeleth from the day " composes Sonnet VII.

> Lo, in the orient when gracious light
> Lifts up his burning head, each under eye
> Doth homage to his new-appearing sight,
> Serving with looks his sacred majesty ;
> And having climb'd the steep-up heavenly hill,
> Resembling strong youth in his middle age,

> Yet mortal looks adore his beauty still,
> Attending on his golden pilgrimage ;
> But when from highmost pitch, with weary car,
> Like feeble age, he reeleth from the day,
> The eyes, 'fore duteous, now converted are
> From his low tract, and look another way.

Shakespeare employed the figure of Phœbus to describe the passage of time.

" Hamlet " (III.2. 165-166) :

> Full thirty times hath Phœbus' cart gone round
> Neptune's salt wash and Tellus' orbed ground.

(Tellus was an old Italian deity representing the earth). The time that has elapsed in the above case is thirty years. The next quotation refers to the daily journey.

"All's Well That Ends Well " (II.1. 164-165) :

> Ere twice the horses of the sun shall bring
> Their fiery torcher his diurnal ring.

The love-sick Juliet, impatient for the night that will unite her to Romeo, cries (III.2. 1-3) :

> Gallop apace, you fiery-footed steeds,
> Towards Phœbus' lodging : such a waggoner
> As Phæthon would whip you to the west.

Phæthon (or Phæton), that is " shining," is sometimes used as another name for the sun. More properly, however, he is the son of the sun-god, who was so presumptuous as to ask his father to allow him to drive his chariot across the sky for one day. Phœbus (or Helios) refused ; but Phæthon's mother, Clymene, added her entreaties, and the sun-god was weak enough to give way. The result was disastrous. Phæthon had not the strength to control the fiery horses, which galloped out of their usual track and nearly set the whole earth ablaze by passing too near it. Zeus (or Jupiter) was very angry and punished Phæthon by slaying him with a flash of lightning.

This picturesque myth is mentioned frequently by Shakespeare. There are two references in " 3 Henry VI." In the first the wounded Clifford groans (II.6. 11-13) :

> O Phœbus, hadst thou never given consent
> That Phæthon should check thy fiery steeds,
> Thy burning car had never scorch'd the earth !

The second occurs in Act I and is also spoken by Clifford (Sc. 4. 33-34) :

> Now Phæthon hath tumbled from his car,
> And made an evening at the noontide prick.
>   (i.e., dial point.)

King Richard II says of himself, " Down, down I come, like glistering Phæton " (III.3. 178). The Duke in " Two Gentlemen of Verona " also shows himself familiar with the old legend (III.1. 153-155) :

> Why, Phæthon,—for thou art Merops' son,—
> Wilt thou aspire to guide the heavenly car,
> And with thy daring folly burn the world.

The words, " Merops' son," refer to the fact that Phæthon was often reproached with being the son, not of Phœbus Apollo, but of Merops, the King of the Ethiopians. The accusation was, however, groundless.

Another synonym for the sun, popular with Shakespeare, is Hyperion. Though more accurately the father of Helios or Phœbus, Hyperion is used by Homer as a name for the sun-god himself, the incarnation of light and beauty. It is in this guise that the poet presents him. " Hyperion's quickening fire " (" Timon of Athens," IV.3. 184), and " Help Hyperion to his horse " (" Henry V," IV.1. 292), are two sentences that acknowledge his solar claims. More illuminating are the following :

" Titus Andronicus " (V.2. 56-57) :

> Even from Hyperion's rising in the east
> Until his very downfall in the sea.

" Troilus and Cressida " (II.3. 206-207) :

> And add more coals to Cancer when he burns
> With entertaining great Hyperion.

Hamlet compares his father to his uncle as Hyperion to a Satyr (I.2. 140) ; and later in the play, during his talk with his mother, Gertrude, in the Queen's closet (III.4. 55-56), he shows her a picture of her first husband, saying, " See what a grace was seated on this brow ; Hyperion's curls, the front of Jove . . . " and so on to the end of the laudatory description.

Another synonym for the sun, used by Shakespeare more often than Hyperion, though not so many times as Phœbus, is Titan.

The name Titanes was generally applied in mythology to the six sons and six daughters of Uranus (Heaven) and Ge (Earth). It was also used, however, as a synonym for the sun-god, and it is in this meaning that Shakespeare employs it. The reflection of " Titan's rays on earth," " Titan's fiery wheels," " Let Titan rise as early as he dare," are typical examples. Two instances occur in the plays associating Titan with a woman's cheek. The first refers to the wronged Lavinia and is used as a simile :

" Titus Andronicus " (II.4. 31-32) :

> Yet do thy cheeks look red as Titan's face,
> Blushing to be encounter'd with a cloud.

The second case is Pisanio's counsel to Imogen on the necessity of disguising herself as a man. He says :

" Cymbeline " (III.4. 162-166) :

> . . . you must
> Forget that rarest treasure of your cheek,
> Exposing it . . . to the greedy touch
> Of common-kissing Titan.

An amusing reference to Titan kissing a dish of butter is made by Prince Hal, when Falstaff enters the tavern after the affair of Gadshill and boasts of his own courage, while dubbing other men rogues and cowards (" 1 Henry IV," II.4. 133).

The foregoing extracts from the plays reveal Shakespeare's attitude toward the sun. There was nothing of the scientist or astronomer in it. Not facts and figures, but beauty, light, and warmth won the adoration of his poet mind. He regarded old Sol as a living, intelligent personality, not as a collection of gases, and decorated his lines with his picturesque legends and classical myths. Now he would word-paint the sun in all its dazzling splendour as it appeared to the eye and appealed to the heart of the nature-lover. Now he would handle it as a simile. Many instances of this have been given, and the following poetic effusion of the King of Navarre, " Love's Labour's Lost " (IV.3. 26-29) may conclude them :

> So sweet a kiss the golden sun gives not
>   To those fresh morning drops upon the rose,
> As thy eye-beams, when their fresh rays have smote
>   The night of dew that on my cheek down flows.

Now it would be in a metaphorical sense that the sun would meet the need of his pen, as in " Julius Cæsar," when he writes of Cassius' death and the defeat of the conspirators, " The sun of Rome is set ! " (V.3. 63). In all his uses Shakespeare's songs of praise for the pulsing life-centre of our universe and his gratitude for its essential blessings are those of the master-poet.

IX.

DAWN AND SUNRISE.

To Shakespeare dawn was the symbol of hope, freshness, youth, renewed strength, action, opportunity. It was the moment when man braced himself to meet his fate, be that good or bad. Hunter observed that the poet likened the new day to a lusty ploughman, brushing away the dew, and going forth to his labour. The first flush of light, chasing away the darkness of night and heralding the coming of the sun, reaches the soul in all of us. It stirred Shakespeare to sublime heights of poesy ; and he has left us descriptive passages of the most entrancing beauty, giving full rein to his unequalled gift of poetic imagery, to honour the risen day.

In a previous chapter we have noted how frequently the dramatist places his scene at daybreak. Often the dawn comes while his characters are speaking. In superb language they describe its coming. Perhaps most famous of such scenes is that poignant parting between Romeo and Juliet. The shrouded, silent hours before the day of battle are a favourite setting, and the morns of Agincourt, Shrewsbury, and Bosworth are described with stirring dramatic force. Real drama, again, enters into the meeting of the conspirators against Cæsar, which takes place in Brutus's orchard in the early hours of morning. More cheering is the passing of night in the garden of Belmont ; while relief is the emotion roused by the daylight at the end of the ghost scene in " Hamlet." Shakespeare, however, did not only use the

87

phenomenon of dawn as a playwright, but turned to it constantly as a poet for expressive and picturesque figures of speech.

Perhaps the play which contains most exquisite writing on the wonder of the dawn is " Romeo and Juliet." The moment, when beams of light triumph over the reign of darkness, is spoken of by Friar Laurence at the door of his cell (II.3. 1-8) :

> The grey-eyed morn smiles on the frowning night,
> Chequering the eastern clouds with streaks of light ;
> And flecked darkness like a drunkard reels
> From forth day's path and Titan's fiery wheels.
> Now, ere the sun advance his burning eye,
> The day to cheer and night's dank dew to dry,
> I must up-fill this osier cage of ours
> With baleful weeds and precious-juiced flowers.

While many of Shakespeare's mornings bring joy and cheerful optimism, that which steals upon Romeo and Juliet in Capulet's orchard is a hated and unwelcome intruder, for it is fated to separate the lovers. Yet the music of Shakespeare's descriptive lines are beautiful indeed. A call of a bird has broken the stillness. Juliet, desperately anxious to keep her lover for a few more precious moments, assures Romeo that it was the nightingale. But he answers (III.5. 6-10 ; 35) :

> It was the lark, the herald of the morn,
> No nightingale : look, love, what envious streaks
> Do lace the severing clouds in yonder east :
> Night's candles are burnt out, and jocund day
> Stands tip-toe on the misty mountain tops.
>
> . . . . . .
>
> . . . more light and light it grows.

The scene, referred to above, where the conspirators call upon Marcus Brutus to mature the plot against Cæsar, is set in the darkest hour before the dawn. The dramatist required to give Brutus and Cassius a few moments of private, whispered conversation, and does so by drawing the other conspirators into a discussion on the sunrise (" Julius Cæsar," II.1. 101-111):

Decius : Here lies the east : doth not the day break here ?
Casca : No.
Cinna : O, pardon, sir, it doth, and yon grey lines
That fret the clouds are messengers of day.
Casca : You shall confess that you are both deceived.
Here, as I point my sword, the sun arises ;
Which is a great way growing on the south,
Weighing the youthful season of the year.
Some two months hence up higher toward the north
He first presents his fire, and the high east
Stands as the Capitol, directly here.

Shakespeare had accurately observed the different points in the heavens at which the sun rose at the different seasons of the year.

The first sign of dawn is described in many beautiful similes by the poet. In " The Tempest " (V.1. 64-65) it is a stealthy comer, " stealing upon the night " and " melting the darkness." In " 3 Henry VI " (II.5. 1-4) it is represented as warring against the shadows :

This battle fares like to the morning's war,
When dying clouds contend with growing light,
What time the shepherd, blowing on his nails,
Can neither call it perfect day or night.

This time of day is described in " Romeo and Juliet," as " an hour before the worshipp'd sun peer'd forth the golden window of the east " (I.1. 125-126).

After the pale light has conquered the darkness and night is in full retreat, the greyness becomes tinged with red,

G

announcing the near approach of Phœbus himself. Horatio in " Hamlet " says, " The morn, in russet mantle clad, walks o'er the dew of yon high eastward hill " (I.1. 166-167). This wonderful moment before the sun appears to view is referred to again in " Richard II " (III.2. 41-43) :

> But when from under this terrestrial ball
> He fires the proud tops of the eastern pines
> And darts his light through every guilty hole. . . .

In describing the journey of Phœbus Apollo we have quoted many beautiful Shakespearian passages on the sunrise itself. A few more are appended here :

" 3 Henry VI " (II.1. 21-25) :

> See how the morning opes her golden gates,
> And takes her farewell of the glorious sun !
> How well resembles it the prime of youth,
> Trimm'd like a younker prancing to his love !

" Titus Andronicus " (II.1. 5-9) :

> As when the golden sun salutes the morn,
> And, having gilt the ocean with his beams,
> Gallops the zodiac in his glistering coach,
> And overlooks the highest-peering hills.

" Midsummer Night's Dream " (III.2. 391-393) :

> Even till the eastern gate, all fiery-red,
> Opening on Neptune with fair blessed beams,
> Turns into yellow gold his salt green streams.

Sonnet CXXXII (5, 6, and 9) :

> And truly not the morning sun of heaven
> Better becomes the grey cheeks of the east.
>
> .   .   .   .   .   .
>
> As those two mourning eyes become thy face.

" Venus and Adonis " (481-484) :

> The night of sorrow now is turn'd to day :
> Her two blue windows faintly she up-heaveth
> Like the fair sun, when in his fresh array,
> He cheers the morn and all the earth relieveth.
>> And as the bright sun glorifies the sky,
>> So is her face illumined with her eye.

Ibid. (853-858) :

> Lo, here the gentle lark, weary of rest,
> From his moist cabinet mounts up on high,
> And wakes the morning, from whose silver breast
> The sun ariseth in his majesty ;
>> Who doth the world so gloriously behold
>> That cedar-tops and hills seem burnish'd gold.

Many of the above are apt literary similes, as when Romeo cries, " It is the east, and Juliet is the sun ! " (II.2. 3). The poet delighted in such flights of fancy.

Not always does the dawn greet a radiant sun. Sometimes he is hidden or dimmed by clouds, and poetry then pictures him as discontented.

" Richard II " (III.3. 62-67) :

> See, see, King Richard doth himself appear,
> As doth the blushing discontented sun
> From out the fiery portal of the east,
> When he perceives the envious clouds are bent
> To dim his glory and to stain the track
> Of his bright passage to the occident.

Sometimes the dramatist gives us a dull morning as more fitting when sorrow or tragedy are uppermost in the thought. The sad story of Romeo and Juliet ends (V.3. 305-307) :

> A glooming peace this morning with it brings ;
> The sun for sorrow will not show his head.

In "Julius Cæsar," again, we read of a "raw-cold morning," " the humours of a dank morning."

Red sky at morning is still an ill weather portent and is mentioned by Shakespeare in "1 Henry IV" (V.1. 1), "How bloodily the sun begins to peer," declares King Henry. It foretells "a tempest and a blustering day." A more striking reference occurs in "Venus and Adonis" (453-456):

> Like a red morn, that ever yet betoken'd
> Wreck to the seaman, tempest to the field,
> Sorrow to shepherds, woe unto the birds,
> Gusts and foul flaws to herdmen and to herds.

A point to note in these references to day's beginning is the distinction made between dawn and sunrise. They are not confused. They do not mean the same to the poet. For example he writes in "Venus and Adonis" (1-2):

> Even as the sun with purple colour'd face
> Had ta'en his last leave of the weeping morn. . . .

Shakespeare was steeped in classical mythology. To the Romans dawn was the goddess Aurora, who rose from her couch at the close of every night and ascended up to heaven in her chariot from the river Oceanus to announce the approach of Phœbus Apollo, the sun, in his car. Aurora saw Phœbus start upon his journey and then bade him farewell. There are two references in the plays to this goddess of dawn, who was called Eos by the Greeks:

"Romeo and Juliet" (I.1. 140-142):

> . . . so soon as the all-cheering sun
> Should in the farthest east begin to draw
> The shady curtains from Aurora's bed. . . .

"Midsummer Night's Dream" (III.2. 379-380):

> . . . night's swift dragons cut the clouds full fast,
> And yonder shines Aurora's harbinger.

In conclusion, an interesting fragment of folk lore may be noted from the first scene of "Hamlet" relating to the

" bird of dawning." This is not the lark, who is the *herald*
of the morn, but the cock. Horatio says :

> I have heard
> The cock, that is the trumpet to the morn,
> Doth with his lofty and shrill-sounding throat
> Awake the god of day, and at his warning,
> Whether in sea or fire, in earth or air,
> The extravagant and erring spirit hies
> To his confine. . . .

And Marcellus continues :

> Some say that ever 'gainst that season comes
> Wherein our Saviour's birth is celebrated,
> The bird of dawning singeth all night long :
> And then, they say, no spirit dare stir abroad.
>
> (149-155 ; 158-161.)

X.

SUNSET.

No part of the day is more beautiful than the sunset. The sky is aglow with gorgeous hues, and fiery rays falling on earth and cloud paint all the colour of red and gold. To the artist the lights and tints whisper of loveliness divine. To the poet the entrancing picture holds a strain of sweet sadness— sadness that our fleeting life is one day nearer to its close, sweet that night brings with it the gift of refreshing sleep.

To Shakespeare the sunset appeared as an old and weary Phœbus, seeking his bed in the ocean. " Ere the weary sun set in the west," we read in " The Comedy of Errors " (I.2. 7) ; and Sonnet VII speaks of him as with weary car, like feeble age, reeling from the day. The same idea is conveyed in the following.

" King John " (V.4. 33-35) :

> . . . . this night, whose black contagious breath
> Already smokes about the burning crest
> Of the old, feeble, and day-wearied sun.

On the eve of Bosworth, Henry of Richmond, studying the sky, repeats the figure of a tired sun, but also mentions a familiar sign of fine weather, which we embody in the jingle, " red sky at night, shepherds' delight."

" Richard III " (V.3. 19-21) :

> The weary sun hath made a golden set,
> And by the bright track of his fiery car
> Gives signal of a goodly day to-morrow.

94

On the other hand, a grey sunset is an evil portent.
" Richard II " (II.4. 21-22) :

> Thy sun sets weeping in the lowly west,
> Witnessing storms to come, woe and unrest.

The sun wages an unequal battle against the oncoming
night : " 2 Henry VI " (IV.1. 1-4) :

> The gaudy, blabbing and remorseful day
> Is crept into the bosom of the sea ;
> And now loud-howling wolves arouse the jades
> That drag the tragic melancholy night.

" Troilus and Cressida " (V.8. 5-8) :

> Look, Hector, how the sun begins to set ;
> How ugly night comes breathing at his heels :
> Even with the vail and darking of the sun,
> To close the day up.

In " Timon of Athens " we read, " Men shut their doors
against a setting sun " (I.2. 150). In " King John " (V.5.
1-4), however, the Dauphin Lewis says :

> The sun of heaven methought was loath to set,
> But stay'd and made the western welkin blush,
> When English measure backward their own ground
> In faint retire.

The sunset presents an obvious symbol for the fall of
human greatness, the end of hope, the defeat of ambitions
and causes, final disaster and death. Shakespeare made free
use of this opportunity for apt simile, of which the following
are typical instances :
" Julius Cæsar " (V.3. 60-64) :

> O setting sun,
> As in thy red rays thou dost sink to night,
> So in his red blood Cassius' day is set,
> The sun of Rome is set ! Our day is gone,

" Romeo and Juliet " (III.5. 127-129) :

> When the sun sets, the air doth drizzle dew,
> But for the sunset of my brother's son
> It rains downright.

Cardinal Wolsey compares his fall from power to the passage of the sun. (The words are probably those of Shakespeare's collaborator, Fletcher).

" Henry VIII " (III.2. 223-225) :

> I have touch'd the highest point of all my greatness ;
> And from that full meridian of my glory,
> I haste now to my setting.

Of the King, however, he says, " That sun I pray, may never set ! " (Ibid. 415).

Shakespeare either makes a solemn, sorrowful, or tragic conclusion coincide with a sunset, poetically described by his characters, or he likens the going-down of the sun to the obliteration of human hopes and aspirations.

XI.

NIGHT.

THE attitude of the human mind to the phenomenon of night is as varied as it well could be. To one it speaks of evil, fear, dread of the unknown and supernatural, crime and vice, disaster and death. To another it conjures up a picture of rest, content, peace, sweet sleep. To the poet it brings the sparkling beauty of a star-gemmed sky. To the lover it tells of romance and joy under the pale light of the moon.

These various aspects of night are reflected in the works of the universal poet. Knowing his fellow creatures as intimately as he did, he was familiar with them all. As a dramatist he makes extensive use of the uncanny, concealing, mysterious impression that night conveys. It is most commonly employed by him to enhance the intensity of his tragic moments, to increase the terror, suspense, and revulsion aroused by wicked deeds, to which darkness is so fitting an accompaniment. Shakespeare, however, could still view night with a more friendly eye, appreciate its gifts of rest and sleep, and honour it as a time of revel and love-making.

It is in its more repulsive character that Shakespeare finds night most effective as a dramatic expedient. During its dark, silent hours horrible ghosts and terrifying supernatural beings are abroad. As Hamlet says (III.2. 406-408):

> 'Tis now the very witching time of night,
> When churchyards yawn, and hell itself breathes out
> Contagion to this world.

97

Hamlet's ghost, Cæsar's shade, the hideous weird sisters in " Macbeth," the host of apparitions in " Richard III," and others, all seek the midnight hours. Only in the shadows can these unearthly creatures move. They disappear on the approach of day, as we learn from the " Hamlet " ghost, who is all anxiety to leave when :

> The glow-worm shows the matin to be near,
> And 'gins to pale his ineffectual fire.
>
> (I.5. 89-90.)

Night, again, is the hour when traitors like the Macbeths and conspirators like the enemies of Cæsar hatch their dastardly plots—" actions blacker than the night." Foul crime and murder are committed under " night's black mantle " by " night's black agents " (" Macbeth ")—and such terrible deeds as the assassination of Duncan, the murder of Desdemona, the slaying of Paris, occur when the sun's face is hid. So, too, do the suicides of Romeo and Juliet. Crime of a lesser kind also hides behind the screening darkness. " Thieves do foot by night " we learn in the " Merry Wives of Windsor " (II.1. 126). Vice of all kinds finds night its native season ; and the most vigorous indictment against its black nature occurs in " The Rape of Lucrece," where lines 117-119 read :

> . . . sable Night, mother of dread and fear,
> Upon the world dim darkness doth display,
> And in her vaulty prison stows the day.

And later in the poem (lines 764-770), we find :

> O comfort-killing Night, image of hell !
> Dim register and notary of shame !
> Black stage for tragedies and murders fell !
> Vast sin-concealing chaos ! nurse of blame !
> Blind muffled bawd ! dark harbour for defame !
> Grim cave of death ! whispering conspirator
> With close-tongued treason and the ravisher !

Night and treason are again associated by Brutus in
" Julius Cæsar " (II.1. 77-79) :

> O conspiracy,
> Shamest thou to show thy dangerous brow by night,
> When evils are most free ?

The horrors and crimes of " Macbeth " are all begotten in
" the foul womb of night." First, the ambitious Lady
Macbeth prays for courage and resolution to carry through her
grim purpose. " Come, thick night," she cries, " and pall
thee in the dunnest smoke of hell " (I.5. 51-52). Macbeth,
outside Duncan's chamber, in those stern waiting moments,
observes (II.1. 49-51) :

> Now o'er the one-half world
> Nature seems dead, and wicked dreams abuse
> The curtain'd sleep.

Macbeth, after the murder of his king, is moved by
irresistible impulse to further crimes. While contemplating
the atrocity against Banquo and Fleance, he exclaims (III.2.
46-50) :

> Come, seeling night,
> Scarf up the tender eye of pitiful day,
> And with thy bloody and invisible hand
> Cancel and tear to pieces that great bond
> Which keeps me pale !

Many other quotations could be given to show the
dramatist's association of night with tragedy, horror, crime,
vice, evil, and death.

A personality frequently mentioned by Shakespeare in
connection with night is Hecate. In classical mythology
Hecate was a mysterious divinity, who gradually acquired
the character of goddess of the dark underworld, the regions
of night. In " Macbeth " she actually makes two appearances
on the stage, but these passages are generally regarded as
interpolated and non-Shakespearian. In the same play,

however, are references to the goddess obviously from Shakespeare's pen. Speaking of night, Macbeth says (II.1. 51-56):

> . . . witchcraft celebrates
> Pale Hecate's offerings ; and wither'd murder,
> Alarum'd by his sentinel, the wolf,
> Whose howl's his watch, thus with his stealthy pace,
> With Tarquin's ravishing strides, towards his design
> Moves like a ghost.

Referring to the coming murder of Banquo and his son, Macbeth declares (III.2. 41-44):

> . . . ere to black Hecate's summons
> The shard-borne beetle with his drowsy hums
> Hath rung night's yawning peal, there shall be done
> A deed of dreadful note.

In "King Lear" (I.1. 112) is the phrase, "the mysteries of Hecate, and the night"; and in "Hamlet" she is mentioned as the goddess of darkness and revenge in the scene where the players act the murder of the elder Hamlet (III.2. 266-271), by pouring poison into his ear :

> Thoughts black, hands apt, drugs fit, and time (i.e., night) agreeing;
> Confederate season, else no creature seeing ;
> Thou mixture rank, of midnight weeds collected,
> With Hecate's ban thrice blasted, thrice infected,
> Thy natural magic and dire property,
> On wholesome life usurp immediately.

The strange attribute, "triple Hecate," which we find in "Midsummer Night's Dream" (V.1. 391), is explained by Hecate's portrayal as a three-fold goddess, or a divinity with three heads.

Among other epithets and descriptive phrases applied by Shakespeare to night are the following : "black-browed," "the scowl of night," "pitchy," "hell-black," "tragic," "melancholy." Night was supposed to defeat the senses ; and such adjectives as "eyeless," "stumbling," "blind,"

" the night's dull ear," were appropriately employed by the poet. The idea of night " screening " an evil deed by throwing " night's cloak " or " night's mantle " over it, was a favourite figure of speech; and the night became sad, ugly, deadly, silent, and so forth. Shakespeare also speaks of the " poisonous damp," " the dusky vapours," or " the cold dew " of night—all expressive phrases of chilly detestation. Nights necessitated " watchdogs," and were, therefore, " long," " tedious," " endless," " lasting." " The heavy gait of night " is a phrase from " Midsummer Night's Dream" (V.1. 375); and in " Henry V " (IV. Chorus. 20-22), we read :

> . . . the crippled tardy-gaited night
> Who, like a foul and ugly witch, doth limp
> So tediously away.

" Swift, swift, you dragons of the night, that dawning may bare the raven's eye," is an invocation from "Cymbeline" (II.2. 48-49). But night does not give way to day without a struggle—" and yet dark night strangles the travelling lamp" (" Macbeth," II.4. 7). Nevertheless, its defeat is inevitable. " Rape of Lucrece " (1079-1082) :

> By this, lamenting Philomel had ended
> The well tuned warble of her nightly sorrow,
> And solemn night with slow sad gait descended
> To ugly hell.

A more picturesque way of expressing the passing of night occurs in "All's Well " (II.1. 166-167), where the setting of Hesperus, the evening star, is named :

> Ere twice in murk and occidental damp
> Moist Hesperus hath quench'd his sleepy lamp.

In the many hundred references to night, which occur in Shakespeare, those which are uncomplimentary far outnumber those which are complimentary. From this we might assume that the poet entertained a decided antipathy to the hours of

darkness, but we must not forget that his soul was thrilled
by the beauty of the stars and the mysterious, silver moonlight. He called night some hard names, but he also applied
to it such epithets as " glimmering " " soft," " still," " peaceful," " silent," " secret." " The sweet of the night " is a very
happy phrase.

One of his pleasant associations with night is that of love.
In the garden scene from " The Merchant of Venice," the
lovers, Lorenzo and Jessica, recall instances when other lovers
plighted their troths on other such lovely nights as theirs.
Most famous of all love-scenes under the stars is that of
Romeo and Juliet. Juliet anticipating the joy of her lover's
embrace, says (III.2. 5, 10-11) :

> Spread thy close curtain, love-performing night.
> . . . Come, civil night,
> Thou sober-suited matron, all in black.

Night as a time of peace and rest also made its appeal to
the poet. " Peaceful night, the tomb where grief should
sleep," is the description of Pericles (I.2. 4-5) ; and in
" Richard III " (V.3. 80-81) Richmond says to Derby :

> All comfort that the dark night can afford
> Be to thy person !

Another association that night brought to Shakespeare's
mind was a time of revelling and feasting. Mark Antony
is one who " revels long o' nights "—" drinks and wastes
the lamps of night in revel," says Octavius Cæsar in "Antony
and Cleopatra " (I.4. 4-5). We hear of night revellings in
" Romeo and Juliet," " The Merchant of Venice," "Othello,"
and other plays. These entertainments, however, though
joyous and riotous, are not free from blame, and lead us to
the conclusion that, despite its beauty, romance, sleep, and
peace, night in the dramatist's view was a fitting accompaniment for all that was wicked, vile, and evil.

XII.

THE MOON.

AT one with all humanity, Shakespeare was moved to praise by the silver beauty of the moon. This, the nearest of our celestial neighbours—it is only 240,000 miles distant—has always held the wondering admiration of mankind. Perhaps our love for the moon is that of parent for child, for it is possible that this close companion, who journeys with us round the sun, was once part of the earth.

Not the cold facts of astronomy, but the loveliness of its pale, gentle light, has endeared the moon to man. From time immemorial its soft argent rays have been associated with dreams of love. It is in this character that it fascinates the poets ; and Shakespeare knew and surrendered to its appeal.

We have had occasion to note before how alluringly the dramatist weds romance and moonlight. That beautiful scene between Romeo and Juliet in Capulet's orchard has been referred to more than once in these pages. So, also, has the entrancing night in the garden of Belmont, when Lorenzo observes to Jessica, " How sweet the moonlight sleeps upon this bank ! Here will we sit." (" Merchant of Venice," V.1. 54). One of the earliest lines in " Midsummer Night's Dream " is, " Thou hast by moonlight at her window sung " (I.1. 30). This play has a close friend in the moon, which shines on the revels of Oberon and Titania and her fairy train, on the wanderings of the lovers, and the adventures of Bottom and his fellow players.

Such instances show that Shakespeare was fully conscious of the value and importance of the clever use of the moon and moonlight as a dramatic aid. He took full advantage of them, despite the crudity of Elizabethan scenery. His language supplied the deficiency, and it is as a poet, therefore, that his praise of Diana is most interesting, for he shows in his lines a wide knowledge of astronomical truth as well as a close acquaintance with mythological legend.

The most noticeable feature of the moon is the constant changes in its appearance—the phases, as we now call them. In olden days the waxing and waning were believed to have good and bad influences on the destinies of man, to affect weather conditions, and to have other far-reaching results. Modern science has exploded these groundless superstitions and explained the phases of the moon in detail. Shakespeare, of course, closely observed lunar phenomena ; and we have a reference to the phases in " Midsummer Night's Dream." " How slow this old moon wanes ! " exclaims Theseus (I.1. 3-4) ; and Hippolyta answers :

> Four days will quickly steep themselves in night ;
> Four nights will quickly dream away the time ;
> And then the moon, like to a silver bow
> New-bent in heaven, shall behold the night
> Of our solemnities.   (I.1. 7-11.)

" The moon is never but a month old," says Dull in "Love's Labour's Lost " (IV.2. 47) in explanation of his riddle. In " The Tempest " Gonzalo makes this sarcastic remark (II.1. 182-184) :

> You are gentlemen of brave mettle ; you would lift the moon out of her sphere, if she would continue in it five weeks without changing.

The frequent changes of the moon naturally suggested the idea of inconstancy, and we find this repeated in a number of

instances by Shakespeare. " Thus change I like the moon "
(" Love's Labour's Lost " V.2. 212); " the moon changes
even as your mind " (" Taming of the Shrew," IV.5. 20).
In Capulet's orchard the lovers converse :

> *Romeo :* Lady, by yonder blessed moon I swear,
> That tips with silver all these fruit-tree tops—
> *Juliet :* O, swear not by the moon, th' inconstant moon,
> That monthly changes in her circled orb,
> Lest that thy love prove likewise variable.
>
> (II.2. 107-111.)

Cleopatra declares ("Antony and Cleopatra," V.2. 239-
241) :

> . . . now from head to foot
> I am marble-constant ; now the fleeting moon
> No planet is of mine.

And Henry V in his charming wooing of Katharine of
France, affirms (V.2. 170-174) :

> A good heart, Kate, is the sun and the moon ; or, rather,
> the sun, and not the moon ; for it shines bright and never
> changes, but keeps his course truly.

The revolution of the moon round the earth is used by the
poet to denote time : " Not many moons gone by " ("Antony
and Cleopatra ") ; " one twelve moons more " and " twice
six moons " (" Pericles ") ; and " 30 dozen moons " for
thirty years (" Hamlet ").

The scientific fact that the moon and planets do not shine
by any light of their own, but by reflected light from the sun,
suggested to Shakespeare the line, " The moon's an arrant
thief, and her pale fire she snatches from the sun " (" Timon
of Athens," IV.3. 440-441). Earlier in the same scene, he
had written (66-69) :

> *Alcib :* How came the noble Timon to this change ?
> *Timon :* As the moon does, by wanting light to give :
> But then renew I could not, like the moon ;
> There were no suns to borrow of.

H

In " Hamlet," again, we read of " thirty dozen moons with borrowed sheen " (III.2. 167).

One of the most important discoveries made in the realm of astronomy was the moon's influence upon the seas as the cause of the tides. This was common knowledge in Shakespeare's day, and there are many references to it, metaphorical and literal.

" Hamlet " (I.1. 118-120) :

> . . . The moist star,
> Upon whose influence Neptune's empire stands,
> Was sick almost to doomsday with eclipse.

" Lear " (V.3. 17-19) :

> . . . and we'll wear out,
> In a wall'd prison, packs and sects of great ones
> That ebb and flow by the moon.

In " The Tempest " Prospero speaks of Caliban's mother as a witch (V.1. 269-271) :

> . . . one so strong
> That could control the moon, make flows and ebbs,
> And deal in her command. . . .

As an instance of the impossible Shakespeare uses the figure in " The Winter's Tale " (I.2. 426-429) :

> . . . you may as well
> Forbid the sea for to obey the moon,
> As or by oath remove or counsel shake
> The fabric of his folly.

The fortunes of those, like thieves, who are governed by the moon, ebb and flow like the sea which she also controls.

" 1 Henry IV " (I.2. 34-36) :

> The fortune of us that are moon's men doth ebb and flow
> like the sea, being governed, as the sea is, by the moon.

From lunar control of the tides came the notion that the moon also ruled the rain clouds. This was a very prevalent idea among Shakespeare's contemporaries. In the "Direction for Health of Magistrates and Students" by a writer named Newton (1574), appears the sentence, "the moone is ladye of moisture." In the Prologue to Lydgate's "Story of Thebes" occur the lines :

> Of Lucina the moone, moist and pale
> That many shoure from heaven may availe.

Shakespeare echoes this conception in such phrases as " the governess of floods," " the watery moon," and

> The moon methinks looks with a watery eye,
> And when she weeps, weeps every little flower.
>> (" Midsummer Night's Dream, III.1. 203-204.)

In " The Winter's Tale " (I.2. 1-2) there is a further interesting reference.

> Nine changes of the watery star hath been
> The shepherd's note since we have left our throne.

What seems to be the explanation of the shepherd's note is found in an old book, translated from the French, entitled, " The Shepherd's Calendar." This dealt with the shepherds' study of the heavens during their night watches over the flocks and described the celestial phenomena noted by them.

It was a widespread misconception that plants improved as the moon increased, and this false deduction prompted such lines as, " as true as plantage to the moon," which we find in " Troilus and Cressida " (III.2. 184). Most people believed that plants gathered during the hours of moonlight possessed an additional efficacy. An example of this occurs in " Hamlet," where Laertes is describing the potency of the poison with which he intends to anoint the point of his foil for the coming duel (IV.7. 142-147). There is no healing herb, not even among those gathered under the moon.

> I bought an unction of a mountebank,
> So mortal that but dip a knife in it,
> Where it draws blood no cataplasm so rare.
> Collected from all simples that have virtue
> Under the moon, can save the thing from death
> That is but scratch'd withal.

The moon's connection with the sea and the rain-clouds provided a ready simile for human tears.

" Richard III " (II.2. 68-70) :

> All springs reduce their currents to mine eyes,
> That I, being govern'd by the watery moon,
> May send forth plenteous tears to drown the world !

The lovely picture of the moon shining on the water came naturally to the poet's mind in this connection.

" Venus and Adonis " (491-492) :

> But hers (her eyes), which through the crystal tears gave light,
> Shone like the moon in water seen at night.

" Love's Labour's Lost " (IV.3. 30-33) :

> Nor shines the silver moon one half so bright
> Through the transparent bosom of the deep,
> As doth thy face through tears of mine give light ;
> Thou shinest in every tear that I do weep.

While the grace and wonder of the moon inspired some of Shakespeare's finest poetry, we find that he was not content to laud its superficial beauty. He observed it much more closely, and noted certain phenomena, which have since occupied the astronomers in the search for scientific explanation. Even in these enlightened days of education, these facts are not generally known. For example, we have a reference in " Love's Labour's Lost " to the moon's " attending star." Biron has loudly sung the praises of Rosaline, the lady-in-waiting, but the King of Navarre, in love with the Princess herself, says (IV.3. 229-231).

What zeal, what fury hath inspired thee now ?
My love, her mistress, is a gracious moon ;
She an attending star, scarce seen a light.

From olden times astronomers had noted and left a record
of a star that was attendant upon the moon.   Later observers
saw what appeared to be a star on the dark part of our satellite.
One theory was of a star passing before the moon ; but
modern science has explained the phenomena as the power of
the lunar mountain Aristarchus to reflect light.

In the same category is another interesting appearance on
the moon, which is known astronomically as *la lumière cendrée*.
It is the ashy light reflected on the unilluminated part of the
moon by the earth, and is sometimes called earthshine.
Falstaff, in boasting vein, uses the simile in " 2 Henry IV "
(IV.-3. 56-59) :

I in the clear sky of fame o'ershine you as much as the full
moon doth the cinders of the element, which show like pins'
heads to her.

Science has no explanation, however, for the strange
apparition in the night sky described in " King John "
(IV.2. 182-184) :

. . . they say five moons were seen to-night;
Four fixed, and the fifth did whirl about
The other four in wondrous motion.

Possibly the poet was giving full reign to his imagination
to create a terrifying celestial portent.

A familiar illusion to all of us is the likeness of a human
face in the moon.   Thiselton Dyer says that the legend of the
man in the moon is a very old one indeed.   He was supposed
to be a man with a bundle of sticks on his back, who was
exiled from the earth many centuries ago and was despatched
so far away that he is beyond the reach of death.   There is
no approach to universal agreement as to who the culprit

was or for what crime he was banished.   Dante identified him with Cain ; and Chaucer banished him for theft and made him carry a thorn-bush.   One belief makes his crime that of Sabbath-breaking, like the man in the Old Testament (Numbers xv, 32), who was caught gathering sticks on the Lord's Day.   As an example to mankind, the man in the moon was, therefore, condemned to carry a bundle of sticks on his back for ever.   Shakespeare adopted the legend and makes his man carry a thorn bush, but he also gives the solitary exile a companion in the shape of a dog.

" Tempest " (II.1. 249) :

> The man i' the moon's too slow.

Ibid (II.2. 140-144) :

> *Caliban :* Hast thou not dropp'd from heaven ?
> *Stephano :* Out o' the moon, I do assure thee : I was the man i' the moon when time was.
> *Caliban :* I have seen thee in her, and I do adore thee : my mistress show'd me thee, and thy dog, and thy bush.

In the interlude played before Theseus and his Court, by Quince, Bottom, and company in " Midsummer Night's Dream " (V.1), one of the players represents moonshine. Says Quince, the Prologue :

> This man, with lanthorn, dog, and bush of thorn,
> Presenteth Moonshine.
>
> (136-137.)

On entering, the player, after vainly trying to describe his appearance in verse, descends to conversational prose (261-264) :

> All that I have to say, is, to tell you that the lanthorn is the moon ; I, the man i' the moon ; this thorn-bush, my thorn-bush ; and this dog, my dog.

Moonshine opens with the line, " This lanthorn doth the horned moon present," on which Demetrius facetiously remarks, he should have worn the horns on his head, while Theseus declares he should be inside his lanthorn. Other references to the horns of the moon occur in the plays.

" Coriolanus " (I.1. 216-218) :

> . . . they threw their caps
> As they would hang them on the horns o' the moon,
> Shouting their emulation.

"Antony and Cleopatra " (IV.12. 45) :

> Let me lodge Lichas on the horns o' the moon.

(Lichas was the companion of Hercules, who brought his master the poisoned garment and was hurled by him into the sea.)

Among the picturesque and appropriate epithets that Shakespeare applies to the moon are " visiting," "wandering," " fleeting," " modest," " chaste," " cold," " fruitless," " blessed," " envious." He also calls it " goddess of the night," " sovereign mistress of true melancholy," and " thrice-crowned queen of night."

The supposed influence of the moon upon mankind we have reviewed in an earlier chapter on astrology. It was generally regarded as baneful, witness such words as lunatic, moon-struck, etc. In " Othello " we read (V.2. 109-111) :

> It is the very error of the moon ;
> She comes more nearer earth than she was wont
> And makes men mad.

Lunar influence is not confined to human beings, but affects other terrestrial creatures. Says Brutus in " Julius Cæsar " (IV.3. 27-28) :

> I had rather be a dog, and bay the moon,
> Than such a Roman.

We have noted how thieves, in Falstaff's words, " go by the moon." " Gentlemen of the shade," he calls them ;

" minions of the moon." The moon seems to have been regarded as befriending scoundrels of all kinds.

"King Lear" (II.1. 40-42):

> Here stood he in the dark, his sharp sword out,
> Mumbling of wicked charms, conjuring the moon
> To stand's auspicious mistress.

As in the case of the sun, Shakespeare uses many synonyms for the moon. He went for them to Greek and Roman mythology, which was familiar to all educated men of his time. The name he introduces most frequently is Dian or Diana, who was identified by the Romans with the Greek goddess, Artemis. To the ancients, Diana, the moon-goddess, was the personification of chastity. She was cold, modest, unmoved by love. She lived, " circled with her nymphs " ("3 Henry VI," IV.8. 21), passionless and austere. Timon of Athens speaks of " the consecrated snow that lies on Dian's lap " (IV.3. 386-387), and the same estimate of the moon's character is repeated in the following lines :

"Midsummer Night's Dream" (I.1. 89-90):

> Or on Diana's altar to protest
> For aye austerity and single life.

Ibid. (II.1. 161-162):

> . . . young Cupid's fiery shaft
> Quench'd in the chaste beams of the watery moon.

"As You Like It" (III.4. 16-19):

> He hath bought a pair of cast lips of Diana : a nun of winter's sisterhood kisses not more religiously ; the very ice of chastity is in them.

" Much Ado About Nothing " (IV.1. 58-59):

> You seem to me as Dian in her orb,
> As chaste as is the bud ere it be blown.

" Merchant of Venice " (I.2. 116-118) :

> If I live to be as old as Sibylla, I will die as chaste as Diana,
> unless I be obtained by the manner of my father's will.

(In the last quotation Portia refers to the Cumæan Sybil,
who was promised by Apollo as many years of life as she
held grains of sand in her hand.)

In " Pericles " Diana herself appears in a vision to the
Prince of Tyre (V.1) ; and the last scene in the play, witness-
ing the happy re-union of Pericles and his wife, Thaisa,
takes place in Diana's temple at Ephesus. Pericles refers to
the goddess as " Celestial Dian, goddess argentine " (V.1.
251) and describes her votaries as clothed in " thy silver
livery " (V.3. 7). Not only is silver the most descriptive
epithet for moonlight, but in astrology, it will be recalled,
silver was allotted to the moon.

Although there were several goddesses Diana, the legends
attaching to them all became associated with the great moon-
goddess. One of these legends is the story of Endymion,
referred to by Portia in the words, " the moon sleeps with
Endymion " (" Merchant of Venice," V.1. 109). Endymion
was a youth of great beauty, who warmed the cold heart of
the moon (Selene or Dian) as he slept on Mount Latmus.
The goddess put him into an eternal sleep that she might lie
by his side and kiss him without his knowledge.

Diana also appeared in the character of huntress, who
followed the chase with her nymphs in the Arcadian mountains. This bent is also noted by Shakespeare in "As You
Like It," where Orlando hangs his love-poems on the trees
of Arden (III.2. 1-4) :

> Hang there, my verse, in witness of my love :
> And thou, thrice-crowned queen of night, survey
> With thy chaste eye, from thy pale sphere above,
> Thy huntress' name that my full life doth sway.

A surname of Diana was Phœbe. This appellation is used in " Midsummer Night's Dream " (I.1. 209-212) :

> To-morrow night, when Phœbe doth behold
> Her silver visage in the watery glass,
> Decking with liquid pearl the bladed grass,
> A time that lover's flights doth still conceal. . . .

Phœbe is mentioned again in " Love's Labour's Lost " in conjunction with two other names for the moon, Luna and Dictynna. Dull puts forward a clever riddle to the two " book-men," Holofernes and Sir Nathaniel (IV.2. 35-41) :

Dull : Can you tell me by your wit,
  What was a month old at Cain's birth, that's not five
    weeks old as yet ?
Hol : Dictynna, goodman Dull . . .
Dull : What is Dictynna ?
Nath : A title to Phœbe, to Luna, to the moon.
Hol : The moon was a month old when Adam was no more,
  And raught not to five weeks when he came to five-score.

XIII.

ECLIPSES.

ASTRONOMY has explained eclipses so completely that to-day even the unlearned may understand them. We know that an eclipse of the sun is caused by the moon passing between it and the earth and wholly or partially obscuring its light. An eclipse of the moon is caused by the earth coming between it and the sun with a similar interruption of its light. In a solar eclipse the moon's shadow, directed to earth, is in the form of a cone. The point of the cone runs over a narrow belt of the earth, never exceeding 170 miles in width. To all within this belt the eclipse is total, while those within 1,000 to 2,000 miles on either side will see a larger or smaller portion of the sun concealed according to their distance from the line of totality. An eclipse of the sun can only occur at new moon, and an eclipse of the moon at full moon.

While the natural astrology of the Middle Ages predicted with accuracy the recurrence of eclipses, judicial astrology, explaining them as portents of evil, obtained the more attentive hearing from the people at large. In the astrological chapter I have described with what terror these phenomena were observed by the ignorant masses, and how they even caused a qualm in the breasts of the learned. We have seen that Shakespeare re-echoed the predictions of the astrologers and saw in eclipses certain signs of coming disaster. Gloucester, in "King Lear," says, "These late eclipses bode no good to us." Antony complains that "our terrene moon is now eclipsed," and portends his fall; Othello declares that "a huge eclipse of sun and moon" would be a fitting accompaniment to the terrible tragedy of Desdemona's end.

Eclipses are spoken of in Sonnet XXXV as staining sun and moon ; and in Sonnet CVII occur the lines (5-6) :

> The mortal moon hath her eclipse endured,
> And the sad augurs mock their own presage.

In " Hamlet " (I.i.   120) Horatio, speaking of the evil omens that foretold Cæsar's death, refers to the moon as " sick almost to doomsday with eclipse."

As in modern language, Shakespeare applies the word " eclipse " figuratively.   In " 1 Henry VI " (IV.5.   52-55) Lord Talbot says to his son John :

> Then here I take my leave of thee, fair son,
> Born to eclipse thy life this afternoon.
> Come, side by side together live and die ;
> And soul with soul from France to heaven fly.

In the third part of this same drama King Henry VI says : " By doubtful fear my joy of liberty is half eclipsed " (IV.6. 62-63).

A strange allusion to the eclipse of the moon occurs in the great incantation scene in " Macbeth " (IV.1).   Among the horrible ingredients cast by the weird sisters into the boiling cauldron are " slips of yew sliver'd (i.e., slipped off) in the moon's eclipse " (27-28).   We have noted that plants gathered in the moonlight were considered to have an added potency. The moon in eclipse, then, would be held as enhancing the strange herbs used for the evil purposes of witchcraft.

The above references to eclipses show that, as a dramatist, Shakespeare was only interested in the old astrological beliefs connected with them.   He does not in his plays touch on the scientific explanations.   The satire on those gullible enough to credit celestial portents, however, which he puts into the mouth of Edmund in " King Lear " (I.2.), proves that science and not superstition appealed to Shakespeare the philosopher.

XIV.

THE STARS.

THE great philosopher Kant said, " Two things strike me dumb ; the starry heavens above and the moral law within." Emerson wrote, " If a man would be alone, let him look at the stars." To Goethe the stars spoke of peace and order, " Like a star, without haste, yet without rest, let each one revolve round his own task." Marlowe penned the lines :

> O, thou art fairer than the evening air,
> Clad in the beauty of a thousand stars.
>
> ("Dr. Faustus.")

To Milton the stars were " innumerable " ; and to all poets they have been sources of inspiration, giving birth to a legion of beautiful passages in our literature.

Their fairness, radiance, and magical influence made a · profound impression upon Shakespeare and drew from him poetry as exquisite as any he lavished on the wonders of nature. Only a few of these can be quoted, typical examples of his gift for perfect word-pictures. In the " Merchant of Venice " (V.1. 58-59) he describes how " the floor of heaven is thick inlaid with patines of bright gold." In " Hamlet " the sky is " this majestical roof fretted with golden fire " (II.2. 313). In " Pericles " he writes of the " field of stars " (I.1. 37) ; and in " Midsummer Night's Dream " of the " spangled starlight sheen " (II.1. 29). In " Romeo and Juliet " (I.2. 25) we read of " earth-treading stars that make dark heaven light"; and in "Antony and Cleopatra" (III.2. 65-66) is the exalted wish, "Let all the number of the stars give light to thy fair way."

Shakespeare conceived of the stars as fire. " Doubt thou the stars are fire," he writes in " Hamlet " (II.2. 116), in the sense that one might as well doubt one's existence. Modern astronomy regards the stars as suns, centres of their separate systems, situated at immense distances from the earth—so immense that in some cases their light takes hundreds of years to reach us. The dramatist had a much narrower conception, for he speaks of them as " these blessed candles " (" Merchant of Venice," V.1. 220) and " those gold candles fix'd in heaven's air " (Sonnet XXI. 12). To Julius Cæsar the sky is " painted with unnumbered sparks," every one of which is fire (III.1. 63-64); and Macbeth, with villainy in his heart, cries, " Stars, hide your fires; let not light see my black and deep desires " (I.4. 50-51).

The poet applies many a picturesque epithet to the stars, such as " twinkling," " blazing," or " glorious." Most of his adjectives, however, bear an astrological significance. Examples are, " lucky," " favourable," " charitable," "happy," " homely "; and, conversely, " malignant," " ill-boding," " thwarting," " angry," " frowning," " inauspicious." An interesting one is " dis-orbed," also from astrology, and suggests an interruption of the ordered progress of the universe—always an ill omen.

Shakespeare's reading of the stars through the spectacles of judicial astrology has been considered in the chapter devoted to that old science. Poetically he frequently turned to the silver sparks of heaven for simile. The obvious and now-hackneyed comparison of eyes to stars was employed by Shakespeare in " Romeo and Juliet " (II.2. 15-22), but more effectively than is possible to a lesser poet :

Two of the fairest stars in all the heaven,
Having some business, do intreat her eyes
To twinkle in their spheres till they return.
What if her eyes were there, they in her head ?
The brightness of her cheek would shame those stars,
As daylight doth a lamp ; her eyes in heaven
Would through the airy region stream so bright
That birds would sing and think it were not night.

Another use of the simile is found in " The Taming of the Shrew " (IV.5. 31-32) :

What stars do spangle heaven with such beauty,
As those two eyes become that heavenly face ?

Rather a different application is that in " Hamlet " (I.5. 17), where the ghost tells his son he could unfold a tale that would make his " two eyes, like stars, start from their spheres."

The use of the word "star" to denote a person of importance, a leading character, which is so familiar in the modern theatre, is found in Shakespeare. On the death of Antony, the guard remarks : " The star is fallen " ("Antony and Cleopatra," IV.14. 106). The King in " Hamlet " likens his relations to his Queen to the star which " moves not but in his sphere." The idea is more fully developed in the following lines from "All's Well " (I.1. 96-100), where Helena speaks of Bertram :

'Twere all one
That I should love a bright particular star
And think to wed it, he is so above me :
In his bright radiance and collateral light
Must I be comforted, not in his sphere.

The adjective " star-like " is used in Cranmer's prophecy of the coming of James I, who from the sacred ashes of Elizabeth's honour " shall star-like " rise. (" Henry VIII," V.5. 47). We also find the expression, " star-like nobleness," in " Timon of Athens."

In a more imaginative metaphorical sense the stars are utilized in " Cymbeline." Belarius, speaking of Cymbeline's sons, declares they are " worthy to inlay heaven with stars " (V.5. 352). An interesting figure occurs in " Pericles," where Thaisa says, " My father's dead," and the Prince expresses the pious wish, " Heaven make a star of him ! " (" Pericles," V.3. 79). The most original of these passages is taken from " Romeo and Juliet " (III.2. 17, 21-25) :

> Come, night, . . .
> Give me my Romeo ; and, when he shall die,
> Take him and cut him out in little stars,
> And he will make the face of heaven so fine,
> That all the world will be in love with night,
> And pay no worship to the garish sun.

Shakespeare pens the phrase " fixed stars " to distinguish those which appear not to change their positions from the wandering planets. Modern astronomy reveals that these stars are not fixed at all, but in motion, some moving at the rate of 200 miles a second through space. But so great is their distance from the earth that centuries must elapse before any change in position can be discerned. For practical purposes, then, to us, versed in recent astronomical discovery, as to Shakespeare, who relied on Ptolemy's deductions, the fixed stars are permanently stationary. The poet has two interesting references.

" Richard II " (II.4. 7-9) :

> 'Tis thought the king is dead. . . .
> The bay-trees in our country are all wither'd,
> And meteors fright the fixed stars of heaven.

" Love's Labour's Lost " (I.1. 88-89) :

> These earthly godfathers of heaven's lights,
> That give a name to every fixed star.

These last lines are satirical. Some thousands of fixed stars are visible to the naked eye, while the telescope, first extensively used in Shakespeare's lifetime, reveals millions of them.

Shakespeare and those of his contemporaries who still embraced the Ptolemaic doctrine, believed that the fixed stars occupied the eighth sphere in the Egyptian's scheme of the universe. Imprisoned within it, they revolved round the earth. Any interruption of their ordered journey was impossible ; and this widespread belief explains such sentences as, " Though you would seek to unsphere the stars with oaths," which occurs in " The Winter's Tale " (1.2. 48).

Of the stars mentioned by the dramatist by name the most important is the North Star, as it was the most important to astronomers, mariners, shepherds, and other observers of his age. The finest mention of the star occurs in the self-laudatory remarks of Julius Cæsar (III.1. 60-66) :

> But I am constant as the northern star,
> Of whose true fix'd and resting quality
> There is no fellow in the firmament.
> The skies are painted with unnumber'd sparks ;
> They are all fire and everyone doth shine ;
> But there's but one in all doth hold his place :
> So in the world. . . .

Another mention is made in " Othello " (II.1. 13-15) :

> The wind-shaked surge, with high and monstrous mane,
> Seems to cast water on the burning bear,
> And quench the guards of the ever-fixed pole.

As a matter of astronomical truth, the polestar is not " ever-fixed," and Shakespeare's error was that of the astronomers of his period. The star is now a little less than $1\frac{1}{2}$ degrees from the celestial pole (i.e., the point in the heavens which the axis of the earth, if extended, would touch),

J

and moves round it very slowly, the movement being perceived only over a long period of time. The motion of the pole of the celestial equator round that of the ecliptic causes the distance between the polestar and north pole gradually to alter. This distance is now decreasing, but there will come a time when the polestar will recede. Two thousand years ago another star of the constellation Ursa Minor stood at the pole; and 12,000 years from now the magnificent star Vega will be the polestar.

In the quotation from "Othello" given above, the "burning bear" is Ursa Minor, of which constellation the polestar is the brightest member. Shakespeare also mentions the Great Bear, Ursa Major. It was commonly called Charles' wain, and was useful to those who told the time by night, like the Carrier in "1 Henry IV" (II.1. 2). Edmund, the rascally villain of "King Lear," records that his "nativity was under Ursa Major" (1.2. 141).

Several references are made to the Pleiades under the description of "the seven stars." Falstaff declares that thieves go by them and the moon (" 1 Henry IV," I.2. 15), and a similar remark comes from Pistol in the Second Part of the drama (II.4. 200). The fool asks a stupid riddle in "King Lear" (I.5. 38-40) about the constellation, which seems to have been one of the best known among the lay observers of the time. The mythological history of the Pleiades as the daughters of Atlas added, no doubt, to the interest taken in them.

Shakespeare mentions few of the stars and constellations individually, being mostly content to describe the expansive beauty of the heavens as a whole.

XV.

THE PLANETS.

SHAKESPEARE'S references to the planets are mainly astrological, interwoven with picturesque details from the lives
of the celebrities of mythology, whose names they bear. I
have devoted a chapter to the widespread belief of planetary
influence in Elizabeth's day. Particularly was the planet,
under which a mortal happened to be born, thought to
influence his life. Numerous instances occur in the plays.
Posthumus of " Cymbeline " was born under Jupiter,
Autolycus of " The Winter's Tale " under Mercury,
Monsieur Parolles of "All's Well That Ends Well " under
Mars, and Conrade of " Much Ado About Nothing " under
Saturn.

The epithets and expressions applied to the planets generally
mostly owe their inspiration to astrology. Typical examples
are, " some ill planet reigns," " ill aspects of planets evil,"
" adverse planets," " the planets of mishap." We read of
" planetary plague " ; and Benedict complains that he was
not born under a " rhyming planet." Even when we get what
appears to be a pure astronomical epithet like " wandering,"
we find that the astrological meaning still predominates :

" 2 Henry VI " (IV.4. 15-16) :

> . . . hath this lovely face
> Ruled, like a wandering planet, over me.

Jupiter was the Lord of Heaven among the Roman
deities, the god of rain, storms, thunder, and lightning ; and,
appropriately enough, his name is conferred on the greatest

of tne planets in our solar system. Jupiter is second only to the sun in size, round which he revolves at a distance of 483,000,000 miles from it, taking 11⅞ years to complete the circuit.

Under the two forms of his name, Jupiter and Jove, Shakespeare refers to him some 120 times in his plays, and takes more notice of him than of Mars, Venus, Mercury, and Saturn combined. But the majority of these references deal with fables that had gathered round his name in the old mythology, particularly as to his over-lordship of the gods, his command of storms and thunder, his Jovian eagle, and his winged herald, Mercury. As Rome was rich in temples to Jupiter, the plays in which Rome figures prominently, " Julius Cæsar," " Coriolanus," "Antony and Cleopatra," " Titus Andronicus," and " Cymbeline," naturally contain many allusions to him. Shakespeare was particularly interested in the Roman period ; and the religion, like every other side of life in the imperial city, was closely studied by him. One of the most expressive adjectives he gives to Jupiter is "multipotent." From phrases such as " Jove bless thee ! " " Jove and my stars be praised ! " and such descriptions as "most gentle," we deduce that Jupiter, unlike most of the planets, was disposed to be kind to mortals and was often a joy-bringing star. The fact that his adjective " jovial " has assumed its present meaning in our language confirms this. Shakespeare uses jovial on three or four occasions, and sometimes in our modern sense : cf. "be bright and jovial " (" Macbeth "). A final interesting point is the frequency with which the dramatist inserts the now popular exclamation, " By Jove ! "

Mars, Rome's great god of war, is cited some three dozen times in Shakespeare, and his character is portrayed in such appropriate epithets as " mailed," " armipotent," " plated,"

" frowning," " valiant," with ample references to his armour, helm, gauntlet, steed, etc. In " Richard II " England is the " seat of Mars," and the Black Prince, " that young Mars." Young Hotspur in " 1 Henry IV " is " Mars in swathling clothes." In " Troilus and Cressida," that drama of the Trojan war, Nestor calls the god, " Mars, the great captain of us all." The derivative, martial, is also freely employed— " a swashing and a martial outside," " warlike and martial," " martial thigh," " martial stalk," " martian scorn," and the surprised exclamation from " 1 Henry IV," " a maid ! and be so martial ! "

Mars the planet, which takes 686 days to go round the sun, and is 141,500,000 miles distant from it, was supposed to influence those born under it towards war, treason, fury, choler, and quarrelling. Among many astrological references is one of astronomy of first interest and importance :

" 1 Henry VI " (I.2. 1-2) :

> Mars his true moving, even as in the heavens
> So in the earth, to this day is not known.

A comparison of these lines with a quotation by Steevens from one of Nash's prefaces to " Gabriel Harvey's Hunt's Up " (1596) is instructive. The quotation runs : " You are as ignorant in the true movings of my muse as the astronomers are in the true moving of Mars, which to this day they could not attain to." This astronomical ignorance was largely dispelled by Kepler's work on Mars, his " De Motibus Stellæ Martis," which was published in 1609.

There is one passage in Shakespeare that suggests the distinctive colour of the red planet.

" Troilus and Cressida " (V.2. 163-165) :

> . . . and that shall be divulged well
> In characters as red as Mars his heart
> Inflamed with Venus.

Venus, the Latin goddess of love, is a fitting name for the lightest and most beautiful and brilliant of all the planets. About the same size as the earth, Venus takes 225 days to circle the sun at a mean distance of 67,000,000 miles. Owing to its position relative to the earth and sun, it is never seen more than 3½ hours before or after the sun. It is, therefore, both the morning and the evening star.

Shakespeare mentions Venus twenty-one times in his works and chiefly in her mythological character—" Venus smiles not in a house of tears " (" Romeo and Juliet," IV.1. 8), " for Venus' sake give me a kiss " (" Troilus and Cressida," IV.5. 49), and " heart inflamed with Venus " in the Martian quotation above. Twice the love planet is contrasted with the grave and gloomy Saturn.

" Titus Andronicus " (II.3. 30-31) :

> Madam, though Venus govern your desires,
> Saturn is dominator over mine.

The second instance, already given in our astrological chapter, occurs in " 2 Henry IV " (II.4. 286), " Saturn and Venus in conjunction ! "

The doves, the traditional birds of love, are named in " Midsummer Night's Dream " (I.1. 169-171, 178) :

> I swear to thee, by Cupid's strongest bow,
> By his best arrow with the golden head,
> By the simplicity of Venus' doves
>
> .   .   .   .   .
>
> To-morrow truly will I meet with thee.

In the " Merchant of Venice " Venus's birds are called " pigeons."

Specific references to the planet are the following, in which its chief quality of brightness is emphasized :

" Midsummer Night's Dream " (III.2. 61) :

> As yonder Venus in her glimmering sphere.

Ibid. (III. 2. 105 - 107). (Oberon's love - spell for Demetrius) :

> When his love he doth espy,
> Let her shine as gloriously
> As the Venus of the sky.

" 1 Henry VI " (I.2. 144-145). (Charles to Joan of Arc):

> Bright star of Venus, fall'n down on the earth,
> How may I reverently worship thee enough ?

When Venus appeared as the evening star, she was known as Hesperus. Shakespeare alludes to her once under this name.

"All's Well " (II.1. 166-167) :

> Ere twice in murk and occidental damp
> Moist Hesperus hath quench'd his sleepy lamp.

In other words, before two nights have passed.

As the morning star Venus's name was Lucifer. In Isaiah xiv, 12, we read : " How art thou fallen from heaven, O Lucifer, son of the morning." The prophet was referring to the King of Babylon, but the church fathers read the passage literally and identified Lucifer with Satan, the prince of darkness. It is thus that Shakespeare uses him. The most significant lines are the following :

" Henry VIII " (III.2. 366-367, 371-372) :

> O, how wretched
> Is that poor man that hangs on princes' favours !
>
> . . . . .
>
> And when he falls, he falls like Lucifer,
> Never to hope again.

" Henry V " (IV.7. 144-147) :

> *Fluellen :* Though he be as good a gentleman as the devil is,
> as Lucifer and Beelzebub himself, it is necessary, look your
> grace, that he keep his vow and his oath,

Mercury, in old mythology the winged messenger of the gods, is the name of the smallest planet, which most swiftly completes its motion round the sun. The journey occupies about eighty-eight days, for Mercury is only some 36,000,000 miles distant from its solar parent.

Shakespeare's interest in Mercury was focussed more upon his importance in mythology than his position in astronomy. Henry V's soldiers are described in their eagerness as " English Mercuries " (II. Chorus 7), and such expressions as " feathered," " winged," " the herald," " like chidden Mercury from Jove," all allude to pagan polytheism. Mistress Quickly, the go-between of Falstaff and his lady-loves, is described by the fat knight as " my good she-Mercury " (" Merry Wives of Windsor," II.2. 81). In astrology Mercury had a close connection with commerce, and Autolycus, who was " littered under Mercury " (" Winter's Tale," IV.3. 25) was a " snapper-up of unconsidered trifles." The planet was the star of rogues and vagabonds. " Mercury endue thee with leasing," is a corroborative line from " Twelfth Night " (I.5. 105), which suggests subtlety and craft. The lively, quick, and tricky god produced the adjective " mercurial," which Shakespeare adopts in " Cymbeline " (IV.2. 310-311) in his description of Posthumus —" his foot Mercurial, his Martial thigh, his Jovial face." Astronomy is conspicuously absent in all the seventeen Shakespearian references to the smallest of the planets.

In Shakespeare's day Saturn was the most distant planet known. It is 886,000,000 miles from the sun and takes $29\frac{1}{2}$ years to circle it. In pagan theology Saturn was the god of seed-time and harvest, and his reign on earth was supposed to have been that halcyon epoch known as the golden age. Astrologers, however, endowed him with a reputation for gloom and melancholy. Shakespeare mentions him fewer times than any other planet, and in two of his five references his is contrasted with Venus—gravity with frivolity (" Titus Andronicus," II.3. 30-31, and " 2 Henry IV," II.4. 286). In " Cymbeline " the lines 10-13 of II.5 illustrate the poet's attitude to the grave god :

> . . . (she) did it with
> A pudency so rosy, the sweet view on't
> Might well have warm'd old Saturn ; that I thought her
> As chaste as unsunn'd snow.

In Sonnet XCVIII, lines 2-4 read :

> . . . proud-pied April, dress'd in all his trim,
> Hath put a spirit of youth in every thing,
> That heavy Saturn laugh'd and leap'd with him.

Those born under Saturn were supposed to be saddled with a saturnine and phlegmatic disposition, hence the point of Don John's remark to Conrade in " Much Ado About Nothing " (I.3. 11-13), " I wonder that thou, being . . . born under Saturn, goest about to apply a moral medicine to a mortifying mischief."

The planet Uranus was discovered by Sir William Herschel in 1781 ; and Neptune, after much close investigation and calculation by many astronomers, was located in 1846. Consequently they were unknown to Shakespeare. As in the case of the planets considered, his interest would have been drawn more towards the old gods after which they were named than to their astronomical importance. Indeed, there are in the plays over twenty references to Neptune as the ancient god of the sea.

XVI.

THE EARTH.

THE words " earth " and " world " are used in many hundreds
of instances in Shakespeare's plays, in very different con-
nections, and with wide varieties of meaning.   The poet
very often speaks of " the earth " when referring to the
people who live on it—mankind, the human race.   Frequently,
when writing " on earth " or " in earth," he has in his mind
the mortal existence in the flesh as opposed to the immortal,
spiritual life in heaven.   He subscribes to the old doctrine
that man is made of the dust of the ground and employs the
word " earth " in this signification also.   Antony addresses
the murdered Cæsar as " thou bleeding piece of earth "
(" Julius Cæsar," III.1. 254).   Perdita is described in " The
Winter's Tale " (V.1. 94-95) as " the most peerless piece
of earth that e'er the sun shone bright on."   Beatrice, in her
heart-whole independence calls man " a piece of valiant
dust " and declares she will not marry " till God make men
of some other metal than earth " (" Much Ado About
Nothing," II.1. 62-63).   The inevitable return of " dust
to dust " is voiced by Warwick in " 3 Henry VI," " I must
yield my body to the earth " (V.2. 9).   " Earth," again, is
several times mentioned by the poet as one of the four
elements or classes of matter recognized by the alchemists,
a point we have fully discussed in a previous chapter.

The foregoing uses of " earth " and " world " are interesting but beyond the scope of our present study.   Our attention
at the moment is focussed on Shakespeare's observations on

the earth as one of the planets in our solar system. He appears
from his poetry to divide his theories between the astronomical
explanation of a sphere suspended in space and the old
biblical conception of a fixed earth resting upon firm foundations, with the underworld below and the vaulted heavens
stretched out above.

Shakespeare, of course, was versed in the astronomical
beliefs of Ptolemy and knew that the earth was a sphere in
space, but it is impossible to ascertain whether he accepted
the new discovery that it revolved round the sun or clung
to the old doctrine that it was the centre of the universe,
round which all the other celestial bodies circled. He writes
of " the round world " in "Antony and Cleopatra " (V.1. 15),
" this terrestrial ball " in " Richard II " (III.2. 41), and of
"the world's diameter" in "Hamlet" (IV.1. 41). In that
terrific storm scene Lear calls to the " all-shaking thunder "
to " smite flat the thick rotundity o' the world ! " (III.2. 7).
There is a quotation from " Troilus and Cressida," which
(as we have noted before) seems to imply Shakespeare's
acceptance of what was then the newest thing in astronomy
(I.3. 85-88).

> The heavens themselves, the planets, and this centre,
> Observe degree, priority, and place,
> Insisture (i.e., constancy), course, proportion, season, form,
> Office and custom, in all line of order.

" This centre " is the earth, and the use of the word
suggests loyalty to the old Ptolemaic theory. But the poet
continues (89-91) :

> And therefore is the glorious planet Sol
> In noble eminence enthroned and sphered
> Amidst the other.

Shakespeare sometimes introduces the word " orb "
as a synonym for earth. In " Hamlet " the First Player,
describing the hush before a storm, says (II.2. 505-508) :

> But as we often see, against some storm,
> A silence in the heavens, the rack (i.e., mass of clouds) stand still,
> The bold winds speechless, and the orb below
> As hush as death.

In " Coriolanus," also, we read, " His fame folds-in this orb o' the earth " (V.6. 126-127).

In " Measure for Measure " we find what, on the surface, is an astronomically-correct description of the suspension of the earth in space.   Claudio shudders at the thought of death, which seems to him may mean (III.1. 124-126) :

> To be imprison'd in the viewless winds,
> And blown with restless violence round about
> The pendent world.

Macbeth's description of night, " Now o'er the one-half world Nature seems dead " (II.1. 49-50), does not imply Shakespeare's agreement with Copernicus as to an earth revolving on its axis, for it fits equally well the old idea of a sun girdling the earth.

In " Troilus and Cressida," a drama notable for some remarkable scientific passages, is mentioned the theory of the magnetic influence or attraction of the centre of the earth. Troilus searching for a good simile to illustrate the strength and fidelity of his love, says (III.2. 184-186) :

> As true as steel, as plantage to the moon,
> As sun to day, as turtle to her mate,
> As iron to adamant, as earth to the centre.

Later in the play Cressida declares (IV.2. 109-111) :

> But the strong base and building of my love
> Is as the very centre of the earth,
> Drawing all things to it.

The old concept of the world contained in the Bible is voiced by Octavius Cæsar in "Antony and Cleopatra." He is anxious to find a basis for a firm friendship with Antony. " If I knew," he says, " what hoop should hold us stanch,

from edge to edge o' the world I would pursue it " (II.2. 116-
118). We find the poet penning the phrase " world's end,"
not only in a time-sense, but in a space-sense as well.

The ancient Hebrew writers and philosophers believed
that the earth stood upon firm and fixed foundations, and
their view is echoed by Shakespeare in such phrases as,
" the huge, firm earth " (" King John," III.1. 72) ; "Thou
sure and firm-set earth " (" Macbeth," II.1. 56) ; " it is
positive as the earth is firm " (" Merry Wives," III.2. 49).
Moreover, we find the concurrent notion of a hell or underworld, where the evil spirits dwelt, in the speech of La
Pucelle (" 1 Henry VI," V.3. 10-12):

> Now, ye familiar spirits, that are call'd
> Out of the powerful regions under earth,
> Help me this once.

" The tongueless caverns of the earth " (" Richard II,"
I.1. 105) and " out of the bowels of the harmless earth "
(" 1 Henry IV," I-3. 61) are two other striking, related
phrases. Among the secrets hidden deep in the earth was
the mineral so precious to man—" treasure in the womb of
the earth " the poet calls it in " Hamlet " (I.1. 137).

When the solidity of the earth's anchorage was threatened,
events of great moment were happening or foreshadowed.
They might be violent death and revenge, such as Queen
Margaret visions when she says of Richard III, " Earth gapes,
hell burns, fiends roar, saints pray, to have him suddenly
convey'd away " (IV.4. 75-76). Glendower declares that
when he was born, " the frame and huge foundation of the
earth shaked like a coward " (" 1 Henry IV," III.1. 16-17).
Florizel in " The Winter's Tale " avows that before so
lamentable a thing comes to pass as the violation of his faith,
" Let Nature crush the sides o' the earth together and mar
the seeds within " (IV.4. 489-490).

The recognition of the earth as " Mother " of mankind, the teeming soil of which provides food and plenty, cheered by the sun, thirsty for the rain, radiant with beauty, is ungrudging in the poet. Even in his dejected mood, Hamlet still called the earth " this goodly frame," although it seemed to him " a sterile promontory " (II.2. 310). While Hotspur rather disrespectfully refers to our planet as " the old beldam," Friar Laurence says (" Romeo and Juliet," II.3. 9-18) :

> The earth, that's nature's mother, is her tomb ;
> What is her burying grave, that is her womb :
> And from her womb children of divers kind
> We sucking on her natural bosom find,
> Many for many virtues excellent,
> None but for some, and yet all different.
> O, mickle is the powerful grace that lies
> In herbs, plants, stones, and their true qualities :
> For nought so vile that on the earth doth live,
> But to the earth some special good doth give.

In " The Tempest " (IV.1. 110-113) Ceres sings :

> Earth's increase, foison plenty,
> Barns and garners never empty :
> Vines with clustering bunches growing ;
> Plants with goodly burthen bowing.

As to the age of the earth, Shakespeare calls it " antique," and makes the Clown in " Twelfth Night " sing : " A great while ago the world begun " (V.1. 414). When it came to figures, he followed the calculation of the Bible—the only computation then available to him. Says Rosalind in "As You Like It," " The poor world is almost six thousand years old " (IV.1. 94-95).

In regard to the size of the world, Shakespeare held an exaggerated idea, or so it seems to us, since modern astronomical research has impressed us with the puny insignificance of the earth compared with the mightiness of space ; and the elimination of time and distance by present methods of communication makes us reject such Shakespearian phrases as " the world's vastidity," " the spacious world," " the world's large space," and Emilia's remark in " Othello," " the world's a huge thing " (IV.3. 69). We must make due allowance for the difference of outlook in an age when a voyage to America and back was an undertaking of several months, and rather admire the spirit that faced the tediousness and discomfort of travel. In that age of adventure it was considered the more sporting :

> To see the wonders of the world abroad,
> Than, living dully sluggardized at home,
> Wear out thy youth with shapeless idleness
> > (" Two Gentlemen of Verona, I.1. 6-8.)

In common with his usual practice, Shakespeare searched classical mythology for a synonym for the earth and called it Tellus. This was an ancient Italian deity, who was goddess of marriage and fertility. In " Pericles " Marina says, " I will rob Tellus of her weed to strew thy green with flowers " (IV.1. 14-15). In " Hamlet " the Player King opens the play, which the Prince has staged, with the words (III.2. 165-166) :

> Full thirty times hath Phœbus' cart gone round
> Neptune's salt wash and Tellus' orbed ground.

—a couplet that we have had occasion to quote more than once in these pages.

XVII.

THE SIGNS OF THE ZODIAC.

THE Zodiac is an imaginary belt encircling the heavens, within which lie the paths of the sun, moon, and planets. It is about sixteen degrees in width and is divided into twelve parts, called " signs," each of which contains a constellation. Two thousand years ago each sign contained the constellation whose name it bore. To-day each constellation is in the sign bearing the name next after its own, a change brought about by the precession of the equinoxes. This process is defined in Funk and Wagnall's dictionary as " a slow motion of the equinoctial points on the ecliptic from east to west, causing the time between successive equinoxes to be appreciably shorter than it otherwise would be."

The names of the twelve signs of the Zodiac are as follows : Aries, the Ram ; Taurus, the Bull ; Gemini, the Twins ; Cancer, the Crab ; Leo, the Lion ; Virgo, the Virgin ; Libra, the Balance ; Scorpio, the Scorpion ; Sagittarius, the Archer ; Capricornus, the Goat ; Aquarius, the Water-carrier ; and Pisces, the Fishes. This division of the Zodiac appears to have been originated by the early inhabitants in that cradle of human progress, development, and civilization, Mesopotamia. From the Chaldeans the old zodiacal system spread to the Greeks, thence to the Egyptians, and so throughout the western world. The Chinese had a different and very complex system of their own.

In the Middle Ages the Signs of the Zodiac were familiar to most people, chiefly on account of their astrological significance. Each sign was supposed to govern a particular part of the body (see Sir Toby and Sir Andrew's dispute about Taurus in "Twelfth Night," I.3. 147-151), and their study was of immense importance in the practice of healing disease. They figured prominently among the early poets, their use being mainly allegorical. Spenser in "The Faerie Queen" (Bk. V. Introd. Stanzas V-VI) notes the movement of certain stars from the sign in which Ptolemy recorded them to the signs in which they were seen by the sixteenth century astronomers.

Shakespeare has two zodiacal references denoting a certain length of time.

"Love's Labour's Lost" (V.2. 804-808):

> . . . but go with speed
> To some forlorn and naked hermitage,
> Remote from all the pleasures of the world ;
> There stay until the twelve celestial signs
> Have brought about the annual reckoning.

"Measure for Measure" (I.2. 169-173):

> . . . but this new governor
> Awakes me all the enrolled penalties
> Which have, like unscour'd armour, hung by the wall
> So long, that nineteen zodiacs have gone round,
> And none of them been worn.

The mention of the Zodiac in "Titus Andronicus" is by way of simile. I have had occasion to quote the passage elsewhere (II.1. 5-9):

> As when the golden sun salutes the morn,
> And, having gilt the ocean with his beams,
> Gallops the zodiac in his glistering coach,
> And overlooks the highest-peering hills ;
> So Tamora . . .

K

Shakespeare seldom mentions the Signs of the Zodiac by name, but three such mentions occur in the one scene from "Titus Andronicus" (IV.3). It is the occasion on which old Titus, crushed by injustice and ingratitude, sends solicitations to the gods by means of arrows shot into the skies by himself, his brother Marcus, his nephew, Publius Lucius, and other gentlemen. Marcus, and Lucius, and the others enter with their bows, and Titus gives them arrows with letters tied to the ends of them (see stage directions at the head of the scene). "Now, masters, draw," orders Titus. They all shoot, and the old man exclaims to his nephew (63-64):

> O, well said, Lucius !
> Good boy, in Virgo's lap ; give it to Pallas.

The constellation Virgo, which gave its name to the Sign, was Astraea, the goddess of justice, who lived among men during the golden age, but owing to their wickedness withdrew to heaven and became a star. Some critics see in this line a reference to the mediæval representation of the Sign as the Madonna and Child.

After Marcus has told Titus Andronicus that he aimed a mile beyond the moon and lodged his letter with Jupiter, Titus turns to Publius (68-72):

> *Titus :* Publius, Publius, what hast thou done ?
> See, see, thou hast shot off one of Taurus' horns.
> *Marcus :* This was the sport, my lord ; when Publius shot,
> The Bull, being gall'd, gave Aries such a knock
> That down fell both the Ram's horns in the court.

The above passages may more properly be read as referring to the constellations themselves rather than to the zodiacal signs which contain them. The reference to Taurus, however, in " Twelfth Night," quoted before, is purely astrological and definitely refers to the Sign of the Zodiac.

In " Troilus and Cressida " (II.3. 205-207) Ulysses con-
demns the suggestion that Ajax should go to the sulking
Achilles and try to cajole him.   He declares :

> That were to enlard his fat-already pride
> And add more coals to Cancer when he burns
> With entertaining great Hyperion.

Cancer was the zodiacal sign of the Summer Solstice.

Another and more obscure reference to the Zodiac occurs
in " 2 Henry IV " (II.4. 288-290), when Prince and Poins
catch Falstaff flirting with Doll Tearsheet.   " Saturn and
Venus in conjunction ! " exclaims the Prince ; and Poins
adds :

> And, look, where the fiery Trigon, his man, be not lisping
> to his master's old tables, his note-book, his counsel-keeper.

Astrologers divided the Zodiac into four " trigons " or
" triplicites."   One consisted of the three " fiery " signs
(Aries, Leo, Sagittarius) ; the others consisted of the three
airy, the three watery, and the three earthy signs.   " When
the three superior planets were in the three fiery signs, they
formed a ' fiery trigon ' ; when in Cancer, Scorpio, and
Pisces, a ' watery ' one, etc." (The Temple Shakespeare,
page 173).

XVIII.

COMETS.

A COMET is a heavenly body moving in a very eccentric orbit under the influence of the sun's attraction. It consists of three parts when perfect—a star-like nucleus, a surrounding envelope or coma, and a tail, which often attains an enormous length. While some comets revolve round the sun in periods ranging from a few years to several centuries, others come from immense stellar distances and seem to pay only one visit to our universe. Records exist of several hundred comets, varying greatly in size, aspect, distance, and intervals of re-appearance.

Astronomy as yet knows little of the laws governing comets, which are still regarded with that superstitious dread that usually accompanies scientific ignorance. Anciently their appearance was viewed with terror, which the gloomy predictions of the astrologers did nothing to alleviate. On the contrary the most alarming prophecies were made by them of disasters that would ensue from these irregular visitants.

Under astrology we saw that the calamity most generally associated with the appearance of a comet was the death of a king. Comets were said to have been sighted at the deaths of Constantine, Attila, Mahomet, and Richard I. Shakespeare introduced this startling phenomena into that night of storm and fury that preceded the fall of Cæsar.

It filled the dictator's wife, Calphurnia, with nameless fear and added desperation to her prayers that her lord would not venture into the Capitol. She declares (" Julius Cæsar," II.2. 30-31) :

> When beggars die, there are no comets seen ;
> The heavens themselves blaze forth the death of princes.

Shakespeare, obviously much moved by Plutarch's account of the fall of Cæsar, returns to these " stars with trains of fire " in " Hamlet," a play he wrote about the same time as his famous Roman tragedy. The comet was said to be Cæsar's spirit and to indicate his reception among the gods.

It was natural that the poet should fasten this strange association of comets with royal disaster to his hero-king, Henry V. I quote again the Duke of Bedford's remarks from " I Henry VI " (I.I. 2-5) :

> Comets, importing change of times and states,
> Brandish your crystal tresses in the sky,
> And with them scourge the bad revolting stars
> That have consented unto Henry's death.

" Stars with trains of fire," or " crystal tresses," are almost perfect descriptions of these phenomena and indicate that the poet had studied them closely. That he had opportunities of doing so, we know. There was a great comet in 1577, as Kepler has himself told us ; and in 1607 what we now know as Halley's comet made one of its periodic appearances. This last event, however, occurred after " Hamlet " and " I Henry VI "—the two dramas containing the above descriptions— were written.

The wonder with which comets were received is reflected in a passage from " I Henry IV " (III.2), where the King, speaking to Prince Hal, says (46-47) :

> By being seldom seen, I could not stir
> But like a comet I was wonder'd at.

And again in " The Taming of the Shrew " (III.2. 96-98) :

> And wherefore gaze this goodly company,
> As if they saw some wondrous monument,
> Some comet or unusual prodigy.

The astrological tenet, that comets were an omen fore-shadowing the fall or death of great men, is accepted again in " 1 Henry VI " (III.2. 29-32) :

> *Bastard of Orleans :* See, noble Charles, the beacon of our friend ;
> The burning torch in yonder turret stands.
> *Charles :* Now shine it like a comet of revenge,
> A prophet to the fall of all our foes !

Shakespeare probably shared the wondering curiosity of the astronomers regarding comets and did not feel the cold clutch of superstitious fear, which laid hold of so many of his ignorant contemporaries whenever these mysterious phenomena invaded the heavens.

XIX.

METEORS AND SHOOTING STARS.

Besides the large congregations of matter known as planets, space contains numberless small bodies, invisible to the eye, even when it is peering through a telescope. Our earth, moving at the rate of thousands of miles an hour, comes into violent collision with these bodies, some of which are not larger than small pebbles or even grains of sand, and are also moving with planetary velocity. The atmosphere around the earth protects us from a ceaseless cannonade by these small bodies. The bodies themselves, on striking the air, are submitted to friction, which first produces intense heat, and then light, rendering the objects visible. The shock dissipates or pulverizes them, and most of them become fused in the upper regions of the air.

These small bodies are called meteors. When the meteor is neither very large nor very brilliant, it is termed a shooting star. The difference is only one of degree, for every day the earth encounters millions of these tiny bodies of varying sizes. Sometimes a meteor escapes complete combustion and dissipation and the nucleus falls on the earth. They are then known as meteorites or aerolites. They can be examined, weighed, and analysed ; and collections of them are to be seen in the British and other museums. The most venerated of all meteorites that " fell from heaven " is to be found in the Great Mosque of Mecca. Known as the Black Stone, it is built into the wall of the Kaaba, and the thousands of pilgrims, who flock to the sacred city, would consider their pilgrimage in vain unless they kissed the stone, or ruby, of heaven.

The old belief was that the stars were little bright bodies fixed into a solid vault called the sky or firmament; and " shooting stars " were thought actually to fall from their places in heaven on to the earth. The Bible seemed to support this conception, especially the Book of Revelation (VI.13) which reads : "And the stars of heaven fell unto the earth, even as a fig tree casteth her untimely figs, when she is shaken of a mighty wind." Shakespeare lived in an age when this idea was still piously accepted by a large majority, who insisted that every statement in Holy Writ was literally true. It is reproduced exactly in the following quotation from " Richard II " (II.4. 18-20) :

> Ah, Richard, with the eyes of heavy mind
> I see thy glory like a shooting star
> Fall to the base earth from the firmament.

The same notion is in the poet's mind in the lines from " Henry VIII " (IV.1. 52-55), where onlookers are discussing the coronation procession of Anne Bullen as it passes them.

> *Second Gent. :* Is that old noble lady, Duchess of Norfolk ?
> *First Gent. :* It is ; and all the rest are countesses.
> *Second Gent :* Their coronets say so. These are stars indeed,
> And sometimes falling ones.

That shooting stars were believed to be real stars, escaped from their spheres, is further supported by these passages :
" Midsummer Night's Dream " (II.1. 150-154) :

> (I) heard a mermaid, on a dolphin's back,
> Uttering such dulcet and harmonious breath,
> That the rude sea grew civil at her song,
> And certain stars shot madly from their spheres,
> To hear the sea-maid's music.

" Titus Andronicus " (II.4. 14-15) :

> If I do wake, some planet strike me down,
> That I may slumber in eternal sleep !

Shooting stars and meteors, suggesting disturbances in the ordered government of the heavens, were regarded gravely by the astrologers as an evil portent. In "King John" (III.4. 157-158) Shakespeare classifies meteors with "prodigies and signs . . . presages and tongues of heaven." It was the appearance of meteors "frighting the fixed stars of heaven" which roused the fears of the superstitious Welsh soldiers, on whose help Richard II was relying. They believed these omens foretold the fall of the king and thereupon disbanded to their homes ("Richard II," II.4.) Such phenomena created great wonder, amazement, and apprehension. In "King John," Lewis the Dauphin declares that he is more amazed at Salisbury's emotion than if he had seen "the vaulty top of heaven figured quite o'er with burning meteors" (V.2. 52-53).

Speaking of the combatants in civil war, King Henry IV compares them to meteors.

" 1 Henry IV " (I.1. 9-13) :

> . . . Those opposed eyes,
> Which, like meteors of a troubled heaven,
> All of one nature, of one substance bred,
> Did lately meet in the intestine shock
> And furious close of civil butchery.

At the end of the same play Henry urges the rebellious Earl of Worcester to :

> . . . move in that obedient orb again
> Where you did give a fair and natural light,
> And be no more an exhaled meteor,
> A prodigy of fear. . . .
>
> (V.1. 17-20.)

The adjective "exhaled" in the above quotation is interesting, for it reveals Shakespeare's views on the scientific explanation of meteors. Further indication is given by

Juliet's remark, when she refused to acknowledge that the growing light is that of the dawn which will separate her from Romeo. She declares, " It is some meteor that the sun exhales " (III.5. 13). Meteors occur in the great storm in " Julius Cæsar," and Brutus declares that he can read his letters by the light of the " exhalations whizzing in the air " (II.1. 44). In the humorous reference to meteors hereunder, the word " exhalations " is used again. The scene is that famous one in the Boar's-Head Tavern in Eastcheap following the practical joke played upon Falstaff and his companions at Gadshill by the Prince and Poins. Falstaff has given a wholly lying account of the affair, making himself out a hero. Prince Hal cross-examines Bardolph and Peto on their cowardly retreat and asks why they ran away when they had the advantage of numbers and weapons on their side : " What instinct hadst thou for it ? "

> *Bardolph :* My lord, do you see these meteors ? do you behold
> these exhalations ?
> *Prince :* I do.
> *Bard :* What think you they portend ?
> *Prince :* Hot livers and cold purses.
> *Bard :* Choler, my lord, if rightly taken.
> *Prince :* No, if rightly taken, halter.
> ("1 Henry IV," II.4. 351-357.)

Although Shakespeare subscribed to the old theory of meteors, which modern astronomy has exploded, his use of them for poetic simile was very effective. A good example occurs in the " Comedy of Errors " (IV.2. 1-6) :

> *Adriana :* Ah, Luciana, did he tempt thee so ?
> Mightst thou perceive austerely in his eye
> That he did plead in earnest ? yea or no ?
> Look'd he or red or pale, or sad or merrily ?
> What observation madest thou, in this case,
> Of his heart's meteors tilting in his face ?

XX.

THE SEASONS.

SHAKESPEARE was intensely aware of the passage of the seasons with their beauty or drabness, their joys or sorrows, their hopes or regrets ; and his works convey the character of each in colourful phrase of picturesque fidelity.

In many cases the dramatist has a distinct mental picture of the time of year at which the action of his drama is passing. He takes the trouble, moreover, to acquaint his audience with it. In " Hamlet," for example, the opening scene on the platform before the castle of Elsinore takes place in winter : " 'Tis bitter cold," says Francisco. When Hamlet watches with the sentries the next night, he declares, " the air bites shrewdly " ; and Horatio agrees that " it is a nipping and an eager air." Plainly Shakespeare visualised a dark, bitter winter night. Later in the play, when poor mad Ophelia gathers her flowers—rosemary, pansies, fennel, columbines, rue, and daisies, and tells us that the violets are all withered some time ago—it is clear that the dramatist imagines his story has carried the time to the end of May or the beginning of June.

In " Julius Cæsar," to take another example, the first three acts take place in February and March. How clearly Shakespeare pictured the seasonable conditions is evidenced in the meeting of the conspirators in Brutus's orchard. There

is a dispute as to the point where day will break.   Casca
says (II.1. 106-110) :

> Here, as I point my sword, the sun arises ;
> Which is a great way growing on the south,
> Weighing the youthful season of the year.
> Some two months hence up higher toward the north
> He first presents his fire.

The correctness of the dramatist's details of setting is
further confirmed by the mighty tempest that shook the
night, for it was evidently one of those equinoctial storms,
so common about this time of year, the Ides, or 15th, of
March.

Shakespeare introduced the seasons into the titles of two
of his dramas—" The Winter's Tale," and "A Midsummer
Night's Dream."   These plays do not, however, best illustrate his extremely accurate knowledge of the different times
of year and their phenomena.   In " The Winter's Tale," it
is true, Camillo in the first few lines does speak of " this
coming summer," but Mamillius's remark in II.1. 25,
"A sad tale's best for winter " is supposed to have suggested
the title.   "A Midsummer Night's Dream," again, is evidently
intended to take place in May rather than at midsummer.
Theseus, when the four lovers, Lysander, Demetrius, Heiena,
and Hermia, are discovered asleep in the wood near Titania's
" flowery bed " and " her close and concentrated bower "
in the hawthorn brake, remarks (IV.1. 137-138) :

> No doubt they rose up early to observe
> The rite of May (i.e., May-day).

Shakespeare's references to the passage of the seasons,
while poetically descriptive, are often metaphoric in their
application.   For example, he compares the change from joy
to sorrow to that of from summer to winter.

" 2 Henry VI " (II.4. 1-4) :

Thus sometimes hath the brightest day a cloud ;
And after summer evermore succeeds
Barren winter, with his wrathful nipping cold :
So cares and joys abound, as seasons fleet.

In "Titus Andronicus," Titus, describing the unfailing tears of sorrow he will shed upon the earth, says (III.1. 19-20) :

In summer's drought I'll drop upon thee still ;
In winter with warm tears I'll melt the snow.

A further figurative use of the seasons occurs in "Love's Labour's Lost" (I.1. 100-107) :

King : Biron's like an envious sneaping frost,
        That bites the first-born infants of the spring.
Biron : Well, say I am ; why should proud summer boast,
        Before the birds have any cause to sing.
        Why should I joy in an abortive birth ?
        At Christmas I no more desire a rose
        Than wish a snow in May's new-fangled shows ;
        But like of each thing that in season grows.

In the quarrel scene between Oberon and Titania ("Midsummer Night's Dream," II.1), the queen of the fairies speaks of the forgeries of jealousy, and complains that "since the middle summer's spring," whenever the fairies have met to dance their "ringlets to the whistling wind," Oberon with his brawls has disturbed their sport. Therefore, she says (107-114) :

The seasons alter : hoary-headed frosts
Fall in the fresh lap of the crimson rose ;
And on old Hiems' thin and icy crown
An odorous chaplet of sweet summer buds
Is, as in mockery, set ; the spring, the summer,
The chiding autumn, angry winter, change
Their wonted liveries ; and the mazed world,
By their increase, now knows not which is which.

Further eccentricities on the part of the seasons is reported in " 2 Henry IV " (IV.4. 123-124) :

> The seasons change their manners as the year
> Had found some months asleep and leap'd them over.

Besides literal descriptions of the different traits of the seasons, the poet uses the common phrases, " in season," " out of season," and so forth, in their less narrow significance.

Of all times of the year that which was most dear to Shakespeare, as it is dear to all those who have any poetry in their souls, was the spring. " The sweet o' the year," Autolycus calls it in " The Winter's Tale (IV.3. 3-4) when " the red blood reigns in the winter's pale." The poet can wish the lovers of " The Tempest," Ferdinand and Miranda, no greater happiness than in the words of Ceres (IV.1. 114-115) :

> Spring come to you at the farthest
> In the very end of harvest.

The joy with which a winter-weary world holds out its arms to the spring is recalled by King Leontes when he greets Florizel and Perdita at his court with the words, " Welcome hither, as is the spring to the earth " (" The Winter's Tale," V.1. 151-152).

In the song with which the serving-wench tries to cheer Queen Katharine, " whose soul grows sad with troubles " (" Henry VIII," III.1. 6-8), she sings of Orpheus :

> To his music plants and flowers
> Ever sprung, as sun and showers
> There had made a lasting spring.

The wonder of the opening buds, when the bare branches clothe themselves once more in all the green luxuriance of their summer garb, is charmingly described by Shakespeare.

He writes of " appearing buds " in early spring as " the new-born infants " ; and in " Pericles " (I.1. 12) Antiochus's fair daughter is described as " apparelled like the spring." The first dabs of colour awake in him a grateful response— " daffodils that come before the swallow dares, and take the winds of March with beauty " (" Winter's Tale," IV.4. 118-120) ; " violets that strew the green lap of the new-come spring " (" Richard II," V.2. 46-47) ; and " pale primroses, that die unmarried, ere they can behold bright Phœbus in his strength " (" Winter's Tale," IV.4. 122-124). While admiring the treasures of the garden, " sweet as a springtime flower," he does not forget the weeds.

" 2 Henry VI " (III.1. 30-32) :

> Now 'tis the spring, and weeds are shallow-rooted ;
> Suffer them now, and they'll o'ergrow the garden,
> And choke the herbs for want of husbandry.

" The flower o' the spring " and " the roses of the spring " did not cause the poet to overlook the spring birds. The swallow is linked with the daffodil in the quotation above. In " Love's Labour's Lost " (V.2) mention is made of another of the migrants—the cuckoo. Says Holofernes the school-master : " This side is Hiems, winter ; this Ver, the spring ; the one maintained by the owl, the other by the cuckoo " (901-903). There follows the song by Spring and Winter ; and Spring sings (904-910) :

> When daisies pied and violets blue
> And lady-smocks all silver-white
> And cuckoo-buds of yellow hue
> Do paint the meadows with delight,
> The cuckoo then, on every tree,
> Mocks married men. . . .

Spring is the time when all creatures mate. " The spring is near, when green geese are a-breeding," says Biron in

"Love's Labour's Lost" (I.1. 97); and the poet knew the call of heart to heart when Nature awoke to smiles after her long winter sleep. What more joyous verse on the season of love has been penned than the following from "As You Like It" (V.3. 17-22)?

> It was a lover and his lass,
>   With a hey and a ho, and a hey nonino,
> That o'er the green cornfield did pass
>   In the spring time, the only pretty ring time,
> When birds do sing, hey ding a ding, ding :
> Sweet lovers love the spring.

The word "spring" is used by Shakespeare in the sense of beginning, birth, dawning. "Shall, even in the spring of love, thy love-springs rot?" asks Luciana of Antipholus in the "Comedy of Errors" (III.2. 2-3). In "Pericles" Gower reads the following inscription on the tomb of Marina (IV.4. 34-35) :

> The fairest, sweet'st, and best, lies here,
> Who wither'd in her spring of year.

Another example of the same use occurs in "Richard II," where the Duke of York says to his son, Aumerle (V.2. 50-51) :

> Well, bear you well in this new spring of time,
> Lest you be cropp'd before you come to prime.

The spring is linked to the fickle month of April, a month especially dear to the poet, for it saw his birth and contained the day of England's patron, Saint George. April was also destined to see Shakespeare's death, but of this he had no prevision as he sang of its glory and loveliness. "Well apparell'd April on the heel of limping winter treads" he writes in "Romeo and Juliet" (I.2. 27-28); and in Sonnet XCVIII, lines 1-4 read :

> From you I have been absent in the spring,
> When proud-pied April, dress'd in all his trim,
> Hath put a spirit of youth in every thing,
> That heavy Saturn laugh'd and leap'd with him.

April as the month of showers and flowers is most delightfully described. "Flora peering in April's front," is a sentence from "The Winter's Tale" (IV.4. 2-3); and in the "Merchant of Venice" a servant of Portia's, announcing the arrival of Bassanio, says (II.9. 93-94):

> A day in April never came so sweet,
> To show how costly summer was at hand.

The well-known character of this alluring month is concisely given in the words, "the uncertain glory of an April day," which we find in the "Two Gentlemen of Verona" (1.3. 85). "Men are April when they woo, December when they wed" is Rosalind's rather cynical assertion in "As You Like It" (IV.1. 147). In "The Tempest" (IV.1. 65) the poet describes the month of rain and sunshine as "spongy April," and in "Titus Andronicus," "youthful April with all his showers" (III.1. 18). "Faster than springtime showers comes thought on thought," is a beautiful figure of speech in "2 Henry VI" (III.1. 337); but few similes could be more deft than the following from "Antony and Cleopatra" (III.2. 42-43):

> The April's in her eyes : it is love's spring,
> And these the showers to bring it on.

From changeable April advancing spring carries us into the entrancing month of May. Of its opening festival Shakespeare has much to say, for May-Day was a happy holiday in the poet's life time and had not degenerated to a verbose date in the political calendar. Stowe says, "In the month of May, namely on May-Day in the morning, every man except impediment, would walk into the sweet meadows

L

and green woods ; there to rejoice their spirits with the beauty and savour of sweet flowers and with the noise of birds, praising God in their kind." To this custom Lysander refers in " Midsummer Night's Dream " (I.1. 166-167), when he says to Hermia, he will wait for her, " where I did meet thee once with Helena, to do observance to a morn of May." In " Henry VIII " (V.4. 14-15) the Porter has as little hope of scattering the noisy crowd as " to make 'em sleep on a May-Day morning," when all sorts of jollities and festivities would be held, including old folk dances—" a morris for May-Day," as we read in "All's Well " (II.2. 25).

An interesting comparison of May to youth occurs in " Henry V " (I.2. 119-120), where the Bishop of Ely says to the King :

> . . . my thrice-puissant liege
> Is in the very May-morn of his youth,
> Ripe for exploits and mighty enterprises.

Of the beauty of May Shakespeare was a wholehearted worshipper. Richard II speaks of his queen, who came from France, as, " adorned like sweet May " (V.1. 79) ; Laertes calls his sister, Ophelia, " Rose of May " ; and Benedict declares that Beatrice exceeds Hero in beauty as " the first of May doth the last of December " (" Much Ado About Nothing," I.1. 194-195).

Love, so fragrant in the spring, sways all to her bidding in the merry month of May. " Love whose month is ever May," writes Shakespeare in " Love's Labour's Lost " (IV.3. 102). "As full of spirit as the month of May " (" 1 Henry IV," IV.1. 101), and " as flush as May " (" Hamlet," III.3. 81) are typical praises with which this moon of lilac and laburnum is honoured.

And so the year passes to " hot June," and we are on the threshold of summer. Shakespeare mentions the mid-year months but seldom in his plays, but the whole summer season is dear to him and, after the spring, the best beloved. He does not robe June, July, and August in the same soft raiment of romance that he bestows on April and May. Nevertheless he writes, " as clear as is the summer's sun " (" Henry V," I.2. 86) and " clear as founts in July " (" Henry VIII," I.1. 154). " Summer is made glorious by the sun," " sweet," " proud," " a sea of glory," " costly." He compares his beautiful women to the loveliness of summer. Pericles describes Thaisa, the daughter of Simonides and afterwards his wife, " as a fair day in summer, wondrous fair " (II.5. 36). Mortimer says of his Welsh wife, the daughter of Owen Glendower (" 1 Henry IV," III.1. 208-210) :

> . . . thy tongue
> Makes Welsh as sweet as ditties highly penn'd,
> Sung by a fair queen in a summer's bower.

In trying to commend the suitor Paris to Juliet, Lady Capulet says, rather extravagantly, " Verona's summer hath not such a flower " (" Romeo and Juliet," I.3. 77).

Possibly Shakespeare disliked the excessive heat and considered it marred the otherwise perfect joys of summer. He writes of the " parching heat," " the scalding heat," and " summer's drought." In " Cymbeline " (IV.4. 29) we read of " hot summer's tanlings," that is, those tanned by the sun ; and in " The Tempest " (IV.1. 134) of " sunburned sicklemen, of August weary." The dying King John cries (V.7. 30-31 ; 35-36. 41) :

> There is so hot a summer in my bosom,
> That all my bowels crumple up to dust.
>
> . . . . . .
>
> Poison'd,—ill fare—dead, forsook, cast off :
> And none of you will bid the winter come
>
> . . . . . .
>
> And comfort me with cold.

Again, the figure of a dry, baking summer is in Bolingbroke's mind when he threatens to " lay the summer's dust with showers of blood " (" Richard II," III.3. 43).

In " Richard III," when the young Prince Edward V declares that if he lives to be a man he'll win " our ancient right in France again," the dramatist puts an old saw in the mouth of the cunning Duke of Gloucester, afterwards the crookback king, " short summers lightly have a forward spring " (III.1. 94).

Though summer is sometimes oppressive and brings scorching heat, drought, and dust, it is yet the season of flowers, and as such Shakespeare did full honour to it. "The leavy summer," he calls it, and sings of " summer-swelling flowers," " the summer's velvet buds," " a chaplet of sweet summer buds," which appears in the " Midsummer Night's Dream " quotation above. Juliet pronounces this charming metaphor (" Romeo and Juliet," II.2. 121-122) :

> This bud of love, by summer's ripening breath,
> May prove a beauteous flower when next we meet.

The rose, the queen of flowers, was to the poet conspicuous in summer's garland of blossom. " Sweet roses in the summer air " he mentions in " Love's Labour's Lost," and coins the following simile in " Richard III " (IV.3. 12-13) :

> Their lips were four red roses on a stalk,
> Which in their summer beauty kiss'd each other.

In that delightful sheep-shearing scene in " The Winter's Tale," undoubtedly copied from similar festivals in the Cotswold country, Shakespeare says of the summer blooms (IV.4. 81-82) :

> . . . the fairest flowers o' the season
> Are our carnations and streak'd gillyvors.

A few lines later Perdita remarks (lines 103-107):

> . . . Here's flowers for you ;
> Hot lavender, mints, savory, marjoram ;
> The marigold, that goes to bed wi' the sun
> And with him rises weeping : these are flowers
> Of middle summer.

In " Pericles " Marina, entering with a basket of flowers, by the sea-shore—her mother was drowned at sea—speaks (IV.1. 14-18) :

> . . . I will rob Tellus of her weed
> To strew thy green with flowers : the yellows, blues,
> The purple violets, and marigolds,
> Shall, as a carpet, hang upon thy grave,
> While summer-days do last.

An exactly similar incident occurs in " Cymbeline " (IV.2. 218-220), where Arviragus, mourning Imogen, who is believed dead, promises :

> With fairest flowers,
> Whilst summer lasts, and I live here, Fidele,
> I'll sweeten thy sad grave.

And after enumerating several flowers, like primrose, azured harebell, and leaf of eglantine, he concludes (228-229) :

> Yea, and furr'd moss besides, when flowers are none,
> To winter-ground thy corse.

(" Winter-ground " means to protect from the inclement weather of winter.)

In " Romeo and Juliet " notice is given to " the gossamer that idles in the wanton summer air " (II.6. 18-19) ; and in "All's Well That Ends Well " the briers are mentioned (IV.4. 31-33) :

> . . . the time will bring on summer,
> When briers shall have leaves as well as thorns :
> And be as sweet as sharp.

The familiar sight of the " summer's corn by tempest lodged " (i.e., beaten down) is a simile in " 2 Henry VI "

(III.2. 176) ; and the poet does not even forget the humble but welcome grass :

"Henry V " (I.1. 65-66) :

> Grew like the summer grass, fastest by night,
> Unseen, yet crescive (growing) in his faculty.

Of the birds of summer Shakespeare makes frequent mention. Autolycus sings of three (" The Winter's Tale," IV.3. 9-12) :

> The lark, that tirra-lyra chants,
> With heigh ! with heigh ! the thrush and the jay,
> Are summer songs for me and my aunts,
> While we lie tumbling in the hay.

In " Timon of Athens " the lords say to Timon : " The swallow follows not summer more willing than we your lordship" (III.6. 31-32) ; and Duncan on that lovely, calm summer's evening ushering in the night of his assassination, remarks on " the temple-haunting martlet, this guest of summer," who makes his " pendant bed and procreant cradle " beneath the eaves (" Macbeth," I.6. 3-4, 8).

Other creatures of summer mentioned by the poet include the " stinging bees," who in " hottest summer's day " are "led by their master to the flowered fields " (" Titus Andronicus," V.1. 14-15). Butterflies appear in a passage in " Coriolanus " (IV.6. 92-95) :

> . . . they follow him,
> Against us brats, with no less confidence
> Than boys pursuing summer butterflies,
> Or butchers killing flies.

The pests of the warm season are referred to again in " 3 Henry VI " in the phrase, " swarm like summer flies " (II.6. 8).

There are a number of interesting allusions throughout the plays to the habits and occupations associated with summer.

In " Love's Labour's Lost " (V.2. 913-16) we hear of shepherds piping on oaten straws and maidens bleaching their summer smocks. Travel was apparently easier in summer and the going on the roads was good. In "The Merchant of Venice " Gratiano exclaims impatiently (V.1. 263-264), " Why, this is like the mending of highways in summer, where the ways are fair enough." The use of the word " summer-house " in " 1 Henry IV " (III.1. 164) is apt to mislead the modern reader. The poet had no vision of a wooden shanty in the corner of the garden. " Summer-house " meant a country house or pleasant retreat.

The inherent sadness of autumn touches the poet in Shakespeare. " Chiding autumn," he calls it, when the summer withers and the leaves all fade. He uses the expression " a cloud in autumn " in " Troilus and Cressida " (I.2. 139) in the sense of a herald of bad weather and metaphorically as a sign of evil times to come. The phrase, " autumn's dust," occurs in " King Lear," where Lear says (IV.6. 199-201) :

> Why, this would make a man a man of salt (tears),
> To use his eyes for garden water-pots,
> Aye, and laying autumn's dust.

The impression of autumn chiding the season of joys and flowers appears to have been a strong one with Shakespeare, for in " The Taming of the Shrew " Petruchio declares he will overbear Katharine " though she chide as loud as thunder when the clouds in autumn crack " (I.2. 95-96).

Autumn brings the thought of harvest, an association that occurred naturally to the country-bred dramatist. In "Antony and Cleopatra " (V.2. 88) he pictures an exceptional spirit of bounty as an autumn " that grew the more by reaping." In " 3 Henry VI," again (V.7. 3-4) he uses this strong simile for the slaughter of battle : " foeman, like to autumn's corn . . . mowed down in tops of all their pride." A line of Shylock's (" Merchant of Venice," I.3. 82) is a reminder that autumn is the mating season of sheep and some other animals.

That phenomenon which we now call an Indian summer, that is, a return of summerlike conditions after autumn has commenced, was noticed by Shakespeare with his wonderful faculty for observing every trick of Nature. In " 1 Henry VI " (I.2. 131-132) La Pucelle (Joan of Arc) exclaims :

> Expect Saint Martin's summer, halcyon days,
> Since I have entered into these wars.

St. Martin's Day is November 11th, and Dr. Johnson gives the following paraphrase of this very appropriate remark by Joan : " Expect prosperity after misfortune, like fair weather at Martlemas, after winter has begun." The same idea appears again in " 1 Henry IV." As he takes his departure, Prince Hal calls out to Falstaff, " Farewell, thou latter spring ! farewell, All-hallown summer ! " (I.2. 178). All-hallow-mas is on the first of November, and the Prince compares the frivolous behaviour of the fat knight at his time of life to the incongruous, unseasonable Indian summer.

Autumn hardens into winter, a season for which Shakespeare reserved some hard epithets. He could not forget, even in the glories of June, that " after summer evermore succeeds barren winter, with his wrathful nipping cold " (" 2 Henry VI," II.4. 2-3). In Sonnet V (5-6) he writes :

> For never-resting time leads summer on
> To hideous winter and confounds him there.

" When great leaves fall, the winter is at hand," observes a London citizen in " Richard III " (II.3. 33) ; and then the dark season descends, graphically described in the words of the exiled Duke in the Forest of Arden ;

"As You Like It " (II.1. 3-11) ;

> Are not these woods
> More free from peril than the envious court?
> Here feel we but the penalty of Adam,
> The seasons' difference; as the icy fang
> And churlish chiding of the winter's wind,
> Which, when it bites and blows upon my body,
> Even till I shrink with cold, I smile and say
> " This is no flattery: these are counsellors
> That feelingly persuade me what I am."

Winter sings of itself in " Love's Labour's Lost " (V.2. 922-927 ; 931-934):

> When icicles hang by the wall,
>   And Dick the shepherd blows his nail,
> And Tom bears logs into the hall,
>   And milk comes frozen home in pail,
> When blood is nipp'd and ways be foul,
>   Then nightly sings the staring owl.
>
>   .   .   .   .   .
>
> When all aloud the wind doth blow,
>   And coughing drowns the parson's saw,
> And birds sit brooding in the snow,
>   And Marian's nose looks red and raw.

Winter is " rough," " howling," " angry," " trembling," " frozen," " biting," " sap-consuming." The poet complains of " the winter's furious rages," and compares man's ingratitude to the piercing blasts and frosts of winter time.

"As You Like It " (II.7. 174-179; 184-189);

> Blow, blow, thou winter wind,
> Thou art not so unkind
>   As man's ingratitude;
> Thy tooth is not so keen,
> Because thou art not seen,
>   Although thy breath be rude.
>
>   .   .   .   .   .
>
> Freeze, freeze, thou bitter sky,
> Thou dost not bite so nigh
>   As benefits forgot;

> Though thou the waters warp,
> Thy sting is not so sharp
> As friend remember'd not.

The weather of winter is " rough " or " foul," " churlish winter's tyranny," and human beings are but " the shrinking slaves of winter " (" Cymbeline," IV.4. 30).   " Winter garments must be lined," declares Touchstone emphatically. "A sad tale's best for winter," is Mamillius's remark already quoted from " The Winter's Tale " (II.1. 25); and Gloucester in " Richard III " speaks of " the winter of our discontent " (I.1. 1).   Bad news is " winterly "; and in " Troilus and Cressida " (IV.5. 24) Achilles, addressing the Trojan girl, Cressida, declares, " I'll take that winter from your lips, fair lady " (with a kiss of greeting).

A happier note is struck in Perdita's reference to winter flowers in " The Winter's Tale " (IV.4. 73-79) :

Perdita :   . . . Reverend sirs,
For you there's rosemary and rue ; these keep
Seeming and savour all the winter long :
Grace and remembrance be to you both,
And welcome to our shearing !
Polixenes :   Shepherdess,
A fair one are you, well you fit our ages
With flowers of winter.

The bird of winter was the owl ; " Then nightly sings the staring owl " we read in the song from " Love's Labour's Lost," quoted above, where Holofernes contrasts him with the spring bird, the cuckoo.

The winter months are named in no kindly spirit by Shakespeare. Arviragus says in " Cymbeline " (III.3. 35-39) :

What should we speak of
When we are old as you ? when we shall hear
The rain and wind beat dark December, how
In this our pinching cave shall we discourse
The freezing hours away ?

The brief hours of daylight allotted to the " dark days before Christmas " are referred to in " The Winter's Tale," where King Polixenes says of his son, Prince Florizel, " He makes a July's day short as December " (I.2. 169). In " Richard II " Bolingbroke asks, " Who can wallow naked in December snow by thinking on fantastic summer's heat ? " meaning that his banishment by his king can be made no easier to bear by thoughts of England and his ultimate return. (I.3. 298).

The cold bleak month of January fares no better at the poet's hands. The " blasts of January " that " blow you through and through " is his description in " The Winter's Tale " (IV.4. 111-112). In " Much Ado About Nothing " Leonato says to Beatrice, " You will never run mad, niece." " No, not till a hot January," is that spirited lady's rejoinder (I.1. 94-95). In the same play (V.4. 40-42) we find a significant reference to February. Don Pedro remarks to Benedick :

> Why, what's the matter,
> That you have such a February face,
> So full of frost, of storm, of cloudiness.

We have already cited Shakespeare's phrase, " the winds of March," and another interesting reference to the month of the war-god occurs in " 1 Henry IV." Sir Richard Vernon has been praising the Prince of Wales (Henry V) to Hotspur, when the young soldier exclaims, " No more, no more : worse than the sun in March, this praise doth nourish agues " (IV.1. 111-112). In " Much Ado " Don John describes Claudio as " a very forward March-chick ! " (I.2. 58)—an amusing way of denoting precocity by comparison to a chicken hatched in March.

So the long winter drags on—" winter's tedious nights," " lagging winters," winter that " tames man, woman, and beast" ("Taming of the Shrew," IV.1. 24). Suffolk speaks of cursing away a winter's night in " 2 Henry VI " (III.2. 335); yet there is nought to be done but, as Posthumus says in " Cymbeline " (II.4. 4-6) :

> Abide the change of time ;
> Quake in the present winter's state, and wish
> That warmer days would come.

At last the frost gives, the snow melts, the buds open, the heavens smile, and on " the heel of limping winter " comes the spring again, and the cycle of time brings a new loveliness to earth and a new joy to the poet's muse.

XXI.

THUNDER AND LIGHTNING.

Few natural phenomena make so determined an attack upon the senses of mortals as the thunder and the lightning. The blinding flashes, the terrifying, crackling roars, have driven the ignorant and superstitious to panic and even disturbed those competent to explain their causes.

In the thunder Shakespeare found a valuable friend, both as a poet and a dramatist. In the next chapter we shall see how he enhanced the horror of his evil and tragic moments, the outbursts of hate and passion, and the hair-raising appearances of the supernatural, by the accompaniment of blinding and deafening storms. With equal effectiveness he employed the thunder in powerful allegory, symbolically, in simile and comparison, and in explanatory and descriptive figures of speech.

Some of Shakespeare's most forcible phrases include allusions to the thunder. It is " the deep and dreadful organ-pipe," " heaven's artillery," " dread rattling," " all-shaking," " deafening." He speaks of tearing " with thunder the wide cheeks of the air," describes in accents of fear the stormy sky where " direful thunders break," and bewails the peace of the heavens broken by the " thunder's crack " or " bursts of horrid thunder."

One of the poet's epithets for thunder is " deep-mouthed." He finds here a strong simile for the human voice when it is angry, threatening, commanding, or imperious. " Thy voice

is thunder," cries Clarence to one of the murderers in
" Richard III " (I.4. 173) ; and the figure is repeated in the
poem in " Love's Labour's Lost " (IV.2. 119), " Thy eye
Jove's lightning bears, thy voice his dreadful thunder." The
grief-laden Constance in " King John " ejaculates, " O,
that my tongue were in the thunder's mouth ! " (III.4. 38) ;
while Chiron in " Titus Andronicus " calls Demetrius a
coward that " thunderest with thy tongue, and with thy
weapon nothing darest perform " (II.1. 58-59). The
phrase, now too familiar, " thunder of cannon," is used by
Shakespeare in " King John." He also describes the meeting
of combatants as a " thundering shock " (Richard II), and
" thunder-like percussion " (" Coriolanus ").

The Romans believed that thunder was the expressed
anger of Jupiter, and the dramatist adopted this mythological
belief for poetic uses. His references to Jove as the thunderer
are, we have seen, much more numerous than those to
Jupiter as the largest of the planets. He calls the all-powerful
Roman god " the great thunder-darter of Olympus," " the
thunder-master," and declares that " great men thunder as
Jove." The following are some of the striking passages in
which " Jove that thunders " is mentioned.

" Troilus and Cressida " (II.3. 208-209) :

> Jupiter forbid,
> And say in thunder " Achilles go to him."

" Coriolanus " (III.1. 255-257) :

> His nature is too noble for the world :
> He would not flatter Neptune for his trident,
> Or Jove for's power to thunder.

" Henry V " (II.4. 99-101) :

> Therefore in fierce tempest is he (i.e., Henry V) coming,
> In thunder and in earthquake, like a Jove,
> That, if requiring fail, he will compel.

Shakespeare adopted the old Roman theory as to thunder because classical mythology was very popular in his age, and all educated people were closely acquainted with the lives and histories of the ancient gods. Whether he understood the real scientific explanation of thunder is not very clear. He makes King Lear ask, " What is the cause of thunder ? " (III.4. 160), but he does not give any reply, though he writes in " Richard II " of tearing " the cloudy cheeks of heaven " (III.3. 57). As a dramatist, of course, he was more concerned with the effect than the cause of thunder.

The lightning also belonged to Jove, and in some of Shakespeare's wonderful descriptive phrases, the name of the god is retained. He calls the familiar electrical phenomenon, for example, " Jove's lightnings," " the precursors o' the dreadful thunder-claps," " momentary," and " sight-outrunning " (" Tempest," I.2. 201-203). " Sulphurous and thought-executing flashes," " swift like lightning," " nimble lightnings," are other notable phrases. The most remarked characteristic of the lightning, which has made it so popular a figure of speech, is well described in the following passages.

" Midsummer Night's Dream " (I.1. 145-149) :

> Brief as the lightning in the collied (i.e., dark) night,
> That, in a spleen, unfolds both heaven and earth,
> And ere a man hath power to say, " Behold ! "
> The jaws of darkness do devour it up :
> So quick bright things come to confusion.

" Romeo and Juliet " (II.2. 118-120) :

> It is too rash, too unadvised, too sudden,
> Too like the lightning, which doth cease to be
> Ere one can say " It lightens."

In "King Lear" we have the phrase "the nimble stroke of quick, cross lightning (IV.7. 33), and in " Julius Cæsar "

" the cross blue lightning seem'd to open the breast of heaven " (I.3. 50-51). Cross lightning is Shakespeare's expression for forked lightning.

The poet was fond of comparisons between the lightning and flashes from the human eye. " Thy eye Jove's lightning bears " we have quoted above from " Love's Labour's Lost "; and Enobarbus says of the angry Antony ("Antony and Cleopatra," III.13. 195), " Now he'll outstare the lightning." Of the duel between Romeo and Tybalt (" Romeo and Juliet," III.1. 177) it is said, " To it they go like lightning." Other metaphorical uses occur.

" Richard II " (III.3. 54-57) :

> Bolingbroke : Methinks King Richard and myself should meet
> With no less terror than the elements
> Of fire and water, when their thundering shock
> At meeting tears the cloudy cheeks of heaven.

" King John " (I.1. 23-26):

> John (despatching an embassy to the French king) :
> Bear mine to him, and so depart in peace :
> Be thou as lightning in the eyes of France ;
> For ere thou canst report I will be there,
> The thunder of my cannon shall be heard.

Shakespeare has a number of references to the " thunder-bolt" or "thunder-stone." In these days, when most people have some acquaintance with electricity, it is common know-ledge that a thunder-bolt is an electrical discharge passing from one part of the heavens to another, or from the clouds to the earth ; and the word refers particularly to such dis-charge striking and damaging a terrestrial object. The old idea was that a solid, heated mass fell with terrific force and buried itself deep in the ground. Shakespeare and his contemporaries believed so, and the references in the plays must be read in the light of this fact. In " King Lear "

(III.2. 5) the old monarch addresses the lightning flashes as " vaunt-couriers to oak-cleaving thunderbolts." The same idea recurs in " Coriolanus," where Volumnia says to her proud son (V.3. 149-153) :

> Thou hast affected the fine strains of honour,
> To imitate the graces of the gods ;
> To tear with thunder the wide cheeks o' the air,
> And yet to charge thy sulphur with a bolt
> That should but rive an oak.

Cordelia, speaking in pity of her aged father, asks (" Lear," IV.7. 31-33) :

> Was this a face
> To be opposed against the warring winds ?
> To stand against the deep dread-bolted thunder ?

In " The Tempest " (II.2. 37-38) Trinculo says of Caliban, " This is . . . an islander, that hath lately suffered by a thunderbolt." In " 1 Henry IV " (IV.1. 119-121) the fiery Hotspur cries :

> Come, let me taste my horse,
> Who is to bear me like a thunderbolt
> Against the bosom of the Prince of Wales.

A rather different use is made of the word by Celia in "As You Like It," as she and Rosalind watch the wrestling match between the champion, Charles, and Orlando. It is thought so certain that Charles will win that Celia declares, " If I had a thunderbolt in mine eye, I can tell who should down." (I.2. 227).

Shakespeare uses thunderstone as a synonym for thunderbolt. Its modern meaning of a certain kind of fossil was unknown to him.

" Cymbeline " (IV.2. 270-1) :

> Fear no more the lightning-flash,
> Nor the all-dreaded thunder-stone.

Cassius, indifferent to the storm, says to the nervous Casca :

" Julius Cæsar " (I.3. 46-49) :

> . . . I have walk'd about the streets,
> Submitting me unto the perilous night,
> And thus unbraced, Casca, as you see,
> Have bared my bosom to the thunder-stone.

The dramatist also uses the word " thunder-stroke " : " They dropp'd, as by a thunder-stroke " (" Tempest," II.1. 204), and the phrase, " to be killed with a thunder-stroke," which occurs in the same play (II.2. 112).

In classical mythology the thunder-bolt was the especial weapon of Jupiter, god of thunder and lord of heaven, who held it in his hand and hurled it as a punishment upon an erring mortal. Shakespeare gives expression to this belief in " Cymbeline," where Jupiter appears on the scene in person, hurls a bolt, and says (V.4. 94-96) :

> How dare you ghosts
> Accuse the thunderer, whose bolt, you know,
> Sky-planted, batters all rebelling coasts ?

Othello has the same idea in mind when he asks, "Are there no stones in heaven but what serve for thunder?" (V.2. 234-235). According to Cleopatra, it is not only the guilty that suffer. " Some innocents," she says, " 'scape not the thunderbolt " ("Antony and Cleopatra," II.5. 77). Prospero, describing the magic powers he has wielded, declares that he has even invaded the prerogatives of the king of the gods and " rifted Jove's stout oak with his own bolt " (" Tempest," V.1. 45).

The mighty thunderstorms, which the poet introduced into his plays with such powerful dramatic effect, are discussed in the following section, devoted to Shakespearian storms.

XXII.

STORMS.

IN our review of natural phenomena on the Shakespearian stage we noted how frequently the dramatist accompanied tragic human history with an outburst of fury on the part of the elements. It is true that simulation of thunder was one of the few effective devices that Elizabethan theatrical producers could employ. Moreover, it was exceedingly popular with certain sections of the audiences. But we must credit Shakespeare with a higher motive than popular showmanship for the introduction of storms into his drama. He was too great a craftsman to be swayed towards the incongruous merely to please the groundlings. The thunder, lightning, darkness, and gales are there because they harmonize with the terror, despair, horror, and wickedness inherent in his grim plots, and are intended to intensify the dramatic and tragic atmosphere.

It is important and interesting to note that Shakespeare introduced storms into his action with greatest effect in those plays written when his genius had fully developed and was at the height of its power. The greatest upheavals of Nature occur in " Julius Cæsar " and " King Lear," two plays belonging to his supreme tragic period, and in " The Tempest " and " Pericles," written at the end of his life. Other spells of rough and tempestuous weather are coincident with dark happenings in " Macbeth " and ' Othello," two more of the great tragedies, and in " The Winter's Tale," also a work of his declining years. Often these are " shipwrecking storms," and losses at sea bechance in a number of the plays mentioned, viz. : " The Tempest," " Pericles," " Othello," and " The Winter's Tale," despite the fact that the " seafaring men provide for storms " (" Comedy of Errors," I.1. 81).

If Shakespeare had been content to rely upon some stage hand producing loud bursts of thunder in the tyring-house to depict the storm which he felt was essential to his story, there would have been little inducement for us to undertake this study, and, indeed, little data for investigation. But, helped though he was by " sounds off," he was faithful to his usual method of describing natural phenomena and gave us vivid and remarkable word-pictures of his hurricanes and thunderstorms, which are as fine examples of forcible descriptive writing as exist in this or any other language.

Turning to " Julius Cæsar " in the first place, we learn that the time of year during which the first three acts take place is February and March. The drama opens on the feast of Lupercal, always held on the 15th February, and the fatal day of Cæsar's assassination is the Ides, or 15th, of March. On the night of March 14th Rome was visited by a particularly violent equinoctial storm. Such an occurrence was seasonable, but on this occasion all records of ferocity were exceeded. At its height Casca and Cicero meet in a Roman street (I.3.) :

> Cicero : Why are you breathless ? and why stare you so ?
> Casca : Are you not moved, when all the sway of earth
> Shakes like a thing unfirm ?   O Cicero,
> I have seen tempests, when the scolding winds
> Have rived the knotty oaks, and I have seen
> The ambitious ocean swell and rage and foam,
> To be exalted with the threatening clouds ;
> But never till to-night, never till now,
> Did I go through a tempest dropping fire.
> Either there is civil strife in heaven,
> Or else the world, too saucy with the gods,
> Incenses them to send destruction.   (I.3. 2-13.)

Here Casca echoes the common belief that storms were the anger of Jupiter and the gods. He continues to tell Cicero of the horrible unnatural sights that have stirred his superstitious fears. Cicero is unmoved by these strange portents, having nothing of the astrologer or star-gazer in his make-up, and being clearly sceptical of the intervention of any supernatural agency.

Cicero takes his departure, and Cassius encounters the troubled Casca. " Cassius, what a night is this ! " he says. " Who ever knew the heavens menace so ? " But Cassius is no more disturbed by the storm than Cicero, and tells his friend that he has walked the streets with his " bosom bared to the thunder-stone."

> And when the cross blue lightning seem'd to open
> The breast of heaven, I did present myself
> Even in the aim and very flash of it.

Casca answers :

> But wherefore did you so much tempt the heavens ?
> It is the part of men to fear and tremble,
> When the most mighty gods by tokens send
> Such dreadful heralds to astonish us.
>
> (Ibid., 50-56.)

Cassius then explains the cause of " the strange impatience of the heavens " on this perilous night :

> Why all these things change from their ordinance,
> Their natures and preformed faculties,
> To monstrous quality,

as a warning to Rome of the dangers that threaten it in the person of Cæsar, who is

> Most like this dreadful night,
> That thunders, lightens, opens graves, and roars
>
> .   .   .   .
>
> . . . fearful, as these strange eruptions are.
>
> (Ibid., 66-68, 74-75, 78.)

" Thunder still " read the stage directions during the dialogue that follows, by which Cassius wins Casca to the conspiracy against Cæsar ; and the chief instigator compares the work they have in hand to the raging tempest . . .

> For now, this fearful night,
> There is no stir or walking in the streets,
> And the complexion of the element
> In favour's like the work we have in hand,
> Most bloody, fiery, and most terrible.
>
> (Ibid., 126-130.)

Cinna, another of the conspirators, enters with the exclamation, " What a fearful night is this ! There's two or three of us have seen strange sights " (I.3. 137-138).

On the same disturbed night Brutus is walking in his orchard. The tempest prevents him from reading the time ' by the progress of the stars." His page, Lucius, brings him a letter, and he finds that " the exhalations whizzing in the air give so much light that I may read by them " (II.1. 44-45). When later the conspirators arrive, " the unaccustomed terror of the night " has evidently abated, for the coming of the grey dawn is described, " raw cold " and " dank."

Cæsar's household has, like every house in Rome, been worried by the storm. " Nor heaven nor earth have been at peace to-night," is the observation of Cæsar himself (II.2. 1). His wife, Calphurnia, has been terrified by the fury of the heavens and reads in them a warning of danger threatening her lord. She implores him to keep to his house, describing some of the ghastly sights that have been witnessed. Cæsar at first yields, but the cunning conspirator, Decius, works upon his vanity and persuades him to go to the Capitol, where he receives, not the kingly crown he expected, but the assassin's dagger.

To the Elizabethans, steeped in astrology and witchcraft,

the appropriateness of the warning storm of " Julius Cæsar," an omen from heaven, was even more apparent than it is to us who have no faith in celestial portents. None the less do we appreciate, however, the triumph of a poetic genius that can describe with such vivid realism this widely-experienced phenomenon.

The great storm in " King Lear " commences as the old ruler, stung by the lack of filial affection and the selfishness and ingratitude of his daughters, Goneril and Regan, rides off in rage on to the bare, exposed heath with his few faithful followers. The Duke of Cornwall says, " Let us withdraw " (i.e., into the castle : they were before the gate) " 'twill be a storm " (II.4. 290), and immediately, according to the stage directions, the tempest rises. Gloucester, loyal to the old king, pleads for greater consideration and kindness. " The night comes on," he says, " the bleak winds do sorely ruffle " (ibid., 303). But the cruel daughters are unmoved. " 'Tis a wild night . . . come out o' the storm " (311-312), are the last words of the Act, uttered by the callous Cornwall.

Through the next Act the storm rages unceasingly, rising to diabolical fury. In the opening lines we hear of the plight of Lear, battered by the merciless elements.

Kent :	Who's there, besides foul weather ?
A Gentleman :	One minded like the weather, most unquietly.
Kent :	I know you. Where's the King ?
Gent. :	Contending with the fretful elements ;
	Bids the wind blow the earth into the sea,
	Or swell the curled waters 'bove the main,
	That things might change or cease ; tears his white hair,
	Which the impetuous blasts, with eyeless rage,
	Catch in their fury, and make nothing of ;
	Strives in his little world of man to out-scorn
	The to-and-fro-conflicting wind and rain.

(III.1. 1-11.)

Kent learns from the Gentleman that Lear is alone with his Fool, and crying, " Fie on this storm ! " goes to seek him.

In the following scene Lear himself harangues the wrathful heavens in words that bring a shudder to the hearer :

> Blow, winds, and crack your cheeks ! rage ! blow !
> You cataracts and hurricanoes spout
> Till you have drench'd our steeples, drown'd the cocks !
> You sulphurous and thought-executing fires,
> Vaunt-couriers to oak-cleaving thunderbolts,
> Singe my white head !   And thou, all-shaking thunder,
> Smite flat the thick rotundity o' the world !
> Crack nature's moulds, all germins spill at once
> That make ungrateful man.   (III.2. 1-9.)

The Fool attempts to get the King into the shelter of a hovel, but Lear continues to address the storm.

> Rumble thy bellyful ! Spit, fire ! spout, rain !
> Nor rain, wind, thunder, fire, are my daughters :
> I tax not you, you elements, with unkindness ;
> I never gave you kingdom, call'd you children,
> You owe me no subscription ; then let fall
> Your horrible pleasure. . . .
> That have with two pernicious daughters join'd
> Your high-engender'd battles 'gainst a head
> So old and white as this.   O! O! 'tis foul !
>   (Ibid., 14-19, 22-24.)

Kent finds his deserted master and is shocked at the old man's pitiful condition, exposed as he is to all the lashing cruelty of the rain and wind and thunder.

> Kent : Alas, sir, are you here ? things that love night
>   Love not such nights as these ; the wrathful skies
>   Gallow the very wanderers of the dark,
>   And make them keep their caves : since I was a man,
>   Such sheets of fire, such bursts of horrid thunder,
>   Such groans of roaring wind and rain, I never
>   Remember to have heard : man's nature cannot carry
>   The affliction nor the fear.

Lear :   Let the great gods,
That keep this dreadful pother o'er our heads,
Find out our enemies now.

(III.2, 41-51.)

Bare-headed and cold, the old man is led by Kent and the
Fool, also drenched and numbed, toward the shelter of the
hovel, for " the tyranny of the open night's too rough for
nature to endure " (III.4. 2-3), and " the contentious storm
invades them to the skin " (6-7). But Lear declares that the
tempest in his mind makes him indifferent to the tempest
without, and he is in no hurry to escape " the pelting of this
pitiless storm." Edgar, feigning madness, is discovered
in the hovel ; and later, Gloucester arrives and exclaims,
" What a night is this ! " Lear, now showing signs of
incipient madness, is at last persuaded into the cover of the
hovel.

The aged and ill-used king loses his reason and descends into
that vacant blackness, heralded by the hideous cruelty of the
storm. Nowhere does Shakespeare so powerfully connect
human tragedy with the scowling front of Nature.

The storm in " The Tempest " takes place at sea and results
in what appears at first to be disastrous shipwreck. The play
opens on board ship with a terrific thunderstorm raging.
Fears that the ship will run aground are acute, and the
Master and his men work feverishly to save her. The
passengers, Alonso, Sebastian, Antonio, Ferdinand, Gonzalo,
and others, get in the sailors' way, and the boatswain, oblivious
of their rank, impatiently orders them below as they " assist
the storm." They comply, but it is all to no purpose, for the
ship seems to be splitting in two (I.1.)

From the island Miranda has seen the vessel sink, and is
grieved for the loss of the souls on board. She says to her
father, Prospero (I.2. 1-5) :

If by your art, my dearest father, you have
Put the wild waters in this roar, allay them.
The sky, it seems, would pour down stinking pitch,
But that the sea, mounting to the welkin's cheek,
Dashes the fire out.

Though Miranda grieves for the ship " dashed all to pieces,"
her father assures her " there's no harm done " and none of
those who sailed in the doomed vessel are drowned. Prospero
is master of the elements on the island and has an airy spirit
called Ariel to do his bidding. The tempest is Ariel's doing,
though the reasons are Prospero's, namely, that his enemies
are aboard the ship. Ariel describes how he carried out his
orders (I.2. 196-206) :

I boarded the king's ship ; now on the beak,
Now in the waist, the deck, in every cabin,
I flamed amazement ; sometime I'ld divide,
And burn in many places ; on the topmast,
The yards and bowsprit, would I flame distinctly,
Then meet and join. Jove's lightnings, the precursors
O' the dreadful thunder-claps, more momentary
And sight-outrunning were not : the fire and cracks
Of sulphurous roaring the most mighty Neptune
Seem to besiege, and make his bold waves tremble,
Yea, his dread trident shake.

Later in the play we hear from Trinculo of " another storm
brewing." He declares (II.2. 19-24) :

I hear it sing i' the wind : yond same black cloud, yond
huge one, looks like a foul bombard that would shed his liquor.
If it should thunder as it did before, I know not where to hide
my head : yond same cloud cannot choose but fall by pail-
fuls. . . .

A little later he cries (Ibid., 39, 42-43) :

Alas, the storm is come again ! . . . I will here shroud
till the dregs of the storm be past.

Throughout the play thunder recurs, and strange sounds and strains of music advertise the magic nature of the island. At the end, however, Prospero surrenders the occult powers he has enjoyed (V.1. 41-51):

> I have bedimm'd
> The noontide sun, call'd forth the mutinous winds,
> And 'twixt the green sea and the azured vault
> Set roaring war: to the dread rattling thunder
> Have I given fire, and rifted Jove's stout oak
> With his own bolt; the strong-based promontory
> Have I made shake, and by the spurs pluck'd up
> The pine and cedar . . .
> . . . But this rough magic
> I here abjure.

The theme of "The Tempest," written about 1611, is believed by commentators to have been suggested to Shakespeare by the wreck of an English vessel on the coast of Bermuda during a terrible storm on 29th July, 1609. The ship, "The Sea-Adventure," commanded by Sir George Somers and Sir Thomas Gates, was carrying colonists to the new settlement at Jamestown, Virginia. The sailors escaped to the island, where they maintained themselves for ten months before they were rescued. Ariel's lines (I.2. 227-229):

> . . . In the deep nook, where once
> Thou call'dst me up at midnight to fetch dew
> From the still-vex'd Bermoothes. . . .

are generally taken as referring to the Bermudas. An account of this event was written by an author named Sil Jourdain and published in 1610 under the title of "A Discovery of the Bermudas, otherwise called the Isle of Devils; by Sir Thomas Gates, Sir George Somers, and Captain Newport, with divers others."

Even before the wreck of the "Sea-Adventure," the Bermuda Islands had a bad name among sailors. Hackluyt gives an account of a voyage by Sir Robert Dudley, the explorer son of the Earl of Leicester, who sailed to the Bermudas in search of the Havannah fleet and returned in 1595. " The fleet," he said, " I found not, but foul weather enough to scatter many fleets." In a pamphlet by Sir Walter Raleigh, dated 1596, the famous colonizer makes the statement, " The rest of the Indies for calms and diseases very troublesome, and the Bermudas a hellish sea for thunder, lightning, and storms." There was also a very popular book, " Silver Watch Bell," by Tymme, in which it is said of Bermuda, " It is called the Isle of Devils, for to such as approach near the same there do not only appear fearful sights of devils and evil spirits, but also mighty tempests, and most terrible and continual thunder and lightning ; and the noise of horrible cries, with screeching do so affright and amaze those that come near the place that they are glad with all might and main to fly and speed them thence with all possible haste they can."

The reputation of the Bermudas and the recent adventure of Somers and his comrades would appeal to Shakespeare as excellent material for a play. The magic nature of Prospero's island, the mysterious sounds and immortal creatures that hovered about it, are certainly in keeping with the popular picture of the Bermudas. Even Caliban is thought by some critics to have been inspired by the sight of American natives brought to England by the explorers. Sir Sidney Lee makes another strong point in favour of such an inception for " The Tempest," when he writes : " The phantom blazes of fire which Ariel in the play scatters about the sinking ship " (see the passage, I.2. 196-205, quoted above) " are very literal remembrances of startling phenomena which sailors imputed to Atlantic storms." Hunter points out strong resemblances between the island of the play and the island of Lampedusa in the eastern Mediterranean. Its geography is more in keeping with the story, and it lies in the seas where the beautiful St. Elmo fires are seen, a phenomenon we shall discuss later, and which Ariel is thought to refer to. The noises and magical properties of Prospero's domicile are, however, more favourable to Bermuda. But, after all, there was nothing to prevent the dramatist from combining characteristic features of the two islands for the purposes of his play.

Storm, high seas, and shipwreck are a material part of the plot of " Pericles," a play for which Shakespeare was only partially responsible, having either collaborated with another dramatist, probably George Wilkins, or re-written portions of this dramatist's work. Though old copies of the play bore Shakespeare's name, it was omitted by the compilers of the First Folio, while close investigation of the internal evidence by a succession of scholars has relieved the poet of the authorship of what Ben Jonson termed a " mouldy tale " and cleared him of a charge of offensiveness, which certain of the scenes justify.

There are two storms in " Pericles." The first is heralded by Gower, as chorus, when speaking the prologue to Act II. Pericles, he tells us, resolved to leave Tarsus and put to sea, but a storm arose (the lines are not Shakespeare's) :

> For now the wind begins to blow ;
> Thunder above and deeps below
> Make such unquiet that the ship
> Should house him safe is wreck'd and split ;
> And he, good prince, having all lost,
> By waves from coast to coast is tost.
>
> (29-34.)

Fortune threw Pericles ashore at Pentapolis. He enters, wet, and cries (II.i. 1-7) :

> Yet cease your ire, you angry stars of heaven !
> Wind, rain, and thunder, remember earthly man
> Is but a substance that must yield to you ;
> And I, as fits my nature, do obey you :
> Alas, the sea hath cast me on the rocks,
> Wash'd me from shore to shore, and left me breath
> Nothing to think on but ensuing death.

It is difficult to find any trace of the Shakespearian music in the above lines, and most critics ascribe them to Wilkins or whoever Shakespeare's collaborator happened to be. On Pericles' second distressing encounter with a storm, during his voyage from Pentapolis to Tyre, when he had his wife, Thaisa, and her nurse, Lychorida, on board, some indifferent lines of prologue by Gower, descriptive of the tempest, are followed by the passage (III.1. 1-6) :

> Thou god of this great vast, rebuke these surges,
> Which wash both heaven and hell ; and thou, that hast
> Upon the winds command, bind them in brass,
> Having call'd them from the deep.   O, still
> Thy deafening dreadful thunders ; gently quench
> Thy nimble sulphurous flashes !

The verse scenes in the last three acts appear to be Shakespeare's contribution to the play.   The scene under consideration continues with the sad death of Pericles' wife, Thaisa, in giving birth to their daughter, Marina. Difficulties arise with the sailors, troubled by the old superstitious dread of ill-fortune through carrying a dead body on board. Pericles, though he declares, " I do not fear the flaw (i.e., stormy wind) ; it hath done to me the worst," would have it calm for the sake of the new-born infant. The first sailor then declares (III.1. 47-49) :

> Sir, your queen must overboard : the sea works high,
> the wind is loud, and will not lie till the ship be clear of the dead.

Pericles replies, " That's your superstition," but the sailors insist they are " strong in custom," and the Prince is forced to yield. Soon afterwards they discover that they are near Tarsus and make for the harbour.

The dramatist does not allow the audience to forget the violent storm with the close of the scene. In the following scene, staged at Ephesus, there enter " Cerimon, a servant, and some Persons, who have been shipwrecked." Cerimon calls for his man, Philemon, and says (III.2. 3-6) :

> Get fire and meat for these poor men :
> 'T has been a turbulent and stormy night.

The servant replies :

> I have been in many ; but such a night as this,
> Till now, I ne'er endured.

Two Gentlemen enter, one of whom declares (III.2. 14-17) :

> Our lodgings, standing bleak upon the sea
> Shook as the earth did quake ;
> The very principals did seem to rend
> And all to topple.

Later in the play (IV.1) Marina describes to Leonine the fierce tempest on the night of her birth when the " wind was north," " never was waves nor wind more violent," and their ship " endured a sea that almost burst the deck " (52 ; 60 ; and 56-57).

Another storm at sea involving tragic shipwreck, in which Antigonus is lost after leaving the baby Perdita on the coast of Bohemia, is the climax of the first part of " The Winter's Tale." Warnings of the approaching hurricane come from the Mariner. " The skies look grimly," he says, " and threaten present blusters . . . The heavens . . . are angry and frown upon us . . . 'tis like to be loud weather "

(III.3. 3-4; 5-11). A short while afterwards Antigonus announces, " The storm begins . . . the day frowns more and more : I never saw the heavens so dim by day. A savage clamour ! " (Ibid., 49. 54-56). Abandoning Perdita, as warned to do in his dream, Antigonus re-embarks, and the ship is caught by the storm. His fate is described by the Clown, viewing it from the shore (III.3. 84-87, 89-96, 99-102) :

> I have seen two such sights, by sea and by land ! but I am not to say it is sea, for it is now the sky : betwixt the firmament and it you cannot thrust a bodkin's point. . . . I would you did but see how it chafes, how it rages, how it takes up the shore ! but that's not to the point. O, the piteous cry of the poor souls ! sometimes to see 'em, and not to see 'em ; now the ship boring the moon with her main-mast, and anon swallowed with yest and froth, as you'ld thrust a cork into a hogshead. . . . But to make an end of the ship, to see how the sea flap-dragoned it ; but, first, how the poor souls roared, and the sea mocked them.

The above incident from " The Winter's Tale " is, perhaps, the most effective description by Shakespeare of the loss of a ship at sea, more dramatically realistic than the wrecks in " The Tempest " or " Pericles."

A very vivid account of a tremendous sea and the scattering of the Turkish fleet is given in " Othello." Montano and two Gentlemen are on an open place near the quay of a sea-port in Cyprus (II.1. 1-19) :

Montano : What from the cape can you discern at sea ?
First Gent. : Nothing at all ; it is a high-wrought flood ;
    I cannot, 'twixt the heaven and the main,
    Descry a sail.
Montano : Methinks the wind hath spoke aloud at land ;
    A fuller blast ne'er shook our battlements :
    If it hath ruffian'd so upon the sea,
    What ribs of oak, when mountains melt on them,
    Can hold the mortise. What shall we hear of this ?

Second Gent. : A segregation of the Turkish fleet :
          For do but stand upon the foaming shore,
          The chidden billow seems to pelt the clouds ;
          The wind-shaked surge, with high and monstrous
            main,
          Seems to cast water on the burning bear,
          And quench the guards of the ever-fixed pole :
          I never did like molestation view
          On the enchafed flood.

Montano :   If that the Turkish fleet
          Be not enshelter'd and embay'd, they are drown'd ;
          It is impossible to bear it out.

Montano's prognostications are correct, for a third Gentleman enters to report (lines 21-24) :

        The desperate tempest hath so bang'd the Turks,
        That their designment halts : a noble ship of Venice
        Hath seen a grievous wreck and sufferance
        On most part of their fleet.

The loss of the Turkish fleet is good news, meaning the end of war, but fears are entertained for the safety of Othello, the noble Moor in the service of Venice, who is sailing to take up the governorship of Cyprus. His lieutenant, Cassio, who has come safely to port himself in another ship, prays (Ibid., 44-6 ; 77-9) :

                O, let the heavens
        Give him defence against the elements,
        For I have lost him on a dangerous sea.
     .   .   .   .

        . . . Great Jove, Othello guard,
        And swell his sail with thine own powerful breath,
        That he may bless this bay with his tall ship.

Othello conquers the tempest and lands in safety. On meeting his wife, Desdemona, he cries (II.1. 186-191) :

N

O my soul's joy !
If after every tempest come such calms,
May the winds blow till they have waken'd death !
And let the labouring bark climb hills of seas
Olympus-high, and duck again as low
As hell's from heaven.

Another storm at sea resulting in suffering and shipwreck is vividly described by Aegeon, the Syracusan merchant, in the " Comedy of Errors " (I.i. 63-78) :

A league from Epidamnum had we sail'd,
Before the always-wind-obeying deep
Gave any tragic instance of our harm :
But longer did we not retain much hope ;
For what obscured light the heavens did grant
Did but convey unto our fearful minds
A doubtful warrant of immediate death ;
Which though myself would gladly have embraced,
Yet the incessant weepings of my wife,
Weeping before for what she saw must come,
And piteous plainings of the pretty babes,
That mourn'd for fashion, ignorant what to fear,
Forced me to seek delays for them and me.
And this it was, for other means was none :
The sailors sought for safety by our boat,
And left the ship, then sinking-ripe, to us. . . .

and he goes on to relate how the children were fastened to " a small spare mast " and he and his wife bound themselves to each end of it before surrendering themselves to the current which bore them towards Corinth. At length the storm dispersed, the sea waxed calm, and the rescue of the shipwrecked was effected.

The upheavals described in " The Winter's Tale," " Comedy of Errors," and " Othello," are not thunderstorms, but violent gales, lashing the seas into fury. These storms take place off the stage. It is when they are staged that Shakespeare makes use of thunder to present a more realistic picture to his audience. We return to thunder again in that flickering storm which hovers over the tragedy of " Macbeth " and rumbles loudly whenever the weird sisters appear. It harmonizes with the bleak Scottish background, the foul crime of murder, and the sinister, uncanny, supernatural influences that pervade the tragedy. The night of the cruel slaying of Duncan is dark and disturbed. On arriving at Macbeth's castle, the young Lord Lennox reports (II.3. 59-61 ; 65-67) :

> The night has been unruly ; where we lay,
> Our chimneys were blown down, and, as they say,
> Lamentings heard i' the air, strange screams of death
> . . . some say, the earth
> Was feverous and did shake.

" 'Twas a rough night," agrees Macbeth ; and Lennox adds, " My young remembrance cannot parallel a fellow to it."

The strange, terrifying happenings of the nocturnal tempest are discussed the next morning between Ross and an old man, who meet outside Macbeth's castle (II.4. 1-7, 10) :

> *Old Man :* Threescore and ten I can remember well :
> Within the volume of which time I have seen
> Hours dreadful and things strange, but this sore night
> Hath trifled former knowings.
> *Ross :* Ah, good father,
> Thou seest, the heavens, as troubled with man's act,
> Threaten his bloody stage : by the clock 'tis day,
> And yet dark night strangles the travelling lamp.
>
> . . . . . .
>
> *Old Man :* 'Tis unnatural.

Storms are indicated or referred to in many other of Shakespeare's plays. Thunder and lightning accompany the attack upon Orleans by the French under Joan la Pucelle. " What tumult's in the heavens ? " says Talbot, one of the English defenders (" 1 Henry VI," I.4. 98). Henry IV and Prince Hal observing the red sky on the morn of the battle of Shrewsbury look forward to " a tempest and a blustering day " (" 1 Henry IV," V.2. 6). Jupiter descends in thunder and lightning in " Cymbeline " and hurls one of his thunderbolts (V.4).

In " Hamlet " we find a reference to that uncanny stillness that often precedes a storm (II.2. 504-508):

> . . . we often see, against some storm,
> A silence in the heavens, the rack stand still,
> The bold winds speechless and the orb below
> As hush as death, anon the dreadful thunder
> Doth rend the region.

Shakespeare often uses a storm in an allegorical sense. John of Gaunt says of the outburst of temper on the part of his nephew, King Richard II, "Small showers last long, but sudden storms are short " (" Richard II," II.1. 35). In " 3 Henry VI " King Edward IV compares the fighting power that Queen Margaret is bringing against him to a gathering storm (V.3. 1-8):

> Thus far our fortune keeps an upward course,
> And we are graced with wreaths of victory.
> But, in the midst of this bright-shining day,
> I spy a black, suspicious, threatening cloud,
> That will encounter with our glorious sun,
> Ere he attain his easeful western bed :
> I mean, my lords, those powers that the queen
> Hath raised in Gallia.

Clarence makes the reassuring reply that " every cloud engenders not a storm " and that a little gale will soon disperse it.

There are many such references in Shakespeare, who employed the figure of the storm as a literary aid with the same facility, ingenuity, and success with which he made it serve his dramatic requirements.

XXIII.

EARTHQUAKES.

It is nearly certain that Shakespeare never travelled abroad, and his experience of earthquakes must consequently have been practically nil. There was, however, a shock felt in London in 1580, and the memory of this may have inspired the Nurse's line in " Romeo and Juliet," " 'Tis since the earthquake now eleven years " (I.3. 23). Hunter, however, calls attention to the great earthquake which occurred in the neighbourhood of Verona in 1570. It destroyed Ferrara and, says the commentator, " would form long after an epoch in the chronological calculations of the old wives of Lombardy."

On the cause of earthquakes an ingenious theory is put forward by Hotspur in " 1 Henry IV " (III.1. 27-32) :

> Diseased nature oftentimes breaks forth
> In strange eruptions ; oft the teeming earth
> Is with a kind of colic pinch'd and vex'd
> By the imprisoning of unruly wind
> Within her womb ; which, for enlargement striving,
> Shakes the old beldam earth and topples down
> Steeples and moss-grown towers.

The above quotation is interesting, since we should expect the poet to content himself with the circumstances and effects of these catastrophic upheavals rather than embark upon an effort to discover their obscure causes.

For dramatic effect Shakespeare does connect these terrifying phenomena with situations of great tensity and importance.   On the night of Duncan's murder, Lennox reports, "Some say, the earth was feverous and did shake" ("Macbeth," II.3. 65).   In that violent storm which preceded the assassination of Julius Cæsar, Casca in awe-struck voice says, "All the sway of earth shakes like a thing infirm." (I.3. 3-4).   In "Pericles" two gentlemen at Ephesus discuss the tempest which buffeted the Prince's ship on which his wife, Thaisa, lay dead.   One of these gentlemen declares (III.2.   13-14):

> Our lodgings, standing bleak upon the sea
> Shook as the earth did shake.

Owen Glendower, the Welsh leader, obsessed with an exaggerated idea of his own importance in the scheme of the universe, tells Hotspur, "At my birth the frame and huge foundation of the earth shaked like a coward" ("1 Henry IV," III.1.   15-17).   Hotspur's reply that the same thing would have occurred if the cat had had kittens, was more true than polite.   Benedick, when warned by Don Pedro that he will shortly quake for Cupid's arrow, replies, "I look for an earthquake too, then" ("Much Ado About Nothing," I.1. 275).

Shakespeare's knowledge of earthquakes not being gathered, as in most cases in connection with natural phenomena, from personal experiences, the poet felt his limitation, and his references in the plays are, therefore, few.   Nevertheless he could not resist availing himself of these shattering disorders for comparison and simile.   In "The Tempest" he writes (II.1.   314-316):

> O, 'twas a din to fright a monster's ear,
> To make an earthquake !   sure, it was the roar
> Of a whole herd of lions.

The catastrophic nature of earthquakes is allegorized.   The victorious Henry V is described to the French king as

" coming in thunder and in earthquake, like a Jove " (II.4. 100). Celia compares the extraordinary coincidence of the meeting of Rosalind and Orlando in the Forest of Arden to mountains that " may be removed with earthquakes and so encounter " (" As You Like It," III.2. 195). Salisbury, who has thrown in his lot with the French, feels the old loyalties warring with the new, and is overcome with emotion. Lewis the Dauphin says to him (" King John," V.2. 40-42):

> A noble temper dost thou show in this ;
> And great affections wrestling in thy bosom
> Doth make an earthquake of nobility.

The Clown in "All's Well That Ends Well," speaking of the lack of good women in the world, declares that if a good woman were born " one every blazing star, or at an earthquake, 'twould mend the lottery well " (I.3. 90-92). Here the poet emphasizes the rarity of the event as far as his own experience went.

XXIV.

THE WINDS.

In his stage storms Shakespeare described in vigorous and graphic language the fury of the whistling gales and the destruction of the tearing hurricane. The puny strength of man left to the mercy of the relentless elements was a favourite picture by which to score dramatic effect and work upon the emotions of his audience. Grief, anger, hate, terror, and tragedy were all echoed in the howling winds. Particularly were helpless mortals exposed to their merciless buffetings when on the open sea. With fear of shipwreck in their minds, they had to meet (as he writes in " 2 Henry IV," III.1. 21-25) :

> . . . the visitation of the winds,
> Who take the ruffian billows by the top,
> Curling their monstrous heads, and hanging them
> With deafening clamour in the slippery clouds,
> That, with the hurly, death itself awakes.

Although the boisterous, earth-shaking tornado may have been most useful to him as a playwright, it would be a mistake to think Shakespeare was less interested in the winds in their more peaceful moods. His epithets are not always turbulent. For example, the wind that carried the exiled Prospero and Miranda to their friendly island in " The Tempest " was a sympathetic wind (I.2. 148-151) :

> There they hoist us,
> To cry to the sea that roar'd to us ; to sigh
> To the winds, whose pity, sighing back again,
> Did us but loving wrong.

The wind may be "merry" ("Comedy of Errors"), or "bounteous" ("Pericles"), or "well-forewarning" as Queen Margaret found it in "2 Henry VI." It may be a gentle zephyr. Lorenzo speaks in "The Merchant of Venice" of a "sweet wind" that "did gently kiss the trees" (V.1. 2). "Gentlest winds of heaven" are prayed for Pericles' voyage (III.3. 38), and in "Cymbeline" the two princely boys are "as gentle as zephyrs blowing below the violet, not wagging his sweet head" (IV.2. 171-172). Other figures of a speech are, "Hear this shower sing in the wind" ("Merry Wives of Windsor," III.2. 38), and "A bubbling fountain stirred with wind" ("Titus Andronicus," II.4. 23).

That the winds were unseen was one of Nature's mysteries that appealed to Shakespeare's fancy. To die is spoken of by Claudio in "Measure for Measure" as "to be imprison'd in the viewless (i.e., invisible) winds" (III.1. 124). The same figure is used by chorus in "Henry V" (III. Pro. 11) where he describes King Harry's ships as "borne with the invisible and creeping wind." The speed of wind is noted in "Midsummer Night's Dream," where Oberon conjures Puck to go about the wood "swifter than the wind" (III.2. 94); and the idea of its unshackled nature is embodied in the phrase from "The Tempest" (I.2. 498-499), "Thou shalt be as free as mountain winds." With freedom is associated the idea of inconstancy, the most pronounced characteristic of the winds. Shakespeare uses the figure in "Romeo and Juliet" (I.4. 100-103):

> . . . more inconstant than the wind, who wooes
> Even now the frozen bosom of the north,
> And, being anger'd, puffs away from thence,
> Turning his face to the dew-dropping south.

The same thought of instability is repeated in "Much Ado

About Nothing " in the trope, " a vane blown with all winds " (III.1. 66).

Many figures of speech in Shakespeare are now every-day expressions. Juliet's sighs for the loss of Romeo are compared to the winds by her father (III.5. 135); and the sentence, " winds and waters, sighs and tears," appears in "Antony and Cleopatra " (I.2. 152). " Sits the wind in that corner ? " says Benedick to himself, when he overhears Pedro, Claudio, and Leonato talking of Beatrice's love for him ("Much Ado," II.3. 101). " Is that the way the wind blows ? " would be the more likely phrasing of the modern Benedick. " Ill blows the wind that profits nobody " writes Shakespeare in " 3 Henry VI " (II.5. 55), which differs little from our very common proverb of to-day. " Something in the wind," another popular saying, appears in " The Comedy of Errors " (III.1. 69), and " words are but wind," the forerunner of our word " windbag " occurs in the same scene (line 75). Many other apt sentences, like " the cool and temperate wind of grace " (" Henry V," III.3. 30), could be quoted to show how generously the poet drew upon the winds for metaphoric needs.

An interesting word that Shakespeare uses frequently is " flaw." A flaw is a sudden puff of wind or a violent but transient wind-storm. Warburton says that some philosophers thought " that the vapours being congealed in the air by cold (which is the most intense in the morning), and being afterwards rarefied and let loose by the warmth of the sun, occasioned those sudden and impetuous gusts of wind which were called flaws." The word is used by the dramatist exactly in this meaning in " 2 Henry IV," where the King speaks of the wayward Prince Hal (IV.4. 34-35) :

> As humorous as winter, and as sudden
> As flaws congealed in the spring of day.

Another reference occurs in " 2 Henry VI " (III.1. 351-354) :

> And this fell tempest shall not cease to rage
> Until the golden circuit on my head,
> Like to the glorious sun's transparent beams,
> Do calm the fury of this mad-bred flaw.

Hamlet talks of patching a wall " to expel the winter's flaw " (V.1. 239); and Coriolanus urges Volumnia to prove invulnerable to shame, " like a great sea-mark, standing every flaw " (V.3. 74). Pericles declares that he does not fear the flaw—in this case a strong wind at sea (III.1. 39). Lady Macbeth, however, exclaims : " O, these flaws and starts ! " (" Macbeth," III.4. 63), meaning storms of human passion.

The practice of forecasting the weather by the direction of the wind is one of great age ; and Shakespeare listened to the prophets and learned from them, particularly the countrymen, who are always more observant of Nature than their brothers of the town. The poet frequently calls a wind by name.

The bitter north wind is viewed with dislike. " The angry northern wind " Titus Andronicus dubs it (IV.1. 104). " 'Tis very cold ; the wind is northerly," says Hamlet, flatly contradicting the silly Osric (V.2. 99). In " The Tempest " it is " the sharp wind of the north " (I.2. 254). Marina describing the terrible conditions in which she was born says, " the wind was north " (" Pericles," IV.1. 52). In " Troilus and Cressida " (I.3. 38) the poet refers to the north wind under its classical name of Boreas. The biting north-easter is cited in " Richard II " (I.4. 6-9) :

> . . . the north-east wind,
> Which then blew bitterly against our faces,
> Awaked the sleeping rheum, and so by chance
> Did grace our hollow parting with a tear.

Further mention of the east wind occurs in " Midsummer Night's Dream " (III.2. 141-142) :

> That pure congealed white, high Taurus' snow,
> Fann'd with the eastern wind.

The south wind brings wet weather—" Like foggy south puffing with wind and rain " ("As You Like It," III.5. 50). Shakespeare refers to the " spongy south " in " Cymbeline," and puts into the mouth of the Prince of Wales in " 1 Henry IV " (V.1. 3-6) :

> The southern wind
> Doth play the trumpet to his purposes,
> And by his hollow whistling in the leaves
> Foretells a tempest and a blustering day.

It was generally believed that the southern winds brought noxious fogs and vapours. An old book, which Shakespeare may have read, said, " This southern wind is hot and moist. Southern winds corrupt and destroy ; they heat, and make men fall into the sickness." In " Troilus and Cressida " " the rotten diseases of the south " are referred to (V.1. 20). In two other instances horrible curses are pronounced. "All the contagion of the south light on you, you shames of Rome ! " cries Marcius in " Coriolanus " (I.4. 30-31) ; and " The south-fog rot him ! " snaps Clotten in " Cymbeline " (II.3. 136). The same curse burst from the lips of Caliban (" Tempest," I.2. 323-324), but it is a south-west wind this time : "A south-west blow on ye and blister you all o'er ! " In contrast to these passages, it was " a prosperous south-wind, friendly," that brought Florizel and Perdita to the court of Leontes in " The Winter's Tale " (V.1. 161).

In an age when navigation was entirely dependent upon the disposition of the winds, the connection between them and sailing was a very close one and present in everybody's mind. "A sailing wind" and a smooth passage over "the wind-obeying deep" were the prayers of England's young race of mariners. "Winds of all the corners kiss'd your sails" is a description of a speedy voyage in "Cymbeline" (II.4. 28); and Polonius's remark to Laertes in "Hamlet" (I.3. 55-56), "Aboard, aboard . . . The wind sits in the shoulder of your sail," denotes a propitious time for putting to sea. All navigators hoped to "sail freely both with wind and stream" ("Othello," II.3. 65) and not to encounter "the winds that sailors rail at" ("Cymbeline," IV.2. 56). Metaphors abound. In "3 Henry VI" York complains that his followers "turn back and fly, like ships before the wind" (I.4. 4). Beatrice in "Much Ado About Nothing" speaks of "the windy side of care" (II.1. 327), that is to "windward of care," the figure being taken from two sailing boats racing.

Two interesting references to the winds of a sporting nature occur in "Hamlet." In the first, shooting is alluded to. Hamlet says : "When the wind is southerly, I know a hawk from a handsaw" (II.2. 397). "Handsaw" means "heron," and Hamlet is referring to the fact that the birds fly with the wind, and when it is from the south, the sportsman has his back to the sun and so is able to distinguish a hawk from a heron. In the second passage it is hunting that supplies the figure of speech. Hamlet says to Rosencrantz and Guildenstern, " Why do you go about to recover the wind of me, as if you would drive me into a toil?" (III.2. 361-362). He likens them to hunters who try to get to windward of their quarry, so that it cannot scent its pursuers and suspect a trap.

With Shakespeare's predilection for classical myth, we shall expect to find a mention of Æolus, the old Greek god who held dominion over the winds. His name occurs in a magnificent speech of the Queen in " 2 Henry VI," of which a partial quotation makes a fitting end to this section (III.2. 82-93):

> Was I for this nigh wreck'd upon the sea,
> And twice by awkward wind from England's bank
> Drove back again unto my native clime?
> What boded this, but well forewarning wind
> Did seem to say, " Seek not a scorpion's nest,
> Nor set no footing on this unkind shore "?
> What did I then, but cursed the gentle gusts,
> And he that loosed them from their brazen caves;
> And bid them blow towards England's blessed shore,
> Or turn our stern upon a dreadful rock?
> Yet Æolus would not be a murderer,
> But left that hateful office unto thee.

XXV.

THE SEA AND ITS TIDES.

In importance the Elizabethan chapter is second to none in the whole maritime history of England. Somewhat behind the other Atlantic nations in exploring the new ocean highways which Columbus and his fellow navigators had unbarred, our country, once she had entered the race for seapower, was destined to outstrip all competitors. In Shakespeare's lifetime, Englishmen, making up in courage what they lacked in experience, definitely challenged the monopoly of Spain and earned the right to sail their vessels on every sea of the globe. The Spaniards, determined to crush this threat to their supremacy, were themselves crushed in one of the most decisive naval battles of all time. England thereafter developed the consciousness of a mighty destiny and began to appreciate the wonderful advantages that must accrue to her by reason of her island position.

English literature reflected the enterprising, self-reliant, and independent spirit of the age, and Shakespeare was foremost among his contemporaries in giving expression to it. Confidence in England's future greatness and recognition of the natural strength of her sea-girt fortress shine through the lines of that famous speech of John of Gaunt in " Richard II " (II.1. 40-49) :

> This royal throne of kings, this scepter'd isle,
> This earth of majesty, this seat of Mars,
> This other Eden, demi-paradise ;

This fortress built by Nature for herself
Against infection and the hand of war ;
This happy breed of men, this little world,
This precious stone set in the silver sea,
Which serves it in the office of a wall,
Or as a moat defensive to a house,
Against the envy of less happier lands.

The same acknowledgment of England's debt to the protecting ocean is echoed in " King John " (II.1. 23-30) :

. . . that white-faced shore,
Whose foot spurns back the ocean's roaring tides
And coops from other lands her islanders,
Even till that England, hedged in with the main,
That water-walled bulwark, still secure
And confident from foreign purposes,
Even till that utmost corner of the west
Salute thee for her king.

Again, the Queen in " Cymbeline," urging the Britons to pay no tribute to Rome, says to the King (III.1. 18-22) :

The natural bravery of your isle, which stands
As Neptune's park, ribbed and paled in
With rocks unscaleable and roaring waters,
With sands that will not bear your enemies' boats,
But suck them up to the topmast.

Though born in the Midlands, as far from the coast as he well could be, Shakespeare felt the stir of the sea in his English blood, the natural attraction and aptitude for seamanship, which were our inheritance from our Viking ancestors and protected and developed through the centuries by our island station. That the poet ever made any voyages himself is extremely unlikely. There is certainly no record of his having done so, though some of his admirers assert that he must at least have travelled to Italy, the centre of art and learning in the Middle Ages, to perfect his education. More probably his personal observation of the sea was obtained from such points along the Kent coast as he was able to reach from London when his writing and acting allowed him the opportunity of a well-earned holiday. That he made the most of these opportunities by the facile exercise of his keen powers of perception is proved by the wealth of imagery suggested to his fertile brain by the sea, which plentifully sprinkles his poetry. A good example of the vivid impressions which he gathered and stored as he trod " the beached margent of the sea " (" Midsummer Night's Dream," II.1. 85), is to be found in that picturesque and faithful description of the Dover cliffs which he puts into the mouth of Edgar in " King Lear " (IV.6. 11-23) :

> Come on, sir ; here's the place : stand still.   How fearful
> And dizzy 'tis to cast one's eyes so low !
> The crows and choughs that wing the midway air
> Show scarce so gross as beetles : half way down
> Hangs one that gathers samphire, dreadful trade !
> Methink he seems no bigger than his head :
> The fishermen that walk along the beach
> Appear like mice ; and yond tall anchoring bark
> Diminished to her cock ; her cock, a buoy
> Almost too small for sight : the murmuring surge
> That on the unnumber'd idle pebbles chafes
> Cannot be heard so high.   I'll look no more,
> Lest my brain turn.

From the captains and sailors, with whom he came in contact, Shakespeare acquired an elementary knowledge of seamanship. We have seen from a few curt sentences in the opening scene of " The Tempest "—" Take in the topsail," " down with the topmast," " bring her to try with main-course (i.e., mainsail), " lay her a-hold," etc.—that he knew a little of how a vessel was handled in a storm and enough to inject realism into his lines. His marine metaphors and similes are numerous, as also are his literal passages descriptive of events afloat. A good example of his figurative

o

use occurs in " 3 Henry VI " (V.4. 1-37) ; where Queen
Margaret says to the dejected Lancastrians before Tewkesbury:

> Great lords, wise men ne'er sit and wail their loss,
> But cheerly seek how to redress their harms.
> What though the mast be now blown overboard,
> The cable broke, the holding-anchor lost,
> And half our sailors swallow'd in the flood ?
> Yet lives our pilot still.   Is't meet that he
> Should leave the helm, and like a fearful lad
> With tearful eyes add water to the sea,
> And give more strength to that which has too much,
> Whiles, in his moan, the ship splits on the rock,
> Which industry and courage might have saved ?
> Ah, what a shame ! ah, what a fault were this !
> Say Warwick was our anchor ; what of that ?
> And Montague our topmast ; what of him ?
> Our slaughter'd friends the tackles ; what of these ?
> Why, is not Oxford here another anchor ?
> And Somerset another goodly mast ?
> The friends of France our shrouds (i.e., sail-ropes) and tacklings
> And, though not skilful, why not Ned and I
> For once allow'd the skilful pilot's charge ?
> We will not from the helm to sit and weep,
> But keep our course, though the rough wind say no,
> From shelves and rocks that threaten us with wreck.
> As good to chide the waves as speak them fair.
> And what is Edward but a ruthless sea ?
> What Clarence but a quicksand of deceit ?
> And Richard but a ragged fatal rock ?
> All these the enemies to our poor bark.
> Say you can swim ; alas, 'tis but a while !
> Tread on the sand ; why, there you quickly sink :
> Bestride the rock ; the tide will wash you off,
> Or else you famish ; that's a threefold death.
> Thus speak I, lords, to let you understand,
> In case some one of you would fly from us,
> That there's no hoped-for mercy with the brothers,
> More than with ruthless waves, with sands and rocks.
> Why, courage, then !

Another sea-faring metaphor is used by Northumberland with reference to the unjust acts of Richard II (II.1. 263-266) :

> But, lords, we hear this fearful tempest sing,
> Yet seek no shelter to avoid the storm ;
> We see the wind sit sore upon our sails,
> And yet we strike not, but securely perish.

There is much of the sea and merchantmen in " The Merchant of Venice " and " Othello," the two plays in which the poet sets many of his scenes in the wave-girt city, which in the Middle Ages was mistress of the Mediterranean. The crossing of the Atlantic and Pacific had transferred supremacy from Venice to the nations on Europe's western seaboard, but the glamour of history still clung to the Adriatic. In the opening scene of " The Merchant of Venice " Salarino says to the preoccupied Antonio (I.1. 9-14) :

> Your mind is tossing on the ocean ;
> There, where your argosies with portly sail,
> Like signiors and rich burghers on the flood,
> Or, as it were, the pageants of the sea,
> Do overpeer the petty traffickers,
> That curt'sy to them, do them reverence,
> As they fly by them with their woven wings.

The sea enters into Shakespearian drama mostly in angry mood. We have discussed the storms and shipwrecks in " The Tempest," " The Winter's Tale, " Othello," " Pericles," etc. The poet knew those seas which the sailors dreaded. He had heard of the evil reputation of the West Indies, especially the Bermudas. Nearer home, he had a wholesome respect for the temper of the Channel, and had listened to tales of the perilous shoals of the Goodwins, " a very danger-ous flat and fatal, where the carcases of many a tall ship lie buried " (" Merchant of Venice," III.1. 3-5).

Shakespeare once more turns to the sea for effectual

imagery in " Troilus and Cressida," where Nestor discusses
the relative worth of courage in different circumstances
(I.3. 34-45).   . . . the sea being smooth,
    How many shallow bauble boats dare sail
    Upon her patient breast, making their way
    With those of nobler bulk !
    But let the ruffian Boreas once enrage
    The gentle Thetis, and anon behold
    The strong-ribb'd bark through liquid mountains cut,
    Bounding between the two moist elements,
    Like Perseus' horse : where's then the saucy boat,
    Whose weak untimber'd sides but even now
    Co-rivall'd greatness ? either to harbour fled,
    Or made a toast for Neptune.

In the above passage the name Boreas is used for the north
wind, of which in classical mythology he was the god. Thetis
was a sea-goddess. Neptune was the chief god of the sea and
provides the poet with a picturesque and universally-under-
stood synonym on which he relies frequently. He speaks of
the sea in " Hamlet " as " Neptune's empire " (I.1. 119).
" Most mighty Neptune," " dreadful Neptune." " Neptune's
salt wash," and " the vessel shakes on Neptune's billow "
are a few of his more striking phrases. "Antony sails o'er
green Neptune's back " ("Antony and Cleopatra," IV.14. 58),
and Cleon says to Pericles (III.3. 36-37) " Then give you
up to the mask'd Neptune and the gentlest winds of heaven "
—" masked " so that its cruel nature might be concealed
during the Prince of Tyre's voyage. In " 2 Henry IV "
(III.1. 50-51), the weary king prays that he may see, among
other strange and wonderful happenings, " the beachy
girdle of the ocean too wide for Neptune's hips." Probably
the most sinister reference to the sea-god is that of Macbeth,
the murderer, when he exclaims (II.2. 60-61) " Will all
great Neptune's ocean wash this blood clean from my hand ? "

In happier vein is the beautiful description of the sunrise in " Midsummer Night's Dream " (III.2. 391-393) :

> Even till the eastern gate, all fiery red,
> Opening on Neptune with fair blessed beams,
> Turns into yellow gold his salt green streams.

And when the day was done, the sun was supposed to sink into the western ocean (" 2 Henry VI," IV.1. 1-2) :

> The gaudy, blabbing, and remorseful day
> Is crept into the bosom of the sea.

In dealing with the sea when rough, restless, or boisterous, Shakespeare dubbed it " vexed," " wild and waste-ful," " raging," " threatening," " breaking," " vaulting," " triumphant," " furrowed." Some of his original expressions are, " mad as the sea," " as hungry as the sea," " the ambitious ocean's swell," " high seas," " the rude seas enraged," " waved like the enraged sea." With the vastness of Neptune's domain in his mind, he called it " boundless," " a wilderness of sea," with a great capacity to receive (" Twelfth Night," I.1. 10). Instancing a hopeless, impossible job in " Richard II," Green is made to say, " The task he undertakes is numbering sands and drinking oceans dry " (II.2. 146). Evaporation is admitted in several instances, notably in " Timon of Athens " (IV.3. 439-440) :

> The sun's a thief, and with his great attraction
> Robs the vast sea.

The sea furnished the poet with yet another simile for tears. "A sea of melting pearl, which some call tears " (" Two Gentlemen of Verona," III.1. 224), " seas of tears," " oceans of his tears," " his face an ocean of salt tears," " add water to the sea," are a representative selection of his expressions.

In the same vein is, " as full of sorrows as the sea of sands," an alliterative simile from the " Two Gentlemen " (IV.3. 33).

It would be impossible to quote all the comparisons to the sea which Shakespeare's poetic fancy dictated. Such phrases as "a sea of glories," "a sea of troubles," constantly occur. A few of the many fine examples of figurative language may be chosen. In "All's Well That Ends Well " Helena remarks that God's greatest purposes are often performed through the weakest minister (II.1. 142-4) :

> . . . great floods have flown
> From simple sources ; and great seas have dried,
> When miracles have by the greatest been denied.

In the " Comedy of Errors," Antipholus of Syracuse, explaining that in the search for a mother and a brother he loses himself, makes this comparison (I.2. 35-38) :

> I to the world am like a drop of water,
> That in the ocean seeks another drop ;
> Who, falling there to find his fellow forth,
> Unseen, inquisitive, confounds himself.

The poet finds a striking simile for glory in " 1 Henry VI " (I.2. 133-135) :

> Glory is like a circle in the water,
> Which never ceaseth to enlarge itself
> Till by broad spreading it disperse to nought.

" The imperious seas breed monsters," writes Shakespeare in " Cymbeline " (IV.2. 35), and of these the ravenous sea-shark is mentioned by the weird sisters in " Macbeth " (IV.1. 24). In " Pericles " (II.1. 25-30) one of the fishermen says :

> Nay, master, said not I as much when I saw the porpus (porpoise), how he bounced and tumbled ? they say they're half fish, half flesh : a plague on them, they ne'er come but I look to be washed. Master, I marvel, how the fishes live in the sea.

Reference is made in " The Merchant of Venice " to Homer's story of Alcides and the sea-monster (III.2. 54).

Lear, again, calls filial ingratitude more hideous than the sea-monster (I.4. 282)—a line that is often taken as meaning the hippopotamus or the whale.

A reference to sea-nymphs occurs in Ariel's curious song of the sea in " The Tempest " (I.2. 396-403) :

> Full fathom five thy father lies ;
> Of his bones are coral made ;
> Those are pearls that were his eyes :
> Nothing of him that doth fade,
> But doth suffer a sea-change
> Into something rich and strange
> Sea-nymphs hourly ring his knell . . .
>   Ding-dong, bell.

Posthumus' servant, Pisanio, offers Imogen a remedy for the distressing malady of sea-sickness in " Cymbeline " (III.4. 192-194) : " If you are sick . . . a dram of this will drive away distemper."

The tides and their importance were fully recognized in this golden age of seamanship, nor was mankind's dependence upon them and the winds appreciated only by the professional mariner. Panthino's remark, "Away, ass ! you'll lose the tide, if you tarry any longer " (" Two Gentlemen of Verona," II.3. 39-40) would appeal to everyone who made his journeys by sailing ship and particularly to an audience drawn from the port of London. Also in the same play are the lines (II.2. 14-16) :

> The tide is now :—nay, not thy tide of tears ;
> That tide will stay me longer than I should.
> Julia, farewell !

There are two Shakespearian passages citing the tides that are among the most famous in all literature. The first occurs in " Julius Cæsar " and is spoken by Brutus (IV.3, 218-224) :

> There is a tide in the affairs of men
> Which taken at the flood leads on to fortune ;
> Omitted, all the voyage of their life
> Is bound in shallows and in miseries.
> On such a full sea are we now afloat,
> And we must take the current when it serves,
> Or lose our ventures. . . .

In the other instance Henry V, planning his campaign in France, impresses upon his counsellors the necessity of protecting the northern border (I.2. 146-149) :

> For you shall read that my great-grandfather
> Never went with his forces into France,
> But that the Scot on his unfurnish'd kingdom
> Came pouring, like the tide into a breach.

The rush of the incoming tide provided the poet with some powerful imagery, of which the following are conspicuous examples, beginning with the Laertes rebellion :

" Hamlet " (IV.5. 99-102) :

> The ocean, overpeering of his list,
> Eats not the flats with more impetuous haste
> Than young Laertes, in a riotous head,
> O'erbears your officers.

" The Tempest " (V.1. 79-82) :

> Their understanding
> Begins to swell ; and the approaching tide
> Will shortly fill the reasonable shore,
> That now lies foul and muddy.

" Richard II " (II.2. 98-100) :

> What a tide of woes
> Comes rushing on this woeful land at once !
> I know not what to do.

" Coriolanus " (V.4. 44-45 ; 50-51) :

> The Volscians are dislodged, and Marcius gone :
> A merrier day did never yet greet Rome.
>
>   .   .   .   .   .   .
>
> Ne'er through an arch so hurried the blown tide,
> As the recomforted through the gates.

A well-known chapter of history is the misfortune which overtook King John in the Wash. He and his train were taking a short cut across the wide stretches of sand, instead of following the more devious route round the shore, when they were surprised by the incoming tide. The dramatist makes Faulconbridge speak of the incident to Hubert in the scene near Swinstead Abbey (" King John," V.6. 39-42) :

> I'll tell thee, Hubert, half my power this night,
> Passing these flats, are taken by the tide ;
> These Lincoln Washes have devoured them ;
> Myself, well mounted, hardly have escaped.

In the quotation from " Coriolanus " above, the wind and tide were in agreement, and the poet may have seen the water so forced through the narrow arches of old London Bridge. More often the sea and the wind are contrary, " old wranglers," as he calls them in " Troilus and Cressida." He finds in their battle a likeness to the struggle between armies, and puts the following lines into the King's speech in " 3 Henry VI " (II.5. 5-13) :

> Now sways it this way, like a mighty sea
> Forced by the tide to combat with the wind :
> Now sways it that way, like the selfsame sea
> Forced to retire by fury of the wind :
> Sometime the flood prevails, and then the wind ;
> Now one the better, then another best ;
> Both tugging to be victors, breast to breast,
> Yet neither conqueror nor conquered :
> So is the equal poise of this fell war.

Henry uses much the same metaphor in the first part of the play, discussing Margaret, his future queen (V.5. 5-9) :

> And like as rigour of tempestuous gusts
> Provokes the mightiest hulk against the tide,
> So am I driven by breath of her renown,
> Either to suffer shipwreck or arrive
> Where I may have fruition of her love.

That brief moment at high tide, when the current is flowing neither in nor out, is responsible for some fine ideas in Shakespeare's lines. In " 2 Henry IV " Northumberland is unable to make up his mind as to his future course of action, whether to fly to Scotland or not. He says (II.3. 62-64) :

> 'Tis with my mind
> As with the tide swell'd up unto his height,
> That makes a still-stand, running neither way.

In "Antony and Cleopatra " Antony says of the beautiful Queen (III.2. 47-50) :

> Her tongue will not obey her heart, nor can
> Her heart inform her tongue, the swan's down-feather,
> That stands upon the swell at full of tide
> And neither way inclines.

Another allusion to the swan, on this occasion to its efforts to swim against the incoming tide, occurs in " 3 Henry VI " (I.4. 19-21), where the Duke of York describes the vain attacks of his faction upon the enemy.

> . . . as I have seen the swan
> With bootless labour swim against the tide
> And spend her strength with over-matching waves.

A reference to the spring tides occurs in " King John," where Constance asks of the day, which the King of France says shall ever be kept a festival in his country (III.1. 84) :

> . . . what hath it done,
> That it in golden letters should be set
> Among the high tides in the calendar ?

In our chapter on the moon we discussed Shakespeare's literary handling of the force of attraction of the earth's satellite upon the tides. The ebb and flow of the sea under this influence are mentioned in a number of passages, many of which have been quoted under that heading. There is a further example in " Troilus and Cressida " where Agamemnon, speaking of the moody Achilles to his friend Patroclus, observes (II.3. 138-141) :

> . . . watch
> His pettish lunes, his ebbs, his flows, as if
> The passage and whole carriage of this action
> Rode on his tide.

The ebbing tide enters into " The Tempest," where Prospero remarks (V.1. 33-36) :

> Ye elves of hills, brooks, standing lakes, and groves ;
> And ye that on the sands with printless foot
> Do chase the ebbing Neptune, and do fly him
> When he comes back. . . .

In " King John " the chastened rebels and their return to allegiance are likened to the receding sea (V.4. 52-57) :

> We will untread the steps of damned flight,
> And like a bated and retiring flood,
> Leaving our rankness and irregular course,
> Stoop low within those bounds we have o'erlook'd
> And calmly run on in obedience
> Even to our ocean, to our great King John.

An interesting remark on the absence of tides in the Black Sea appears in " Othello " (III.3. 453-456) :

> Like to the Pontic Sea,
> Whose icy current and compulsive course
> Ne'er feels retiring ebb, but keeps due on
> To the Propontic and the Hellespont.

Steevens has suggested that Shakespeare owed his information to the following passage in Pliny's Natural History, as translated by Philemon Holland : "And the sea Pontus ever more floweth and runneth out from Propontes, but the sea never retireth back again within Pontus." The " Propontic " is the Sea of Marmora.

Shakespeare mentioned a number of other seas by name. The Mediterranean is reported by Ariel as the " flote " on which he dispersed Alonso's fleet (Tempest," I.2. 234), and cited again in " Love's Labour's Lost," where the fantastical Armado uses the oath, " By the salt wave of the Mediterraneum ! " (V.1. 61). The Channel is given its own name in " 2 Henry VI " (IV.1. 114), " Waft me safely across the Channel." Generally it is described as " the narrow seas "—" Falconbridge commands the narrow seas " (" 3 Henry VI," I.1. 239) and " Edward from Belgia, . . . hath passed in safety through the narrow seas, and . . . doth march amain to London (ibid., IV.8. 1-4). " The swelling Adriatic seas " are noted in " The Taming of the Shrew " (I.2. 74) ; and the Ionian Sea is a scene of the duel between Antony and Octavius Cæsar in "Antony and Cleopatra " (III.7. 23).

XXVI.

CLOUDS.

SOME of Nature's most entrancing pictures are the gifts of the clouds. All admirers of the beautiful are familiar with the white bows, the snowy billows, the mighty banks, the swelling thunder-cloud, the filmy, gauze-like vapours blown hither and thither by the wind, and a sky ribbed like sand on the sea-shore. The glory of every sunset is enhanced when fleecy clouds are there to reflect the burning rays. Every dawn has a more radiant sunrise when there are clouds to herald Phœbus. Scurrying masses over our heads are inspiring ; restful is a roof of still patterns.

It is a curious fact that Shakespeare has little to say on the attractive aspect of a cloud-strewn heaven. Its beauties did not, apparently, move him sufficiently to cause him to forget that clouds were veils to the brilliance of the sun and forerunners of tempest. He does speak of Ariel riding on " the curl'd clouds " in " The Tempest " (I.2. 192) and describes the dawn as " chequering the eastern clouds with streaks of light " (" Romeo and Juliet," II.3. 2). But for the most part clouds to him are sinister phenomena, " black, suspicious, threatening," the couriers of storm, the carriers of darkness, and omens of evil for humanity. In " Richard II " (I.1. 41-42) he writes :

> . . . the more fair and crystal is the sky,
> The uglier seem the clouds that in it fly.

Although the poet calls the clouds " lazy-paced " in "Romeo and Juliet " and " slippery " in " 2 Henry IV," in " King John " they become " the invulnerable clouds of heaven " (II.1. 252). King Edward IV in " 3 Henry VI " compares the forces marshalled against him by the Queen to gathering storm-clouds and is not much comforted by Clarence's assurance that " every cloud engenders not a storm " (V.3. 13). The truth that even the greatest happiness is tinged with care is expressed by Shakespeare in the familiar words, " Thus sometimes hath the brightest day a cloud " (" 2 Henry VI," II.4. 1).

The rainclouds provided the poet with an obvious simile for human tears—" the weeping clouds " he calls them in " 2 Henry IV " (I.3. 61). In " 2 Henry VI " the Queen says (III.2.38 3-385) :

> . . . mourn I not for thee,
> And with the southern clouds contend in tears,
> Theirs for the earth's increase, mine for my sorrows ?

Besides acknowledging the beneficial effect of the rains, the poet here makes another reference to the south as the region of moisture, a point we noticed in relation to the south wind (Section XXIV).

In that poignant scene in "Antony and Cleopatra," where the fallen Queen of Egypt applies the poisonous asp to her breast and arm, Charmian cries (V.2. 302-303) :

> Dissolve, thick cloud, and rain that I may say
> The gods themselves do weep !

Cloud and sorrow thus became closely associated in Shakespeare's mind. He uses the very expression, " the cloud of sorrow," in " Love's Labour's Lost." " Cloudy melancholy " (" Titus Andronicus "), " cloud my joys " (" 2 Henry VI "), " Edward's sun is clouded " (" 3 Henry VI "), and, " Hath clouded all thy happy days " (Richard II "), are typical sentences. " How is it that the clouds still hang on you ? " asks Claudius of the gloomy Hamlet (I.2. 66). In " Romeo and Juliet " we get a passage in which the clouds of sorrow are added to the clouds of a grey morning. Montague speaking of Romeo says (I.1. 137-140) :

> Many a morning hath he there been seen,
> With tears augmenting the fresh morning's dew,
> Adding to clouds more clouds with his deep sighs.

Later in this play, when Juliet has lost her Romeo and her parents are trying to force a husband upon her, she sighs, " Is there no pity sitting in the clouds ? " (III.5. 198).

Not only sorrow, but anger is described as " a cloudy brow " or " cloudy countenance." In "Antony and Cleopatra " we find the phrase, " he has a cloud in his face " (III.2. 51).

Shakespeare's quarrel with the clouds was their habit of veiling the sun and hiding the smiling face of heaven. He compares Richard II to a discontented sun (III.3. 65-67) :

> When he perceives the envious clouds are bent
> To dim his glory and to stain the track
> Of his bright passage to the occident.

The same figure is repeated in " 1 Henry IV " (I.2. 221-223) where Prince declares :

> . . . I will imitate the sun,
> Who doth permit the base contagious clouds
> To smother up his beauty from the world.

Titus Andronicus uses the same metaphor (III.1. 212-214) :

> . . . with our sighs we'll breathe the welkin dim,
> And stain the sun with fog, as sometime clouds
> When they do hug him in their melting bosoms.

Macbeth, in the midst of his great feast to his nobles, is confronted by the ghost of the murdered Banquo and

completely loses his equanimity and presence of mind.   It
has overcome him, he says, like " a summer's cloud " (III.4.
111).

The dispersing of the clouds, both literally and figuratively,
was to the poet a happy consummation, much to be desired.
Whether it were the wind, " A little gale will soon disperse
that cloud " (" 3 Henry VI," V, 3. 10), or the coming of
morning, as Puck says in " Midsummer Night's Dream,"
" Night's swift dragons cut the clouds full fast " (III.2. 379),
or the sun's rays dissolving them, " To the brightest beams
distracted clouds give way " ("All's Well," V.3. 33-34),
it mattered not, so long as the blue sky were clear of the
offending vapours.   Says Petruchio in " The Taming of the
Shrew " (IV.3. 175-176) :

> And as the sun breaks through the darkest clouds,
> So honour peereth in the meanest habit.

In " Richard III," the Duke of Gloucester congratulates
himself that "All the clouds that lour'd upon our house "
are " in the deep bosom of the ocean buried " (I.1. 3-4).

The height of the clouds is employed to denote tall terrestrial objects like " cloud-capped towers " (" Tempest ")
and " mountains turned into clouds " (" Midsummer Night's
Dream ").   We also find the old religious belief that heaven
was a locality situated above the clouds.   Friar Laurence
says (" Romeo and Juliet," IV.5. 73-74), " She is advanced
above the clouds, as high as heaven itself."

The sometimes astonishing beauty of the cloudy formations
seems to have been rather ignored by Shakespeare, but he
noticed the fantastic shapes, with their likenesses to earthly
figures, which are commonly seen.   There is, of course, that
famous scene in " Hamlet," where the Prince, feigning
madness, mercilessly pulls Polonius's leg (III.2. 392-398):

Hamlet : Do you see yonder cloud that's almost in shape of a camel ?

Polonius : By the mass, and 'tis like a camel, indeed.

Hamlet : Methinks it is like a weasel.

Polonius : It is backed like a weasel.

Hamlet : Or like a whale ?

Polonius : Very like a whale.

Hamlet was not serious, but Antony in the following passage describes in effective language the wonderful shapes we often view, if we look upward.

"Antony and Cleopatra " (IV.14. 2-7) :

> Sometime we see a cloud that's dragonish,
> A vapour sometime like a bear or lion,
> A tower'd citadel, a pendent rock,
> A forked mountain, or blue promontory
> With trees upon 't, that nod unto the world
> And mock our eyes with air.

P

XXVII.

RAIN.

THE rain assisted Shakespeare to many a happy turn of phrase, the best known being probably that famous simile from the trial scene of " The Merchant of Venice " (IV.1. 184-186) :

> The quality of mercy is not strain'd,
> It droppeth as the gentle rain from heaven
> Upon the place beneath :

In " Richard II " Bolingbroke turns to the elements to find a comparison for the relations between King Richard and himself. He says (III.3. 58-60) :

> Be he the fire, I'll be the yielding water :
> The rage be his, whilst on the earth I rain
> My waters.

Enobarbus, speaking of Cleopatra to Antony, declares that her passions are greater storms than almanac can report. It cannot be that she is pretending. " If it be," he continues, " she makes a shower of rain as well as Jove " ("Antony and Cleopatra," I.2. 157).

Rain plays its part, as we have seen, in Shakespeare's storms, particularly in " King Lear," where it is described as the " to-and-fro-conflicting wind and rain " (III.1. 11), and " the pelting of this pitiless storm " (III.4. 29), and " groans of roaring wind and rain " (III.2. 47). " The rain came to wet me once and the wind to make me chatter " says the pathetic old king after the tempest was over (IV.6.

102). " Rain and wind beat dark December " we read in
" Cymbeline " (III.3. 38) ; and Pericles prays, " Wind,
rain, and thunder, remember earthly man " (II.1. 2).

Shakespeare had observed, however, that rain often kept
off until the thunder had ceased or a high wind had dropped.
In " 1 Henry VI " (III.2. 59) Joan la Pucelle, after a fierce
harangue by Talbot, says, " If Talbot do but thunder, rain
will follow." In " 3 Henry VI " occur the lines (I.4. 145-
146) :

> For raging winds blow up incessant showers,
> And when the rage allays, the rain begins.

In " Troilus and Cressida " the same thought is repeated
by Pandarus (IV.4. 55-56) :

> Where are my tears ? rain, to lay this wind,
> or my heart will be blown up by the root.

" Small showers last long, but sudden storms are short,"
from " Richard II " (II.1. 35), further confirms Shakespeare's
close observation of matters meteorological. In " Lear "
he refers to smiles and tears in the words, " You have seen
sunshine and rain at once " (IV.3. 19-20).

As in the case of clouds, the poet finds similes on the rain
a natural way of describing human grief. In " Richard III "
Gloucester relates how, when the sad story of his father's
death was told, " All the standers-by had wet their cheeks,
like trees bedash'd with rain " (I.2. 163-164). In " Love's
Labour's Lost " (V.2. 819-820), the Princess speaks of . . .

> Raining the tears of lamentation
> For the remembrance of my father's death.

Her sincerity is open to doubt, however, if we believe a
line in the Induction to " The Taming of the Shrew "
(Sc. 1. 125), which affirms that it is " a woman's gift to
rain a shower of commanded tears." Prince Henry turns to

the simile to point the contrast between grief within the palace of Westminster, where the King is dying, and the smiling weather outside : " How now ! rain within doors, and none abroad ! " (" 2 Henry IV," IV.5. 9).

Two interesting notes on the effect of persistent rain are to be found in the plays. In the first Shakespeare, referring to King Edward IV's trial of his persuasive powers upon Lady Grey, writes, " He plies her hard ; and much rain wears the marble " (" 3 Henry VI," III.2. 50). In " Titus Andronicus " we find the exact opposite (II.3. 139-141) :

> . . . let it be your glory
> To see her tears, but be your heart to them
> As unrelenting flint to drops of rain.

A rainy night was a dismal, unpleasant affair to the poet, and his dramatic associations with it are similarly dismal. The night on which Banquo was murdered was dark and wet. " It will be rain to-night," says Banquo. " Let it come down," retorts the murderer (" Macbeth," III.3. 16). In " Much Ado About Nothing " (III.3) Borachio and Conrade had a miserable night, which " drizzled rain " (line 111), when they were arrested by the watch and their plot against Hero frustrated. Of a different nature is the soldierly " grouse " of the sentries in " 1 Henry VI " (II.1. 6-7), " constrain'd to watch in darkness, rain and cold," while " others sleep upon their quiet beds."

An echo of the poet's boyhood days in the country is heard in the lines commenting on the influence upon his supporters of Coriolanus's appearance, " They will out of their burrows, like conies after rain, and revel all with him " (IV.5. 225-227). Also smacking of the countryside is Rosalind's remark to Orlando : " I will be more jealous of thee than a Barbary cock-pigeon over his hen, more clamorous than a parrot against rain " ("As You Like It," IV.1. 150-152).

In conclusion, we must note the song, " For the rain it raineth every day," with which " Twelfth Night " ends (V.1. 398-401) :

> When that I was and a little tiny boy,
>   With hey, ho, the wind and the rain,
> A foolish thing was but a toy,
>   For the rain it raineth every day.

An adaptation of the same song is sung by the Fool in " King Lear " (III.2.) His version runs (75-78) :

> He that has and a little tiny wit,—
>   With hey, ho, the wind and the rain,—
> Must make content with his fortunes fit,
>   For the rain it raineth every day.

In our chapter on the spring we dealt with the refreshing showers of April without which, as Shakespeare says in " Midsummer Night's Dream," the roses of June would fade (I.1. 128-131) :

> *Lysander :* How now, my love ! why is your cheek so pale ?
>   How chance the roses there do fade so fast ?
> *Hermia :* Belike for want of rain, which I could well
>   Beteem them from the tempest of my eyes.

XXVIII.

THE RAINBOW.

As we should expect in a poet, Shakespeare's attitude toward
the rainbow is one of admiration for its beauty rather than a
desire to investigate its scientific cause. His few references
to it deal with its most obvious characteristic, the semi-circle
of radiant hues.

The rainbow is mentioned in a charming passage from
"King John," which we have had occasion to quote elsewhere in this study (IV.2. 11-16) :

> To gild refined gold, to paint the lily,
> To throw a perfume on the violet,
> To smooth the ice, or add another line
> Unto the rainbow, or with taper-light
> To seek the beauteous eye of heaven to garnish,
> Is wasteful and ridiculous excess.

In connection with a mention of the rainbow in "Lucrece,"
Shakespeare introduces the word "water-gall," which is
the secondary rainbow so often visible in the sky. The lines
are as follows (1586-89) :

> And round about her tear-distained eye
> Blue circles stream'd like rainbows in the sky .
> These water-galls in her dim element
> Foretell new storms to those already spent.

In Homer's "Iliad" the messenger of the gods is Iris.
In ancient mythology, as in the story of Noah in Genesis,
the rainbow was believed to be a promise from heaven to
man. Iris was the personification of this rainbow, and she

appears as such in the masque presented by Prospero for the two lovers in " The Tempest." Ceres, another of the masque's characters, addresses Iris thus (IV.1. 76-82) :

> Hail, many-colour'd messenger, that ne'er
> Dost disobey the wife of Jupiter;
> Who, with thy saffron wings, upon my flowers
> Diffusest honey-drops, refreshing showers;
> And with each end of thy blue bow dost crown
> My bosky acres and my unshrubb'd down,
> Rich scarf to my proud earth. . . .

The two other mentions of the rainbow are more commonplace. In " The Winter's Tale " the pedlar, Autolycus, has " ribbons of all the colours i' the rainbow " (IV.4. 205); in " Merry Wives of Windsor," Falstaff declares, after his thrashing, that he was beaten " into all the colours of the rainbow " (IV.5. 118).

XXIX.

HAIL.

SHAKESPEARE'S references to hail are few compared with those to other natural phenomena of a similar kind. It is clear, nevertheless, that he had noted the circumstances in which such falls occurred, for he makes clever figurative use of them in his poetry. When Antony puts the question to Cleopatra, " Cold-hearted toward me ? " she replies ("Antony and Cleopatra," III.13. 158-162) :

> Ah, dear, if I be so,
> From my cold heart let heaven engender hail,
> And poison it in the source, and the first stone
> Drop in my neck : as it determines, so
> Dissolve my life.

(" Determines " in this line means, " comes to an end.")

The black sky that accompanies a hailstorm is in the poet's mind when he makes the King of France in "All's Well That Ends Well " say (V.3. 32-34) :

> I am not a day of season,
> For thou mayst see a sunshine and a hail
> In me at once.

The dissolving effect of the sun on the hailstone was used on two occasions by Shakespeare for effective simile. In the first the proud patrician, Coriolanus, scornfully attacks the common people of Rome, rioting for lack of bread (I.1. 176-178) :

> . . . you are no surer, no,
> Than is the coal of fire upon the ice,
> Or hailstone in the sun,

The second instance occurs in that amusing middle-class comedy, "The Merry Wives of Windsor." Despatching his love-letters to Mistress Ford and Mistress Page, the old rascal Falstaff says, "Rogues, hence, avaunt! vanish like hailstones, go " (I.3. 90).

Shakespeare most generally utilizes the word "hail" in the sense of showering down blessings or evils. Helena says in "Midsummer Night's Dream" (I.1. 242-245):

> For ere Demetrius look'd on Hermia's eyne,
> He hail'd down oaths that he was only mine;
> And when this hail some heat from Hermia felt,
> So he dissolved, and showers of oaths did melt.

Cleopatra asking the messenger for news of Antony (II.5. 44-45) promises that if the tidings be good: "I'll set thee in a shower of gold, and hail rich pearls upon thee." Our final quotation comes from the "Merry Wives of Windsor," from the scene where Falstaff is finally undone. The fat knight exclaims (V.5. 20-24):

> Let the sky rain potatoes; let it thunder to the tune of Green Sleeves (an old popular ballad, still extant), hail kissing-comfits (i.e., sugar-plums), and snow eringoes (sea-holly); let there come a tempest of provocation, I will shelter me here!

XXX.

SNOW.

SHAKESPEARE was chiefly indebted to snow for furnishing a poetic simile for chastity and purity. "As pure as snow" is a phrase that occurs in "Macbeth" (IV.3. 53) and "as chaste as unsunn'd snow," in "Cymbeline" (II.5. 13). In "The Tempest" Ferdinand, Miranda's lover, assures her father, Prospero (IV.1. 54-56):

> I warrant you, sir;
> The white cold virgin snow upon my heart
> Abates the ardour of my liver.

Hamlet, at cross-purposes with the world, and disdainful of all mankind, says to Ophelia whom he had loved (III.1. 140-142): "Be thou as chaste as ice, as pure as snow, thou shalt not escape calumny. Get thee to a nunnery, go: farewell."

Diana was the cold goddess of chastity, and Shakespeare introduces her into Timon's speech where he addresses the gold (IV.3. 384-387):

> Thou ever young, fresh, loved, and delicate wooer,
> Whose blush doth thaw the consecrated snow
> That lies on Dian's lap.

In "Coriolanus" the drama's hero, speaking of Valeria, calls her (V.3. 65-67):

> The moon of Rome; chaste as the icicle
> That's curdied by the frost from purest snow
> And hangs on Dian's temple.

Snow as a pattern of perfect whiteness or beauty occurs easily to a poet. Shakespeare uses it frequently in this sense. " Snow-white hand " (" Love's Labour's Lost ") and Florizel's words to Perdita in " The Winter's Tale " (IV.4. 373-376) are typical examples :

> I take thy hand, this hand,
> As soft as dove's down and as white as it,
> Or Ethiopian's tooth, or the fann'd snow that's bolted
> By the northern blasts twice o'er.

Othello, contemplating his terrible crime against Desdemona, declares (V.2. 3-5) :

> Yet I'll not shed her blood,
> Nor scar that whiter skin of hers than snow
> And smooth as monumental alabaster.

In " Midsummer Night's Dream " Demetrius awakes to set eyes on Helena, with whom he finds himself hopelessly in love, owing to Puck's mistake in anointing him with the love potion instead of Lysander. " O Helen ! " he cries, " to what shall I compare thine eyne ? " and continues (III.2. 139-143) :

> O, how ripe in show
> Thy lips, those kissing cherries, tempting grow !
> The pure congealed white, high Taurus' snow,
> Fann'd with the eastern wind, turns to a crow
> When thou hold'st up thy hand.

In " Hamlet " the guilty Claudius hopes that the mercy of heaven is great enough to wipe the murderer's stain from his hands (III.3. 43-46) :

> What if this cursed hand
> Were thicker than itself with brother's blood,
> Is there not rain enough in the sweet heavens
> To wash it white as snow ?

We find the expression, "his beard was white as snow," in " Hamlet " (IV.5. 195) in one of Ophelia's snatches of song. Another disconnected line she hums is, "white his shroud as the mountain snow" (ibid., line 34). Such a description in regard to clothes and material is repeated by Autolycus in the sentence, " Lawn as white as driven snow " (" Winter's Tale," IV.4. 220).

In " Titus Andronicus " we hear of a " snow-white steed " (II.3. 76). Perhaps the most original figure in this connection is that used by Juliet (III.2. 17-19) :

> Come, night, come, Romeo, come, thou day in night ;
> For thou wilt lie upon the wings of night
> Whiter than new snow on a raven's back.

The white falls of winter must have been early boyhood memories of the poet, when he wandered over the Cotswold country. " Winter's drizzled snow," he calls them in the " Comedy of Errors." Recollection of the cold, biting atmosphere stirs in the lines of " Richard II " (I.3. 298-299), where he asks who can—

> . . . wallow naked in December's snow
> By thinking on fantastic summer's heat ?

In " King John " we get another simile from the snow covered landscape, when he says that a few French reinforcements would call English sympathisers to their side " as a little snow, tumbled about, anon becomes a mountain" (III.4. 176-177). A more pointed war simile, however, occurs in the speech of the French King, when he urges his countrymen to attack the conquering Henry V (III.5. 50-52) :

> Rush on his host, as doth the melted snow
> Upon the valleys, whose low vassal seat
> The Alps doth spit and void his rheum upon.

The plight of the animal kingdom in winter time won the sympathy of the poet. " Birds sit brooding in the snow " is a line from Winter's song in " Love's Labour's Lost " (V.2.

933). In "Antony and Cleopatra," Octavius Cæsar, apostrophizing Antony and calling upon him to "leave his lascivious wassails," reminds him of the hardships he once was willing to undergo for victory and honour (I.4. 63-66):

> . . . Thy palate then did deign
> The roughest berry on the rudest hedge;
> Yea, like the stag, when snow the pasture sheets,
> The barks of trees thou browsedst.

Snow out of season is mentioned in " Richard III," where the crookback is described as kind "as snow in harvest" (I.4. 249); and again in "Love's Labour's Lost," where Biron avers (I.1. 105-106):

> At Christmas I no more desire a rose
> Than wish a snow in May's new-fangled shows.

An interesting simile occurs in "All's Well That End's Well," where Parolles, speaking scornfully of certain soldiers, declares, "Half . . . dare not shake the snow from off their cassocks, lest they shake themselves to pieces " (IV.3. 191-193).

Two references to snowballs occur. "As cold as a snowball " is a phrase in " Pericles " (IV.6. 148); and Falstaff, after he has been thrown in the river, calls for drink, " Come, let me pour in some sack to the Thames water; for my belly's as cold as if I had swallowed snowballs for pills to cool the veins" ("Merry Wives of Windsor," III.5. 22-24).

The melting of the snow under the influence of the sun's rays or fire heat lends itself easily to figurative treatment. " Cold snow melts with the sun's hot beams," says Queen Margaret in " 2 Henry VI "; "Henry my lord is cold in great affairs . . . and Gloucester's show beguiles him" (III.1. 223-226). Reminiscent of the snow-man is Richard II's wish (IV.1. 260-262):

> O that I were a mockery king of snow,
> Standing before the sun of Bolingbroke,
> To melt myself away in water-drops !

The much-wronged Titus Andronicus affirms that so great is his grief, " In winter with warm tears I'll melt the snow " (III.1. 20). Demetrius in " Midsummer Night's Dream " confesses, " My love to Hermia, melted as the snow " (IV.1. 170-171).

In the Casket Scene of " The Merchant of Venice " Portia asks Bassanio to confess what treason is mixed with his love, and the handsome young suitor vigorously replies (III.2. 30-31) :

> There may as well be amity and life
> 'Tween snow and fire, as treason and my love.

Much the same idea is expressed by Julia in " Two Gentlemen of Verona " (II.7. 19-20) :

> Thou wouldst as soon go kindle fire with snow
> As seek to quench the fire of love with words.

Snow to Shakespeare's mind was symbolical of purity, chastity, coldness, self-possession, indifference—the opposite of the passionate, pulsating, impulsive, volatile nature that he knew so well. While he was busy, dramatically, in bringing " oil to fire " and " snow to colder moods " (" King Lear," II.2. 83), thereby emphasizing the traits of different characters, he was equally happy to change those aloof temperaments by the gentle influence of love, as the snows of winter are thawed by the spring sunshine.

XXXI.

FROST AND ICE.

THE frost and ice, the prominent features of wintry conditions, won considerable attention from the poet, though little of love and admiration. We have seen that his whole attitude towards winter was one of dislike and resignation. Where others could see beauty in naked trees, bare landscapes, and snow-crowned hills, Shakespeare reserved some of his hardest epithets for the season from which these treasures of Nature are inseparable. The fairy patterns and crystal creations of King Frost do not appear to have had influence enough to detract the poet's attention from the cruel, bitter weather on which their existence depended. It would almost seem as if Shakespeare was intensely sensitive to the cold and felt it more keenly than most people do.

Frost enters into many of his most lucent word-paintings descriptive of winter. Some phrases we have noted already. Examples of these are, "the freezing hours" of "dark December" ("Cymbeline," III.3. 39), and Benedick's "February face, so full of frost, of storm, and cloudiness" ("Much Ado About Nothing," V.4. 41-42), "Old Hiem's icy crown" ("Midsummer Night's Dream," II.1. 109), Winter's "icy fingers" ("King John," V.7. 37), and "the icy fang . . . of the winter's wind" ("As You Like It," II.1. 6-7)—all phrases suggestive of a shivering world. The prospect of "six frozen winters" in banishment was the ugly one that King Richard presented to unhappy

Bolingbroke (" Richard II," I.3. 211). Freezing cold seemed
to Shakespeare an apt simile for man's ingratitude " ("As
You Like It," II.7. 184-189) :

> Freeze, freeze, thou bitter sky,
> That dost not bite so nigh
>   As benefits forgot :
> Though thou the waters warp,
> Thy sting is not so sharp
>   As friend remember'd not.

In the " Tempest " Prospero considers that Ariel, in
grateful remembrance of all that he has done for the sprite,
should be glad to do him business even " in the veins o'
the earth when it is baked with frost " (I.2. 255-256). In
the song of Winter, which closes " Love's Labour's Lost,"
there is a picture of frosty conditions, " when icicles hang by
the wall," the "milk comes frozen home in pail, and "blood
is nipp'd " (V.2. 922, 925, and 926). Biting cold is suggested
by " the mountain tops that freeze " (" Henry VIII," III.1.
4); while, for an unpleasant duty, that of a watchman on a
frosty night could hardly be excelled (see " Titus Andronicus,"
III.1. 5).

Ice-pictures occur in many instances. In " Timon of
Athens " Apemantus speaks of the " cold brook, candied with
ice " (IV.3. 225-226), and Claudio in "Measure for Measure"
of " thrilling region of thick-ribbed ice " (III.1. 123).
The smoothness of the ice is referred to in " King John "
(IV.2. 13), where the expression " to smooth the ice " is
used alongside " to paint the lily " and " to add another hue
unto the rainbow " to express superfluity. Another very
effective metaphor is used by Shakespeare in " Henry V,"
where the poet writes, " You may as well go about to turn
the sun to ice with fanning in his face with a peacock's
feather " (IV.1. 211-213).

Shakespeare employs the phrase, " frozen to death," on two or three occasions, notably in " Richard III," where King Edward, speaking of himself and Warwick, says (II.1. 114-117):

> . . . when we both lay in the field
> Frozen almost to death, how he did lap me,
> Even in his own garments, and gave himself,
> All thin and naked, to the numb cold night.

" My blood froze " (" Comedy of Errors "), springs from this idea and is used figuratively. " I could a tale unfold " that would " freeze thy young blood," declares the Ghost to Hamlet (I.5. 16). Juliet fastens on the same metaphor (IV.3. 15-16):

> I have a faint cold fear thrills through my veins,
> That almost freezes up the heat of life.

As in the case of snow, ice suggested a cold temperament, and hence chastity, to Shakespeare. It is, perhaps, his most frequent metaphorical use of the phenomenon and found in such expressions as, " the very ice of chastity is in them " ("As You Like It," III.4. 18), " chaste as ice " (" Hamlet," III.1. 140), and " chaste as the icicle that's curdied (i.e., congealed) by the frost," (" Coriolanus," V.3. 65-66). In " All's Well That Ends Well " Lafeu says of the young courtiers who decline the offer of Helena as a wife, " These boys are boys of ice, they'll none have her " (II.3. 99). In " The Taming of the Shrew " the following conversation takes place between Curtis and Grumio about Petruchio, their master, and his wife, Katharina the Shrew (IV.1. 18-25):

> *Curt* : Is my master and his wife coming, Grumio ?
> *Gru* : O, ay, Curtis, ay ; and therefore fire, fire ; cast
> on no water.
> *Curt* : Is she so hot a shrew as she's reported ?
> *Gru* : She was, good Curtis, before this frost ; but, thou
> knowest, winter tames man, woman, and beast.

Q

From the above quotations it will be seen that ice was not only a synonym for chastity but also for coldness, indifference, or an unloving, stony-hearted nature. Another instance of this use occurs in " Two Gentlemen of Verona," where the foolish Thurio complains to the Duke that his daughter, Silvia, has no eyes for him when Valentine is nigh. The lover is, therefore, banished, but Thurio complains that since his exile Silvia's attitude towards himself has worsened. " I am desperate of obtaining her," he groans. The Duke answers (III.2. 6-10) :

> This weak impress of love is as a figure
> Trenched (i.e., carved) in ice, which with an hour's heat
> Dissolves to water, and doth lose its form.
> A little time will melt her frozen thoughts,
> And worthless Valentine shall be forget.

In " The Taming of the Shrew," Katharina, now docile and obedient, tells the widow (V.2. 137-139) :

> . . . dart not scornful glances from those eyes,
> To wound thy lord, thy king, thy governor ;
> It blots thy beauty as frosts do bite the meads.

In " Henry VIII " the Lord Chamberlain at the banquet in York Place divides ladies who are sitting next to each other, saying, " Nay, you must not freeze ; Two women placed together makes cold weather " (I.4. 21-22). In " Timon of Athens " Timon calls an upright and continent life learning " the icy precepts of respect " (IV.3. 258). The ice of chastity should be guarded from all flames of passion, but the ice of indifference should be broken. In " The Taming of the Shrew " Baptista refuses to allow suitors to approach his fair younger daughter, Bianca, until the elder, Katharina, is wed. But Katharina is a shrew, and Petruchio is flattered into believing that he is the only man who can

tame her.   Says Tranio, servant to Lucentio who is in love
with Bianca (I.2. 265-70) :

> . . . you are the man
> Must stead us all and me amongst the rest ;
> And if you break the ice and do this feat,
> Achieve the elder, set the younger free
> For our access, whose hap shall be to have her
> Will not so graceless be to be ingrate.

It is not only in the kingdom of love that the figure of ice
is employed by the poet.   It may describe the general trend
of an individual's temperament and even depict national
character.   Such an example is found in " Henry V," where
the Constable of France, speaking of the English and con-
trasting their coldness and calmness with his more fiery and
hot-blooded countrymen, exclaims (III.5. 15-25) :

> Dieu de batailles ! where have they this mettle ?
> Is not their climate foggy, raw and dull,
> On whom, as in despite, the sun looks pale,
> Killing their fruits with frowns ?   Can sodden water,
> A drench for sur-rein'd jades, their barley-broth,
> Decoct their cold blood to such valiant heat ?
> And shall our quick blood, spirited with wine,
> Seem frosty ?   O, for honour of our land,
> Let us not hang, like roping icicles
> Upon our houses' thatch, whiles a more frosty people
> Sweat drops of gallant youth in our rich fields !

The above passage not only gives us Shakespeare's conception of the English character in brief space, but also his
acknowledgment of the influence of climate on disposition.
    Lack of enthusiasm, loss of zeal and loyalty, are also
portrayed by recourse to winter frosts for the provision of
significant figures.   " This act   . . .   shall cool the hearts
of all his people and freeze up their zeal," we read in " King
John " (III.4. 149-150).   Young Clifford in " 2 Henry VI,"

on the battlefield of St. Albans, where his father is killed and
his side routed, cries, " O war . . . throw in the frozen
bosoms of our part hot coals of vengeance ! " (V.2. 35-36).
Hotspur speaks of a laggard ally as a " frosty-spirited rogue "
(" I Henry IV," II.3. 21); and Buckingham, sending Catesby
to sound Lord Hastings as to his willingness to join their
faction, tells him to handle him tactfully and break off his
talk, " if he be leaden, icy-cold, unwilling " (" Richard III,"
III.1. 176).

" Cold hearts freeze allegiance in them," declares Queen
Katharine in describing to Henry VIII how unpopular are
Wolsey's heavy taxes among his subjects (I.2. 61).   Richard
III tries to win Buckingham's consent to the death of the
little Princes.   The Duke tries to temporize, and the King
exclaims impatiently, " Tut, tut, thou art all ice ; thy kindness
freezeth ! " (IV.2. 22).

In " Coriolanus " the ice provides the poet with a simile
for instability when he makes his hero compare the fickle
Roman mob to a " coal of fire upon the ice " (I.1. 177).
In " Timon of Athens " we get a picture of flint-like feelings,
when Timon sends his steward, Flavius, to borrow money
from gentlemen to whom Timon has been most generous
in the past.   There was no warm-hearted response.   Flavius
returns empty-handed, loaded with the so-called friends'
excuses, and tells his lord (II.2. 221-222) :

> With certain half-caps (i.e., grudging salutations) and cold-
>   moving nods
> They froze me into silence.

Our final quotation on this aspect of Shakespeare's use of
frost and ice as a literary figure is taken from " Hamlet."
The Prince has been speaking very frankly to his mother and
condemning her for what he regards as her surrender to

her immoral promptings. He concludes on a sarcastic note
(III.4. 85-88) :

> . . . proclaim no shame
> When the compulsive ardour gives the charge,
> Since frost itself as actively doth burn,
> And reason panders will.

Frost and old-age had an affinity in Shakespeare's imagination, and in several cases the two are connected. "Frosty
head " for grey hairs is a figure in " 2 Henry VI " (V.1. 167).
Marcus in " Titus Andronicus " speaks of " my frosty signs
and chaps of age " (V.3. 77). Old Adam in "As You Like
It," declares his "age is as a lusty winter, frosty, but kindly "
(II.3. 52-53). In " The Taming of the Shrew," Tranio
taunts Gremio with, " Greybeard, thy love doth freeze "
(II.1. 340).

In " 1 Henry IV " Worcester describes bad news as that
which " bears a frosty sound " (IV.1. 128). Rather similar
is the remark of the Prince of Morocco in " The Merchant of
Venice," when he has wrongly chosen the golden casket and
lost his chance of marrying Portia : " Then, farewell, heat,
and welcome, frost ! " (II.7. 75). In " Richard II," when
the aged John of Gaunt bitterly criticizes his nephew, the
angry young king exclaims (II.1. 117-118) : " Darest with
thy frozen admonition make pale our cheek."

The influence of the frosts upon the flowers was well
known to Shakespeare, and his knowledge was the cradle of
several fine lines. The most significant of his figures is that
of a cruel, untimely frost nipping the young buds as they open.
In " Love's Labour's Lost " the King says of Biron (I.1. 100-
101) :

> Biron is like an envious sneaping frost,
> That bites the first-born infants of the spring.

In " 2 Henry IV " Lord Bardolph observes (I.3. 37-41) :

> . . . a cause on foot,
> Lives so in hope, as in an early spring
> We see the appearing buds ; which to prove fruit,
> Hope gives not so much warrant as despair
> That frosts will bite them.

Speaking of the dead Juliet, Capulet declares (IV.5. 28-29) :

> Death lies on her like an untimely frost
> Upon the sweetest flower of all the field.

Perhaps the finest lines on this theme are those from " Midsummer Night's Dream," which the poet puts into the mouth of Titania (II.1. 107-108) :

> The seasons alter : hoary-headed frosts
> Fall in the fresh lap of the crimson rose.

In the following passage from " Henry VIII " the fallen Wolsey compares the state of man (III.2. 352-357) :

> . . . to-day he puts forth
> The tender leaves of hopes ; to-morrow blossoms,
> And bears his blushing honours thick upon him ;
> The third days comes a frost, a killing frost,
> And, when he thinks, good easy man, full surely
> His greatness is a-ripening, nips his root.

Above we have remarked upon Worcester's description of bad news having a frosty sound. In " Titus Andronicus " Saturninus, on receipt of evil reports, affirms, " These tidings nip me . . . as flowers with frost " (IV.4. 70-71).

There are two striking similes in the plays which refer to the effect of frosts upon the animal kingdom. In the first, found in " 2 Henry IV," Morton asserts, " This word, rebellion, it had froze them up, as fish are in a pond " (I.1. 199-200). The second occurs in " Titus Andronicus," where

Marcus refers to the kiss the maimed Lavinia gives to Titus (III.1. 251-252):

> Alas, poor heart, that kiss is comfortless,
> As frozen water to a starved snake.

Shakespeare uses frost and ice, or more properly, frosty and icy, as a geographical indication. In " The Merchant of Venice " the Prince of Morocco refers to the cold regions of the north in the words (II.1. 4-5):

> Bring me the fairest creature northward born,
> Where Phœbus' fire scarce thaws the icicles.

" The frozen bosom of the north " is alluded to again in " Romeo and Juliet " (I.4. 101).

Russia was the chief region connected with ice, snow, and frost in Shakespeare's mind. When the King of Navarre and his companions dress up as Russians in " Love's Labour's Lost," the Princess addresses them as " my frozen Muscovits " (V.2. 265). " The frosty Caucasus " is mentioned in " Richard II " (I.3. 295); and the icy currents of the Pontic (Black) Sea in " Othello" (III.3. 453). In "Hamlet" Horatio recalls the victory of the elder Hamlet over " the sledded Polacks on the ice " (I.1. 63).

Among other countries, whose frigid climate impressed the poet, was Switzerland, and " the frozen ridges of the Alps " is a description in " Richard II " (I.1. 64). The remark, " an icicle on a Dutchman's beard," found in " Twelfth Night " (III.2. 29-30), may refer to the discovery of Northern Nova Zembla by the Dutchman, Barenz, in 1596.

XXXII.

MIST AND FOG.

Fair is foul, and foul is fair ;
Hover through the fog and filthy air.

THESE sinister lines occur in the opening scene of " Macbeth," where the three Weird Sisters appear in thunder and lightning to convey that atmosphere of gloom and horror which enfolds this terrible but magnificent tragedy. The lines also reveal Shakespeare's own feelings in regard to obscuring and confusing mists and fogs. It was one of unrelieved detestation, as is proved beyond question by the study of selected passages from his works.

On the cause of these phenomena the poet had ascertained certain facts. He puts the following curse into Lear's mouth after his cruel treatment at the hands of Goneril (" King Lear," II.4. 168-170) ;

Infect her beauty,
You fen-sucked fogs, drawn by the powerful sun
To fall and blast her pride.

In " Midsummer Night's Dream " he blames the winds for the fogs (II.1. 88-90) :

Therefore the winds . . .
. . . have suck'd up from the sea
Contagious (i.e., pestilential) fogs. . . .

It is Shakespeare's most serious complaint against the fogs that they " stain the sun " (" Titus Andronicus," III.1. 213). The sun permits " the base contagious clouds to smother up

his beauty from the world " (" 1 Henry IV," I.2. 222-223),
but at length he breaks "through the foul and ugly mists of
vapours that did seem to strangle him " (lines 226-227).

The fall of the misty darkness of night is described in
" 2 Henry VI," where the captain, mourning the departure
of daylight, observes (IV.1. 3-7):

> And now loud-howling wolves arouse the jades
> That drag the tragic melancholy night ;
> Who, with their drowsy, slow and flagging wings,
> Clip dead men's graves, and from their misty jaws
> Breathe foul contagious darkness in the air.

Morning mists are remarked upon by Romeo : " Jocund
day stands tiptoe on the misty mountain tops " (" Romeo
and Juliet," III.5. 9-10). In contrast to the clouds that
crown the towering peak are the vapours that fill the valleys,
and the poet speaks of the " misty vale " in " Titus
Andronicus" (V.2. 35) as a "lurking-place" where murder
" can couch for fear." In the same play we come across
another mental association of mist with facts forbidding.
He writes (II.3. 236), "As hateful as Cocytus' misty mouth."
Cocytus was the river supposed to be connected with the
lower world and sometimes spoken of as flowing through
those infernal regions.

Shakespeare accepts the verdict that England's climate is
foggy, and in " Henry V " makes the Constable of France
say in comment upon the élan of the English enemy (III.5.
16-17):

> Is not their climate foggy, raw, and dull,
> On whom, as in despite, the sun looks pale ?

Our prevailing south-west wind was supposed to be the
cause of our weather. We have seen that moist and misty
conditions were associated with the south. " Like foggy
south, puffing with wind and rain," is a remark of Rosalind

("As You Like It," III.5. 50). The same idea is echoed in a conversation between citizens of Rome in " Coriolanus " (II.3. 29-37) :

> *Third Citizen :* Nay, your wit will not so soon out as another man's will ; 'tis strongly 'wedged up in a blockhead ; but if it were at liberty, 'twould, sure, southward.
> *Second Citizen :* Why that way ?
> *Third Citizen :* To lose itself in fog ; where being three parts melted away with rotten dews, the fourth would return for conscience sake, to help to get thee a wife.

The impenetrability of fogs suggested to the poet expressions for physical obscuration and mental confusion. In " Midsummer Night's Dream " Oberon gives the following instructions to Puck (III.2. 354-359) :

> Thou see'st these lovers seek a place to fight :
> Hie, therefore, Robin, overcast the night ;
> The starry welkin cover thou anon
> With drooping fog, as black as Acheron ;
> And lead these testy rivals so astray,
> As one come not within another's way.

In the " Comedy of Errors," Antipholus of Syracuse is completely muddled by the complications that have arisen, and does not know whether he is awake or asleep, mad or sane. He decides to take his cue from others :

> I'll say as they say, and persever so,
> And in this mist at all adventures go.
>
> (II.2. 217-218.)

In " Cymbeline " Imogen declares confidently that she is able to see her way clearly through the uncertain and obscure events present and foreshadowed. She says to Pisanio (III.2. 80-82) :

> I see before me, man : nor here, nor here,
> Nor what ensues, but have a fog in them,
> That I cannot look through.

The traditional comparison of ignorance to fog is cited in
the Clown's words to Malvolio in " Twelfth Night " (IV.2.
46-48) : " There is no darkness but ignorance ; in which
thou art more puzzled than the Egyptians in their fog "—
a reference to the plague of darkness.

Romeo uses an original metaphor when in Friar Laurence's
cell. A knocking is heard, and the holy man urges in his
anxiety, " Good Romeo, hide thyself," but the unhappy
lover replies (III.3. 72-73) :

> Not I ; unless the breath of heart-sick groans
> Mist-like infold me from the search of eyes.

Lastly, we have one of the terrible curses that the dramatist
puts into Lear's mouth, which incidentally throws a light on
his own feelings. After the insufferable behaviour of
Albany and Goneril, the ex-king cried out, " Blasts and fogs
upon thee ! " (I.4. 321).

XXXIII.

DEW.

To quote the "New English Dictionary," dew is "the moisture deposited in minute drops upon any cool surface by condensation of the vapour of the atmosphere; formed after a hot day, during or towards night, and plentiful in the early morning." This scientific explanation of the presence of dew is of comparatively recent date. The old idea was that the dew fell from the air. Shakespeare shared this theory with others. It had been current since a very early age, from the days of Aristotle at least, and continued to hold ground as late as Wordsworth's lifetime.

Shakespeare expresses this general conception, or rather, misconception, in "Romeo and Juliet," where he makes Capulet say, "When the sun sets, the air doth drizzle dew" (III.5. 127). King John, again, uses the words, "Before the dew of evening fall" (II.1. 285). In "Midsummer Night's Dream," the Fairy, in response to Puck's question, replies (II.1. 8-9):

> And I serve the fairy queen,
> To dew her orbs upon the green.

(In this passage "orbs" are the rings of fresh green grass, which the superstitious believed were caused by the fairies.) Dew, descending at night, is linked in the poet's mind with sleep, and thus we read of "the golden dew of sleep" in "Richard III" (IV.1. 84) and "the honey-heavy dew of slumber" in "Julius Cæsar" (II.1. 230).

"Midsummer Night's Dream" is a play containing many references to the dew, and in Act III (sc. I, line 204) Titania says, "When she (the moon) weeps, weeps every little flower." Commenting on this passage, Steevens writes that Shakespeare "means that every little flower is moistened with dew, as if with tears, and not that the flower itself drizzles dew." The modern and correct notion could be picturesquely described as every little flower weeping, but the poet lived long before this discovery was made.

Dew falling from the sky gave the poet a perfect simile for tears. He even writes of "dewy tears" in "Richard III." In the "Rape of Lucrece" are the lines (1226-1229):

> . . . as the earth doth weep, the sun being set,
> Each flower moisten'd like a melting eye,
> Even so the maid with swelling drops 'gan wet
> Her circled eyne.

Montague speaks of Romeo as "with tears augmenting the fresh morning's dew" ("Romeo and Juliet," I.1. 138); and we read of tears as "vain dew" in "The Winter's Tale" (II.1. 109), and "honourable dew" in "King John" (V.2. 45-46):

> Let me wipe off this honourable dew
> That silverly doth progress on thy cheeks.

The dews of the morning appeared to the poet as the beauty of freshness. In "Hamlet" Laertes speaks of "the morn and liquid dew of youth" (I.3. 41). Petruchio says he will flatter the difficult Katharina and tell her "she looks as clear as morning roses newly wash'd with dew" (II.1. 173-174). "As fresh as morning dew distill'd on flowers" is a line in "Titus Andronicus" (II.3. 201). The King in "Love's Labour's Lost" finds the simile a useful one in the verses he composes to the Princess (IV.3. 26-29):

> So sweet a kiss the golden sun gives not
> To those fresh morning drops upon the rose,
> As thy eye-beams, when their fresh rays have smote
> The night of dew that on my cheek down flows.

The benefit of the dew to the flowers provides a metaphor for the Lords of Scotland, marching to the overthrow of the tyrant, Macbeth (V.2. 28-30):

> *Caithness:* And with him (Malcolm) pour we, in our country's purge,
> Each drop of us.
> *Lennox:*   Or so much as it needs
> To dew the sovereign flower and drown the weeds.

It is before the sun has dried "night's dank (i.e., moist) dew" ("Romeo and Juliet," II.3. 6) that Shakespeare saw it as drops of pearl. He speaks of a moonlight night in "Midsummer Night's Dream" in these terms (I.1. 209-11):

> . . . when Phœbe doth behold
> Her silver visage in the watery glass,
> Decking with liquid pearl the bladed grass.

In the same play the Fairy says (II.1. 14-15):

> I must go seek some dewdrops here,
> And hang a pearl in every cowslip's ear.

And again, Oberon (IV.1. 58-59):

> And that same dew, which sometime on the buds
> Was wont to swell, like round and orient pearls.

In "Coriolanus" Shakespeare writes of "the dews of flattery"; and in "Antony and Cleopatra" there is a pretty example of the poet's original fancy in Euphronius's remark about Antony (III.12. 8-10):

> I was of late as petty to his ends
> As is the morn-dew on the myrtle leaf
> To his grand sea.

It appears, however, that dew was not always refreshing, pearly, and fairy-like. In some passages it seems to take on a somewhat sinister significance. It is "raw and cold" ("Richard III"), or "rotten" ("Coriolanus"), and associated with clouds and dangers ("Julius Cæsar"). Hamlet wishes that "this too, too solid flesh would melt, thaw and resolve itself into a dew!" (I.2. 129-130). "Dews of blood" is an expression from the same play. In "Cymbeline" (IV.2. 283-285), where Belarius enters with the body of Cloten, we read:

> Here's a few flowers, but 'bout midnight more:
> The herbs that have on them cold dew o' the night
> Are strewings fitt'st for graves.

Dew, it seems, was sometimes endowed with magical properties. Ariel relates how Prospero once called him up at midnight "to fetch dew from the still-vex'd Bermoothes" ("The Tempest," I.2. 228). In the same play Caliban delivers himself of this vicious curse (I.2. 321-323):

> As wicked dew as e'er my mother brush'd
> With raven's feather from unwholesome fen
> Drop on you both!

There remains the question of the honey-dew, which Shakespeare mentions in the following touching simile from "Titus Andronicus" (III.1. 111-113):

> When I did name her brothers, then fresh tears
> Stood on her cheeks, as doth the honey-dew
> Upon a gather'd lily almost wither'd.

The poet was ignorant of the real nature of honey-dew. Doubtless he obtained his facts from the classical writers. Pliny stated that honey-dew was the saliva of the stars, or a liquid produced by the purgation of the air. Actually the sweet, glutinous substance is a secretion deposited upon the flowers in dewlike drops by various insects of the Aphis family.

XXXIV.

THE ECHO.

THE delightful custom of ancient mythology of personifying and weaving skilful fables around natural phenomena has a good example in the echo. According to the classical writers, Echo was a nymph, who engaged Hera's attention by talking to her incessantly while her husband, Zeus, sported with other nymphs. When the goddess saw through the trick that was being played upon her, in her anger she punished Echo by changing her into the familiar voice of the rocks. Later, Echo fell in love with the handsome Narcissus. Her love was not returned, and in sorrow she pined away until nothing but her voice remained.

This story was well known to Shakespeare, but only once does he mention the nymph by name. Juliet, calling after the departing Romeo, prays (II.2. 159-164):

> O, for a falconer's voice,
> To lure this tassel-gentle (i.e., male hawk) back again !
> Bondage is hoarse, and may not speak aloud ;
> Else I would tear the cave where Echo lies,
> And make her airy tongue more hoarse than mine,
> With repetition of my Romeo's name.

The use of Echo as the name of one of the Lord's hounds in the Induction to " The Taming of the Shrew " has no connection with the nymph, since he is spoken of in the masculine gender.

The most poetic description of the character of the echo is contained in the following lines from " Twelfth Night," where Viola declares to Olivia she wishes to—

> Halloo your name to the reverberate hills,
> And make the babbling gossip of the air
> Cry out " Olivia ! "   (I.5. 291-293.)

" Babbling " is the epithet chosen also in " Titus Andronicus " (II.3. 17-19) :

> . . . the babbling echo mocks the hounds,
> Replying shrilly to the well-tuned horns,
> As if a double hunt were heard at once.

In " King John " the English and French have failed to agree on terms of peace. The Dauphin Lewis is defiant, and Faulconbridge retorts (V.2. 167-173) :

> . . . do but start
> An echo with the clamour of thy drum,
> And even at hand a drum is ready braced
> That shall reverberate as loud as thine ;
> Sound but another, and another shall
> As loud as thine rattle the welkin's ear
> And mock the deep-mouth'd thunder.

In " 2 Henry IV " we find an apt comparison of unreliable rumour to the echo (III.1. 97-98). Warwick says :

> Rumour doth double, like the voice and echo,
> The numbers of the fear'd.

Macbeth, praying the Doctor to cure the diseased mind of his wife, promises that if he succeeds, " I will applaud thee to the very echo, that should applaud again " (V.3. 53-54).

Shakespeare's other uses of the word " echo " are commonplace and require no mention here.

XXXV.

FIRE AND FLAME.

THE awe-inspiring and all-devouring phenomena of fire and flame are mentioned hundreds of times in Shakespeare's plays, but perhaps the poet was not so happy nor so picturesque in his fire metaphors as in those suggested by other wonders of Nature. In one mood fire appears to him as " raging," " fierce," " wrathful," " flashing," " revenging." With the licking flames in his mind, he speaks of it as " climbing " and " quick." " The violent speed of fire " is one of his phrases ; " as red as new-kindled fire," another. He sees bullets as " wrapped in fire." But " violent fires soon burn out themselves " (" Richard II," II.1. 34); and we get fire in another mood when it is " idle," " dead," or " drowsy." "A rash fierce blaze of riot " (ibid., line 33) can render man helpless, while " a little fire is quickly trodden out ; which being suffered, rivers cannot quench " (" 3 Henry VI," IV.8. 7-8).

So prominent a phenomenon was bound to suggest a host of metaphors to the universal poet, and particularly do we find comparisons between fire and the human emotions. " The fire of love," " the flame of love," " the fire of passion," " the quick fire of youth," " flaming youth," " the flame of fair eyes," are all examples of this use. Says the Duchess to old John of Gaunt in " Richard II " (I.2. 10) : " Hath love in thy old blood no living fire ? " Next we get enthusiasm compared to fire in such expressions, now

commonplace, as—" to be on fire," " to fire the blood,"
" to set the blood on fire." In " Julius Cæsar " Brutus speaks
of "fire enough to kindle cowards " (II.1. 120-121), and
in " 3 Henry VI " King Edward IV, addressing his soldiers
at Tewkesbury and explaining the task that lies before them,
says (V.4. 70-72) :

> I need not add more fuel to your fire,
> For well I wot ye blaze to burn them out :
> Give signal to the fight.

Anger is another abstract idea which the poet emphasizes
by a fiery simile. " The fire's extreme rage," " flaming wrath,"
" the fire of rage," " hasty as fire," and the following lines
from " The Taming of the Shrew " (II.1. 133-136), are
illustrations :

> . . . where two raging fires meet together
> They do consume the thing that feeds their fury.

And he adds :

> Though little fire grows great with little wind,
> Yet extreme gusts will blow out fire and all.

The passage describes in metaphor the coming clash
between the tempers of Katharina and Petruchio.

The finest instance of Shakespeare's dramatic use of fire
upon the stage, apart from the lightning of his thunderstorms,
is that pathetic scene in " King John," where Prince Arthur
pleads with Hubert, who has been commissioned to burn
out his eyes. The pathos is intensified by the dying brazier
over which the cruel instruments of torture are being heated
(IV.1. 106-117) :

> *Arthur :*   . . . the fire is dead with grief,
> Being create for comfort, to be used
> In undeserved extremes : see else yourself ;
> There is no malice in this burning coal ;
> The breath of heaven hath blown his spirit out
> And strew'd repentant ashes on his head.

Hubert : But with my breath I can revive it, boy.
Arthur : And if you do, you will but make it blush
              And glow with shame at your proceedings, Hubert .
              Nay, it perchance will sparkle in your eyes ;
              And, like a dog that is compell'd to fight,
              Snatch at its master that doth tarre (i.e., incite) him on.

Lucifer matches did not come into general use until the beginning of the nineteenth century, and the people of Shakespeare's day had to rely on flint and tinder-box. This homely article provided the poet with many an ingenious and puissant turn of phrase, of which the following are representative :

" Julius Cæsar " (IV.3. 110-113) :

        O Cassius, you are yoked with a lamb,
        That carries anger as the flint bears fire,
        Who, much enforced, shows a hasty spark
        And straight is cold again.

" Timon of Athens " (I.1. 22-25) :

             . . . the fire i' the flint
    Shows not till it be struck ; our gentle flame
    Provokes itself, and, like the current, flies
    Each bound it chafes.

" Troilus and Cressida " (III.3. 255-258) :

   There was wit in this head, and 't would out : and so there
is ; but it lies as coldly in him as fire in a flint, which will not
show without knocking.

Belief in hell-fire was almost universal in the Middle Ages, and is echoed by Shakespeare in such sentences as, " set hell on fire," " burn in everlasting fire," " sulphurous and tormenting flames," and the ejaculation, " fire and brimstone ! " In " Henry V " a flea on Bardolph's nose is said to have been compared by Falstaff to a black soul burning in hell-fire " (II.3. 43) ; the Porter in " Macbeth " talks of "the primrose way to the everlasting bonfire" (II.3. 21-22).

(Bonfire is a word which occurs several times in Shakespeare.)
Old King Lear cries out in his madness (IV.7. 45-48):

> You do me wrong to take me out o' the grave;
> Thou art a soul in bliss; but I am bound
> Upon a wheel of fire, that mine own tears
> Do scald like molten lead.

There are many references to fire as an element, a meaning
that has been discussed elsewhere.

Several allusions of an unusual character require brief
mention. Shakespeare on four occasions uses the adjective
"fire-new." In modern parlance we should substitute
"brand new." The poet had in mind coins fresh from the
mint. In "1 Henry IV" (III.3. 53) Falstaff, always poking
fun at Bardolph's red nose, compares it this time to a sala-
mander, which he declares he has maintained with fire, in
other words, with sack, for thirty-two years. The sala-
mander is a lizard which was once popularly supposed to live
in fire, and so became the sprite embodying fire. "A sea-
coal fire," an expression that occurs in "2 Henry IV" (II.1.
95) and "Merry Wives of Windsor" (I.4. 9), relates to
fires made with coal, in those days imported into England
by sea. A coal fire was something of a novelty in Elizabethan
times, when nearly all fires were of wood.

Ariel's activities on the sinking ship in "The Tempest"
include a handling of that strange manifestation of nature
known as St. Elmo's Fire. In his report to Prospero the
sprite says (I.2. 196-201):

> I boarded the king's ship; now on the beak,
> Now in the waist, the deck, in every cabin,
> I flamed amazement: sometime I'ld divide
> And burn in many places; on the topmast,
> The yards and bowsprit, would I flame distinctly,
> Then meet and join.

We have seen that Sir Sidney Lee explains this passage as a reference to " startling phenomena which sailors imputed to Atlantic storms." Thiselton Dyer and other commentators interpret it as alluding to the widely-known St. Elmo's Fire. A tip of light appears on the ends of pointed objects such as masts and yards of ships, spires, and even the extremities of the fingers, and is accompanied by a crackling noise. The glow is caused by the slow discharge of electricity from the atmosphere to earth. St. Elmo (St. Erasmus, a martyred bishop of Italy, who died in 304) was adopted by the sailors of the Mediterranean as their patron saint, and the appearance of the fire was afterwards accepted as proof of his protection. The phenomenon was familiar to the ancient Greeks, and Pliny mentions it in his " Natural History." When it appeared as a single flame, it was Helena of Trojan war fame, and an omen of ill luck. As a double flame it was called Castor and Pollux, the guardians of sailors among the classical gods, and, therefore, a good sign. Dyer writes : "According to some, it never appears but after a tempest, and is supposed to lead people to suicide by drowning. Shakespeare in all probability consulted Batman's ' Golden Books of the Leaden Goddes,' who, speaking of Castor and Pollux—' They were figured like two lampes or cresset lightes—one on the toppe of a maste, the other on the stemme or foreshippe.' He adds that if the first light appears in the stem or foreship and ascends upwards, it is a sign of good luck ; if ' either lights begin at the topmast, bowsprit,' or foreship, and descend towards the sea, it is a sign of tempest. In taking, therefore, the latter position, Ariel had fulfilled the commands of Prospero and raised a storm."

A passage in Hakluyt's " Voyages " (1598) describes St. Elmo's Fire and strikingly illustrates the above speech of Ariel. It runs : " I do remember that in the great and

boysterous storme of this foule weather, in the night, there
came upon the toppe of our maine yarde and maine maste,
a certaine little light, much like unto the light of a little
candle, which the Spaniards called the Cuerpo-Santo, and
said it was St. Elmo, whom they take to bee the aduocate of
sailers . . . This light continued aboord our ship about
three houres, flying from maste to maste, and from top to
top; and sometimes it would be in two or three places at
once." The Italian "corpo santo" is the origin of the word
"corposants," by which the fires were known to English
sailors.

Further on in "The Tempest" we find Ariel playing the
part of another curious phenomenon, known as "Jack-o'-
lantern" or "will-o'-the-wisp." The sprite has led Stephano
and his drunken companions "through tooth'd briers, sharp
furzes, pricking goss, and thorns," and left them "i' the filthy-
mantled pool"; (IV.1. 180-182), and the disgusted butler
exclaims to Caliban, "Monster, your fairy, which you say is
a harmless fairy, has done little better than play the Jack with
us " (lines 197-198). Paraphrasing this passage, Dr. Johnson
says that Ariel " has played ' Jack-with-a-lanthorn,' has led
us about like an ignis fatuus, by which travellers are decoyed
into the mire."

The scientific explanation of the ignis fatuus (Jack-o'-
lantern or will-o'-the-wisp) is " a phosphorescent light seen in
the air over marshy places, supposed to be caused by the
evolution and spontaneous combustion of some highly
inflammable gas " (Funk and Wagnall's New Standard
Dictionary). Shakespeare, perhaps, believed that the ignis
fatuus and St. Elmo's Fire were the same thing, or had a like
cause, since he makes Ariel impersonate both phenomena.

In "Midsummer Night's Dream" Puck, "that shrewd
and knavish sprite call'd Robin Goodfellow " or "Hobgoblin"

(II.1. 33-34; 40), plays the part of will-o'-the-wisp, and, in harmony with the rural folk lore of the time, loves to "mislead night-wanderers, laughing at their harm" (II.1. 39). " Sometime a horse I'll be," he says ; " sometime a hound . . . sometime a fire " (III.1. 111-112). Jack-o'-lantern or Kit-with-the-canstick (candlestick), as he was sometimes called, was supposed to misguide belated travellers with his swinging, illusory lantern.

In " King Lear " the Fool, seeing Gloucester's torch in the distance, cries, " Look, here comes a walking fire," and Edgar answers, " This is the foul fiend Flibbertigibbet: he begins at curfew and walks till the first cock " (III.4. 119-121). Hunter thought that Flibbertigibbet was another name for Will-o'-the-wisp, since his fire would be seen in the dark hours between the curfew and cock-crow. Yet another name was fire-drake, which is used in " Henry VIII " (V.4. 45). Falstaff, however, rejects picturesque synonyms and uses the classical term, ignis fatuus, in " 1 Henry IV." Describing how Bardolph of the red face ran into the darkness, when they were set upon by Prince and Poins, the fat knight says (III.3. 42-46) :

> When thou rannest up Gadshill in the night to catch my horse, if I did not think thou hadst been an ignis fatuus or a ball of wildfire, there's no purchase in money.

With " Fire and Flame " our study of " Shakespeare and Science " reaches its conclusion. If this book has enabled the lover of Shakespeare to understand the master-poet better than he did before, to appreciate him more fully, and to regard him with more reverence and enthusiasm, it has fulfilled its purpose. For our final quotation we may go to " The Tempest," Shakespeare's swan song, where,

with his imagination and poetic genius ripened to its fullest,
he rises to spiritual prophecy. The beauties of Nature
which he has loved, the goddess whom he has worshipped,
are seen in his closing years to be possessed of eternal life,
and the finite chains which shackle them to the earth melt
into the haloes of the life to come. Our erring, mortal vision
will fade, and we shall see the truth as it really is in all its
infinite and everlasting loveliness.

> These our actors,
> As I foretold you, were all spirits, and
> Are melted into air, into thin air :
> And, like the baseless fabric of this vision,
> The cloud-capp'd towers, the gorgeous palaces,
> The solemn temples, the great globe itself,
> Yea, all which it inherit, shall dissolve,
> And, like this insubstantial pageant faded,
> Leave not a rack behind. We are such stuff
> As dreams are made on ; and our little life
> Is rounded with a sleep.
>
> (IV.i. 148-158).

INDEX

Æolus, god of the winds, 197.
"Alchemist, The" (Ben Jonson), 63-4.
Alchemy, 4, 60-69, 130.
"Almagest, The" (Ptolemy), 27.
Apollo (*see also*, Phœbus), 78, 81, 92, 113.
"Apology for Poetry" (Sidney), 11.
Archer, William, author, 10.
Aries, sign of Zodiac, 51, 136, 138-9.
Aristarchus, 26.
Aristarchus (lunar mountain), 109.
Aristotle, 34, 244.
Astrology, 4, 37-59, 140, 145.
Astronomy, 4, 26-36, 37-8.
Aurora, goddess of dawn, 32, 92.
Autumn, 159-60.

Bacon, 1-2, 33-4, 42.
Batman, Stephen, physician and author, 74, 254.
Bible, The, 5, 29, 34, 110, 127, 132-4, 144, 222.
Boreas, the north wind, 195, 204.
Brahe, Tycho, astronomer, 41.
Browne, Sir T., antiquary, 42.
Bruno, Giordano, 29-30.

Cancer, sign of Zodiac, 136, 139.
"Canterbury Tales," 60.
"Castle of Knowledge, The" (Recorde), 30.
Celestial Pole, The, 121.
Charles' Wain (The Great Bear), 35, 122.
Chaucer, 40, 60, 110.
Clouds, 213-17.

Cocytus, river, 241.
Comets, 17, 32, 52-3, 140-42.
Copernicus, 4, 28-31, 33, 38, 41-2, 78, 132.
Copernicus, System of astronomy, 28-31, 33, 78, 132.

Dante, 110.
Dawn, 32, 87-93.
De Alveto, alchemist, 64.
Dee, John, astrologer and alchemist, 31, 42, 64.
De Glanville, Bartholomew, friar, 74.
"De Magnete" (Gilbert), 31.
"De Motibus Stellæ Martis" (Kepler), 29, 125.
"De Proprietatibus Rerum" (de Glanville), 74.
"De Revolutionibus Orbium Cœlestium" (Copernicus), 29.
Dew, 244-7.
Diana, 32, 104, 112-14, 226.
Dictynna, 114.
Digges, Thomas, astronomer, 31.
"Directions for Health of Magistrates and Students" (Newton, 1574), 107.
"Discovery of the Bermudas, A" (Jourdain), 179.
"Doctor Faustus" (Marlowe), 33, 117.
Dyer, Thiselton, commentator, 109, 254.

Earth, 26-8, 78, 130-35.
Earthquakes, 189-91.
Echo, 248-9.
Eclipses, 54-5, 115-16,